1. Individual sponge flans

# CAKES AND BAKING

**HAMLYN**
LONDON · NEW YORK · SYDNEY · TORONTO

Published by
The Hamlyn Publishing Group Limited
LONDON · NEW YORK · SYDNEY · TORONTO
Hamlyn House, Feltham, Middlesex, England

© Copyright Paul Hamlyn Ltd. 1962
First Published 1962
Revised edition 1970

ISBN 0 600 00576 3

Printed in Czechoslovakia by PZ Bratislava
520019

# CONTENTS      LIST OF COLOUR PLATES

1. Individual sponge flans
2. Boiled fruit cake
3. Walnut cherry gâteau
4. Chocolate swiss roll
5. American apple cake
6. American bride's cake
7. Golden shortcake
8. Christmas cake
9. Celebration cake
10. Danish layer cake
11. Apple strudel
12. Banana chocolate flan
13. Chocolate gâteau
14. Gingerbread squares
15. Meringue baskets
16 & 17. Lemon fingers/Yeast tea ring
18. Brownies
19. Peanut crackers
20. Rich fruit bread
21. Battenburg and hot cross buns
22. Wiltshire lardy cake
23. Mocha shell cake
24. Hazelnut and chocolate gâteau

# INTRODUCTION

It has given me particular pleasure to edit this book on home
baking, which includes a great variety of recipes for cakes,
biscuits, bread and scones, as well as many suggestions for
decorating them.

I know from my demonstrations throughout the country and on
television that there is still a great interest in home baking. I
think nothing is more rewarding than delicious home-made cakes
or a loaf of crusty bread coming out of the oven. Those of us
who have particularly busy lives, running a home as well as a
career, know that it is a very 'comfortable' feeling to have a rich
Dundee cake or some meringues tucked away in a tin—ready to
serve an unexpected visitor or to bring out when we are unusually
rushed.

In every part of the country there are traditional recipes which
have been in use for many years, and I have tried to include a
good selection of these. On the other hand my post-bag is full of
letters which say, 'Please may we have NEW ideas', so you will
find in this book some ideas for very new cakes—perhaps a
combination of flavours that is unusual, or a new and particularly
speedy way of producing a cake or loaf.

Every country has recipes that are particularly its own—the
meringue Pavlova cakes from Australia, the very light chiffon
cakes from America, Linzer Torte from Austria—and you will
find a chapter containing these cakes from other countries. I do
hope you will try them, and I am quite sure they will become as
popular in your family as they are in the families of their country
of origin.

Many people speak of bread making as if it were a most difficult
form of cooking—it isn't, you know. After all it wasn't such a
long time ago that bread was made in most homes, and today it
should be much easier with our heat regulated ovens. In case you
are nervous of cooking with yeast, though, in the bread section
there are a number of breads which can be made without it.

When you have tried these I would urge you to get some yeast,
and make a batch of bread. I am sure you will enjoy not only the
results, but the handling of the dough as well. While home baking
is particularly rewarding, it is probably the form of cooking
where more things can go wrong than any other. That is why you
will find in most chapters a section which points out the 'pitfalls'
to avoid.

I should like to thank the many people who have worked hard to
produce the large selection of pictures in this book—I am sure
you will agree they make the book a pleasure to read as well as
easier to follow.

# OVEN TEMPERATURES

In most recipes in this book reference has been given to the oven temperature or the gas setting. This is an approximate guide only. Different makes of cooker vary and it is a fact even the same make of cooker can give slightly different individual results at the same temperature or setting.

If in doubt as to whether the temperature given is EXACTLY right for your particular cooker, then do at all times refer to your own manufacturer's temperature chart. It is impossible in a general book to be exact for every cooker, but you will find that the following are a good average in every case.

| Oven | Electricity °F | Gas Regulo | °C |
|---|---|---|---|
| COOL | 225–250 | 0–½ | 107–121 |
| VERY SLOW | 250–275 | ½–1 | 121–135 |
| SLOW | 275–300 | 1–2 | 135–149 |
| VERY MODERATE | 300–350 | 2–3 | 149–177 |
| MODERATE | 375 | 4 | 190 |
| MODERATELY HOT | 400 | 5 | 204 |
| HOT | 425–450 | 6–7 | 218–233 |
| VERY HOT | 475–500 | 8–9 | 246–260 |

# CARE OF CAKE TINS, MOULDS, ETC.

1. When the tins are new wipe out carefully, then oil or grease very efficiently – lard and cooking fat are both excellent for greasing tins. Put the tins into a warm oven only and heat gently. Remove from the oven and wipe away surplus fat with a soft cloth or kitchen tissue. Put the tins away.

2. After using the tins try NOT to wash them; instead wipe out with a soft cloth or kitchen tissue immediately you take out the cake.

3. If it has been necessary to wash the tins, wipe them very dry then put into a warm place (over the cooker or in the warming drawer of the cooker) for several hours before putting them into a cupboard. This prevents their becoming rusty.

4. Always wait just a minute or two before attempting to take cakes from tins or moulds – this allows them to shrink slightly away from the bottom and sides of the tin. They are then much easier to remove, and you are less likely to find cakes 'sticking'.

# WEIGHTS AND MEASURES

English weights and measures have been used throughout this book. In case it is wished to translate these into their American counterparts the following tables give a comparison:

## LIQUID MEASURE

ONE PINT of liquid may be regarded as equal to TWO American measuring cups for all practical purposes. (American cups are standard '½-pint' measuring cups, but the American pint is slightly smaller than the British and American ½-pint cups are actually equivalent to two-fifths of a British pint.)

3 teaspoonfuls equal 1 tablespoonful.

The average English teacup is ¼ pint or 1 gill.

The average English breakfast cup is ½ pint or 2 gills.

When cups are mentioned in the recipes in this book they refer to a B.S.I. measuring cup which does hold ½ pint.

## FRENCH WEIGHTS AND MEASURES

It is difficult to convert to French measurements with absolute accuracy, but 1 oz. is equal to approximately 30 grammes, 2 lb. 3 oz. to 1 kilogramme.

For liquid measure approximately 1¾ pints may be regarded as equal to 1 litre. 1 demilitre is half a litre, and 1 decilitre is one-tenth litre.

## SOLID MEASURE

| ENGLISH | INGREDIENTS | AMERICAN |
|---|---|---|
| 1 pound | Butter or other fat | 2 cups |
| 1 pound | Flour | 4 cups |
| 1 pound | Granulated or Castor Sugar | 2 cups |
| 1 pound | Icing or Confectioners' Sugar | 3 cups |
| 1 pound | Brown (moist) Sugar | 2⅔ cups |
| 1 pound | Golden Syrup or Treacle | 1 cup |
| 1 pound | Rice | 2 cups |
| 1 pound | Dried Fruit | 2 cups |
| 1 pound | Soft Breadcrumbs | 4 cups |
| ½ ounce | Flour | 1 level tablespoon* |
| 1 ounce | Flour | 1 heaped tablespoon |
| 1 ounce | Sugar | 1 level tablespoon |
| ½ ounce | Butter | 1 tablespoon smoothed off |
| 1 ounce | Golden Syrup or Treacle | 1 level tablespoon |
| 1 ounce | Jam or Jelly | 1 level tablespoon |

* must be standard measuring tablespoon

# SUCCESSFUL CAKE MAKING

## 1 Successful cake making

1 Weigh ingredients carefully.

2 Follow the recipe exactly for the first time, before you make any modification.

3 Remember all ovens vary a little so treat the oven number or temperature given as an approximate guide only.

4 Always check the temperature given by the manufacturer's instruction book.

5 Test cakes carefully before bringing out of the oven (see below).

6 Spongy type cakes and light fruit cakes are cooked when they feel firm in the centre if you press with your finger, and have shrunk from tin.

7 Rich fruit cakes are cooked when they no longer 'hum' and have shrunk from the sides of the tin. You can test with a warm skewer but this is NOT as good as listening.

8 Allow light cakes to cool for 1 or 2 minutes before turning out of the tin. A rich Christmas or wedding cake should cool in its tin, otherwise the weight of the fruit might cause it to break.

9 Always store cakes away from pastry, bread or biscuits. Keep them in airtight tins.

10 Allow rich fruit cakes a reasonable time to mature before cutting.

Successful cake making also depends on the way you handle the ingredients. Various terms are used in cake making, and it is essential to interpret these correctly.

**To melt** means you heat the ingredients steadily until the fat has dissolved, but do not go on cooking.

**To rub in** means you mix the fat with the flour (or dry ingredients) with the tips of your fingers until the mixture looks like fine crumbs.

**To cream** means you blend fat and sugar (and other ingredients given in the recipe) until very soft and light. Your hand is the best utensil for this, particularly if the fat is hard or the weather cold. Many people, however, find this unpleasant, so use a wooden spoon.

**To whip or whisk** means you beat the ingredients, preferably with a proper egg whisk or electric mixer, until they reach the right consistency. Do not try whisking eggs and sugar for sponges with a fork, as it would take far too long.

**To fold** means a gentle 'flicking' movement to blend the ingredients. You can tell if you are 'folding' correctly as your hand and wrist should just turn gently. Do this with a metal spoon or knife.

## 2 Choosing the right ingredients

Ingredients play a big part in the success of all recipes, particularly when baking.

**Choice of flour:** Most recipes in this book are worded as follows: 4 oz. flour (with plain flour use 1 level teaspoon baking powder). The flour referred to means self-raising.

There are a few recipes in which you will find the amount of baking powder suggested with plain flour seems either more or less than usual (the average amount being 1 level teaspoon to 4 oz. plain flour, which makes it equivalent to most self-raising). The reasons for these changing proportions of plain flour are either because the cake is heavy in fruit, honey or other ingredients, which means less baking powder is ideal; or where a high percentage of baking powder is used, it is to give a particularly light, puffy result.

If a recipe has given self-raising flour as an alternative you will get a good result with self-raising flour, but a more perfect result with plain flour and the amount of baking powder stated.

Some recipes, however, simply mention the word 'flour' without specifying whether you need any baking powder if using plain flour. In these cases plain flour quite definitely gives a better result and the raising agent in self-raising flour is unnecessary either (a) because it is a biscuit type cake or (b) because yeast is being used.

**Choice of fat:** This is often important. In some cases butter is stressed, in others margarine, some cooking fat or, as it is often known, vegetable shortening. There are various types of margarine on sale—luxury or superfine have the advantage of being richer and creaming more readily. The modern whipped up cooking fats are also easy to handle in rubbing in or creaming.

Spoon measures should be level—but if a recipe specifically mentions LEVEL then it means extra care must be taken in measuring. REMEMBER ABOVE ALL: OVENS VARY, SO USE THE TEMPERATURES GIVEN AS A GUIDE AND CHECK WITH YOUR OWN OVEN CHART.

## 3 Choosing the right equipment

*An electric mixer*

We have not listed all the equipment desirable for cake making in this book, since there is such a wide variety available that it would be impossible, and so much depends on your own personal wishes.

Certain things, however, are worth mentioning.

An electric mixer saves you the time of creaming, whisking, etc., and also kneading when making bread or yeast cakes. Illustrated is one of the up-to-date electric mixers. Follow the directions for method of mixing recommended by the makers.

When buying cake tins choose the best quality you can, for they will repay you, not only by lasting a long time, but by giving better baking results.

There are a great variety of shaped tins to add interest to your baking and if you make rather delicate cheese cakes, light sponges, etc. a Spring release cake tin is invaluable to remove the cake without breaking.

Ring tins are also extremely useful for Angel cakes, Devil's Food cakes and even an ordinary mixture which can be baked in a shorter time.

LOOK AFTER YOUR TINS and equipment, dry them well after being washed, and wherever possible DO NOT WASH THE TINS after being used. Instead wipe out while still warm with a soft cloth or kitchen paper.

## 4 To keep cakes fresh and moist

1 Store carefully—IN A SEPARATE CONTAINER from bread, biscuits or pastry.

2 Wrap in foil or greaseproof paper.

3 Line cake tins with greased greaseproof paper, and keep this paper on the cakes until ready to ice or serve.

4 Take care not to overcook cakes. Test carefully—see directions in Number 1.

5 Do not omit the golden syrup if this is an ingredient in a cake recipe; it helps to keep it very moist for quite a long time.

6 Prick rich fruit cakes and spoon over small quantities of sherry or brandy or rum, allow this to soak into the cake, so giving a moist texture.

## 5 When cakes have become dry

1 Brush the outside rather liberally with milk and put the cake into a moderately hot oven for about 10 minutes. This freshens the cake temporarily but it must be eaten the same day.

2 Slice fruit cakes thinly, butter, and serve as rich tea bread.

3 Use in Russian cake—see Recipe 598, or as filling in Mock Maids of Honour (Recipe 270).

In most families there are cakes which, over the years, have proved very popular, and of course there are traditional cakes that will always be made and served. These cakes we give you in the following pages.

Elsewhere in the book you will find a great variety of new recipes, but here are the old favourites in well tested and tried form.

## 6 Family fruit cake

8 oz. flour (with plain flour
    use 3 level teaspoons
    baking powder)
pinch salt
4 oz. margarine

6 oz. currants
4 oz. castor sugar
1 egg
5 tablespoons milk

Sieve the flour, salt and baking powder, if used, into a basin. Rub in the margarine until the mixture is as fine as breadcrumbs. Add the cleaned fruit and sugar, and mix well. Beat the egg and add the milk and mix with the dry ingredients to a consistency that will drop from the spoon. Prepare a 2-lb. loaf tin or a 6-inch cake tin by lining with greased greaseproof paper. Turn the mixture into the prepared cake tin and bake in the middle of a moderate oven (375°F.—Gas Mark 4) for 1¼ to 1½ hours. When cooked the cake should be well browned and feel firm in the centre. Cool on a cake rack.

## 7 Economical rock buns

Follow the same recipe and method as for family fruit cake (Recipe 6) but use only 2 tablespoons milk to mix to a stiff dough. Pile the mixture into rough heaps on a greased baking tin, using 2 forks for shaping. Bake near the top of a hot oven (425–450°F.—Gas Mark 6–7) for approximately 12–15 minutes.

## 8 Rich rock buns

Method of mixing as family fruit cake (Recipe 6), but increase the amount of margarine to 5 or 6 oz. and the sugar to 6 oz.

Mix with 2 eggs, and only 1 tablespoon milk. Add about 8 oz. mixed fruit. Pile the mixture into rough heaps on a greased baking tin, using 2 forks for shaping. Dust with castor sugar and bake for approximately 12 minutes near the top of a hot oven (425°F.—Gas Mark 6). As these are very short and crisp allow to cool for a few minutes before removing from the baking tin.

## 9 Chocolate and orange rock cakes

| | |
|---|---|
| 8 oz. self-raising flour | rind 1 orange, finely grated |
| pinch salt | 4 oz. milk chocolate |
| 3 oz. castor sugar | 1 egg |
| 3 oz. cooking fat | 1 tablespoon milk |

Sieve the flour, salt and sugar into a basin. Add the cooking fat and orange rind and rub in until mixture resembles fine breadcrumbs. Chop the chocolate fairly coarsely and stir into dry ingredients. Lightly beat the egg and milk together and stir into the mixture. Place the mixture in heaped dessertspoonfuls on a baking sheet brushed over with melted cooking fat. Bake near the top of a hot oven (425°F.—Gas Mark 6) for 20 minutes. Cool on a cake rack.

## 10 Stand-by cake mixture

| | |
|---|---|
| 1 lb. self-raising flour | 8 oz. cooking fat |
| 1 level teaspoon salt | |

Sieve the flour and salt into a basin and rub in the cooking fat until the mixture resembles fine breadcrumbs. This can then be put in a screw-top jar or any airtight container and stored in a cool, dry place ready for use. In this way it can be kept for up to three months, and when making cakes or puddings you can just weigh out the amount given in the recipe. The weight of the stand-by mixture is the total weight of flour, salt and cooking fat, when rubbed together.

## 11 Marmalade cake

12 oz. stand-by cake mixture (Recipe 10)
3 oz. castor sugar
2 rounded tablespoons marmalade
1 egg
3 tablespoons milk

Topping
1 rounded tablespoon marmalade
1 rounded teaspoon sugar
½ oz. browned almonds, chopped

Place the stand-by mixture in a basin and stir in the sugar and marmalade. Beat the egg and milk together and stir into the dry ingredients. Mix well and place in a 7-inch square tin lined with greaseproof paper and brushed with melted cooking fat. Bake in a moderate oven (375°F.—Gas Mark 4) in the middle of the oven for 50–60 minutes. Turn out on a cake rack.
For the topping, heat the marmalade and sugar to boiling, brush over the top of the hot cake and sprinkle with the almonds. When cold cut into fingers or squares.

*Marmalade cake*

## 12 Lardy jacks

| | |
|---|---|
| 8 oz. flour (with plain flour | 4 oz. lard* |
| use 2 level teaspoons baking | 2 oz. dried fruit |
| powder) | 3 tablespoons sugar |

*\* Try to use real lard and not cooking fat*

Sieve together flour and baking powder, if used. Rub in 1 oz. lard then mix with water as for pastry. Roll out into oblong shape then spread with 1 oz. lard and part of the fruit and sugar. Fold into three, turn and re-roll. Do this until all lard, sugar and fruit are used. Cut into fingers, brush tops with little milk. Bake in a hot oven (450°F.—Gas Mark 7) for 10–15 minutes.

## 13 Dundee cake (rich recipe)

| | |
|---|---|
| 6 oz. margarine or butter | 2 oz. glacé cherries |
| 6 oz. sugar | 1 lb. mixed dried fruit |
| 3 eggs | 2 oz. chopped candied peel |
| 8 oz. plain flour | 2 tablespoons milk |
| 1½ level teaspoons baking | 2 oz. split almonds |
| powder | |
| 1 teaspoon spice | *To glaze* |
| 2 oz. almonds, chopped | egg white left in egg shells |

Cream the margarine and sugar together until soft and light. Add the beaten egg. Sieve dry ingredients together. Mix the chopped almonds, floured cherries, fruit and peel together. Stir in the flour and enough milk to make a slow dropping consistency, then lastly put in the fruit. Put into a greased and floured 8-inch cake tin. Cover with the split almonds and brush with a little egg white to glaze. Bake for 2–2½ hours in the centre of a very moderate oven (325–350°F.—Gas Mark 3) reducing the heat after 1½ hours to 300°F.—Gas Mark 2. Cool slightly in tin before turning on to a wire rack.

## 14 Chocolate Dundee cake

| | |
|---|---|
| 6 oz. margarine | 2 oz. glacé cherries |
| 6 oz. sugar | 12 oz. mixed dried fruit |
| 2 eggs | 2 oz. chopped candied peel |
| 7 oz. flour (with plain flour | 4 tablespoons milk |
| use 1½ level teaspoons | 2 oz. split almonds |
| baking powder) | |
| 1 oz. cocoa | *To glaze* |
| 1 teaspoon spice (optional) | egg white left in egg shells |
| 2 oz. almonds, chopped | |

Cream the margarine and sugar together until soft and light. Add the beaten eggs. Sieve dry ingredients together. Mix the chopped almonds, floured cherries, fruit and peel together. Stir in the flour and enough milk to make a slow dropping consistency, then lastly put in the fruit. Put into a greased and floured 8-inch cake tin. Cover with the split almonds, and brush with a little egg white to glaze. Bake for 2–2¼ hours in the centre of a very moderate oven (325–350°F.—Gas Mark 3), reducing heat after 1½ hours to 300°F.—Gas Mark 2. Cool slightly in tin before turning on to a wire rack.

## 15 *Economical Dundee cake*

Ingredients as Dundee cake (Recipe 13), but reduce the amounts of margarine and sugar to 4 oz., the fruit to 8–10 oz. and the eggs to 2. Bake in a 7 or 8-inch tin in the centre of a moderate oven (375°F.—Gas Mark 4) for 1¼–1½ hours.

*Economical dundee cake*

## 16 *Modern mix fruit cake*

8 oz. margarine
8 oz. castor sugar
1 lb. flour (with plain flour 4
   level teaspoons baking
   powder)
2 rounded teaspoons mixed
   spice

1 lb. mixed fruit
4 eggs
4 tablespoons milk

Place all ingredients in a large mixing bowl. Mix together with a wooden spoon (pressing margarine to side of basin if refrigerated). Then beat for 1–2 minutes. Place in an 8-inch square cake tin, bottom lined with greaseproof paper and brushed all round with margarine. Smooth top evenly. Bake in the middle of a very moderate oven (350°F.—Gas Mark 3) for 2–2¼ hours. Cool on a cake rack.

*Modern mix fruit cake*

## 17 *Golden fruit cake*

6 oz. butter *or* margarine
6 oz. castor sugar
8 oz. plain flour
1½ level teaspoons baking
   powder
3 eggs
4 oz. sultanas

4 oz. mixed peel
4 oz. glacé cherries
2 oz. desiccated coconut
6 oz. walnuts *or* Brazil
   nuts, coarsely chopped
little milk

Cream butter and sugar very well. Sieve dry ingredients. Add well beaten eggs gradually to butter mixture, then stir in dry ingredients, all fruit etc., and lastly just enough milk to give a soft consistency. Put into a 7-inch tin, lined with greased paper, and bake for approximately 2¼–2½ hours in centre of a very moderate oven (325–350°F.—Gas Mark 3). After 1½ hours, if cake is becoming rather brown, lower the heat slightly. Test carefully—see Number 1.

## 18 *Pineapple fruit cake*

*To decorate*
sieved apricot jam

glacé cherries
pineapple rings

Ingredients as for golden fruit cake (Recipe 17), but add 3 oz. VERY WELL DRAINED, chopped, canned pineapple or glacé pineapple. If using canned pineapple use slightly less milk than in the golden fruit cake.

Brush the top of the cake with sieved apricot jam, and cover with the pineapple and glacé cherries.

## 19 *Luncheon cake*

8 oz. flour (with plain flour
   use 2 level teaspoons
   baking powder)
5 oz. margarine *or* 3 oz.
   margarine and 2 oz. lard
4–5 oz. sugar
6 oz. mixed dried fruit

2 oz. mixed peel
1 egg
little milk
1 oz. almonds (optional)
1 dessertspoon glacé cherries
   (optional)

Sieve flour and baking powder, if used, together, rub in margarine, add sugar, dried fruit and peel, then beaten egg and enough milk to make a sticky consistency. Put into a well greased and floured loaf tin and bake for just an hour in centre of a moderate oven (350–375°F.—Gas Mark 3–4). If using almonds and cherries, blanch and dry almonds then put on top of cake with halved cherries, before baking.

## 20 Fruit gingerbread

2 oz. cooking fat
1½ oz. brown sugar
8 oz. syrup
¼ pint milk
4 oz. plain flour
pinch salt
1 level teaspoon mixed spice
3 level teaspoons ground
  ginger

4 oz. wholemeal flour
1 oz. chopped candied peel
2 oz. sultanas
1 egg
1 level teaspoon bicarbonate
  of soda
few blanched almonds

Melt fat, sugar and syrup together in a saucepan. Add milk and leave to cool. Sieve plain flour, salt and spices, stir in wholemeal flour, fruit and egg. Mix bicarbonate of soda with melted ingredients and stir into dry mixture. Mix well, pour into a 7-inch square tin brushed with melted fat and lined. Bake in centre of a moderate oven (375°F.—Gas Mark 4) for 40–45 minutes. Cool on a cake rack. Cut into squares and place a blanched almond on each square.

*Fruit gingerbread*

## 21 Marmalade bars

4 oz. margarine
2 oz. sugar
3 tablespoons marmalade
8 oz. flour (with plain flour use
  2 teaspoons baking powder)

2 eggs
grated rind 1 orange
orange juice to mix

Cream together margarine, sugar and marmalade. Sieve flour and baking powder, if used, together. Beat eggs well. Add eggs and flour alternately to margarine mixture, together with orange rind and enough juice to make a soft mixture. Line a tin measuring 8 × 5-inches with greased greaseproof paper and put in cake mixture. Bake for about 40 minutes in middle of a moderately hot oven (400°F.—Gas Mark 5). When cold cut into fingers and either dust with icing sugar or cover with orange-flavoured frosting or water icing (Recipes 401, 371).

## 22 Vinegar cake

6 oz. fat
12 oz. flour (with plain flour
  use 3 level teaspoons
  baking powder)
6 oz. sugar

8 oz. fruit
1 teaspoon bicarbonate of
  soda
2 tablespoons vinegar
½ pint milk

Rub the fat into the flour, add sugar and fruit. Stir the bicarbonate of soda and vinegar into the milk and add to the other ingredients. Put mixture into a greased, floured tin and bake in centre of a moderate oven (375°F.—Gas Mark 4) for approximately 1½ hours.

## 23 Economical Genoa cake

4 oz. margarine
4 oz. castor sugar
8 oz. flour (with plain flour
  use 2 level teaspoons
  baking powder)
2 eggs

1 teaspoon grated lemon rind
milk to mix
6 oz. dried fruit
2 oz. chopped candied peel
little sugar

Method as for Madeira cake (Recipe 44). Mix in fruit after adding flour, etc. and bake for just over 1¼ hours at 375°F.—Gas Mark 4.

## 24 Rich Genoa cake

6 oz. butter
6 oz. sugar
8 oz. flour (with plain flour
  use 1½ level teaspoons
  baking powder)

4 eggs
grated rind 1 lemon
8 oz. mixed fruit
2 oz. chopped candied peel
sugar to decorate

Cream together the butter and sugar until soft and light. Sieve flour and baking powder, if used, together. Beat eggs. Add eggs and flour alternately to butter mixture, then lemon rind, fruit and peel. Put into greased and floured 8-inch cake in, sprinkling a little sugar on top. Bake for just on 1½ hours in the centre of a very moderate oven (350°F.—Gas Mark 3).
This is a medium rich type of cake, which keeps reasonably well.

## 25 Cherry loaf

6 oz. flour (with plain flour
  use 1½ level teaspoons
  baking powder)
3 oz. castor sugar
pinch salt
3 oz. cooking fat
1 egg

½ teaspoon vanilla essence
2 tablespoons milk
4 oz. glacé cherries, cut into
  halves

Sieve flour, sugar and salt into a basin. Add fat, egg, vanilla and milk, and beat for about 1 minute until ingredients are well mixed. Stir in cherries thoroughly, saving three halves to place along top of loaf for decoration. Place in a 1-lb. loaf tin, brushed with melted fat. Gently press cherries into top of loaf. Bake in the middle of a moderate oven (375°F.—Gas Mark 4) for 1–1¼ hours. Turn out, and cool on a cake rack.

## 26  *Boiled fruit cake*

½ pint water *or* cold tea
3 oz. lard
3 oz. sugar
3 oz. dried fruit
2–3 oz. glacé cherries
10 oz. flour (if using plain flour add 3 level teaspoons baking powder)

1 teaspoon mixed spice
pinch salt
1 teaspoon bicarbonate of soda
granulated sugar, glacé cherries and angelica leaves, to decorate

Boil liquid, fat, sugar and fruit together in a pan for 2 or 3 minutes. Allow to cool slightly. Meanwhile, sieve together dry ingredients. Add liquid and beat thoroughly. Pour into greased and floured 8-inch cake tin. Bake in centre of moderately hot oven (400°F.—Gas Mark 5) for 45 minutes, then lower heat to Gas Mark 4—350°F. for a further 30–45 minutes. Cool on a cake rack. Sprinkle the top with a little granulated sugar and decorate with glacé cherries and angelica leaves. An exceptionally economical cake that does not dry easily.

(*Illustrated in colour plate 2*).

## 27  *Eggless fruit cake*

3 oz. margarine
3 oz. sugar
8 oz. flour (with plain flour use 1½ level teaspoons baking powder)

1 teaspoon bicarbonate soda
1 teaspoon spice
generous ¼ pint milk
12 oz. mixed dried fruit
2 oz. chopped candied peel

Cream margarine and sugar until soft. Sieve flour, soda, baking powder, if used, and spice. Work into margarine together with milk. Lastly add fruit and peel. Leave in bowl overnight. Next day stir again and put into 7-inch cake tin lined with greased and floured paper. Bake for 2½ hours in very moderate oven (350°F.—Gas Mark 3).

## 28  *Rich raisin cake*

6 oz. margarine
6 oz. sugar
3 eggs
8 oz. flour (with plain flour use 1½ level teaspoons baking powder)

1 teaspoon spice (optional)
2 oz. almonds, chopped (optional)
1 lb. raisins
2 tablespoons milk *or* sherry

Cream the margarine and sugar together until soft and light. Add the beaten eggs. Sieve dry ingredients together. Mix together almonds and raisins. Stir in flour and milk or sherry, then lastly stir in fruit. Put into a greased and floured 8-inch cake tin. Bake 2–2¼ hours in very moderate oven (350°F.—Gas Mark 3).

## 29  *Rich gingerbread*

5 oz. butter *or* margarine
4 oz. brown sugar
6 oz. black treacle *or* golden syrup
1 tablespoon water

7 oz. flour (with plain flour use level teaspoons baking powder)
2 teaspoons ground ginger
1 teaspoon grated lemon rind
2 eggs

Put butter, sugar, treacle and water into pan and heat gently until butter has melted. Sieve all dry ingredients together. Pour melted ingredients on to dry mixture and beat hard until thoroughly mixed. Make sure no mixture is left in pan. Add lemon rind and eggs. Beat once again, then pour into a 7-inch square tin lined with greaseproof paper and bake for 1–1¼ hours in centre of a very moderate oven (350°F.—Gas Mark 3). Test by pressing gently in centre of cake. If no impression is left by your finger the cake is cooked. Cool for about 30 minutes in tin, then turn out carefully on to a wire rack.

*Rich gingerbread*

## 30 Lemon gingerbread

3 oz. fat
3 tablespoons golden syrup *or* black treacle
3 oz. sugar
6 oz. flour (with plain flour use 1½ teaspoons baking powder)
1 teaspoon mixed spice
1 level teaspoon bicarbonate of soda
1–1½ teaspoons ground ginger

grated rind 1 lemon
1 egg
¼ pint water
1 tablespoon lemon juice

*To decorate*
lemon glacé icing (Recipe 374)
finely grated rind 1 lemon

Put fat, syrup and sugar into a saucepan and heat until fat has melted. Sieve together all dry ingredients. Add lemon rind. Beat in melted fat and egg, continue beating until very smooth. Bring lemon juice and water to boiling point in saucepan previously used for fat. Pour over cake mixture and beat well. Line a 7-inch cake tin or an oblong tin measuring 8 × 6-inches with greased and floured greaseproof paper, pour in mixture and bake for 1 hour in centre of very moderate oven (350°F.—Gas Mark 3) if using an oblong tin, or a little longer for round tin. Cool in tin, coat with thin lemon glacé icing (Recipe 374) and before it sets sprinkle over finely grated lemon rind.

## 31 Grantham gingerbreads

1 lb. flour
6 oz. margarine
12 oz. castor sugar
½ oz. ground ginger

1 teaspoon nutmeg
2 small eggs
juice 1 lemon
ground rice

Sift flour, rub in fat, make well in centre and add sugar, ginger and nutmeg. Mix to firm dough with eggs and lemon juice. Leave in a cool place for some hours. Roll out ½-inch thick (using ground rice to 'flour' the board). Cut into rounds with 3-inch cutter. Put on greased tins and bake in centre of a moderate oven (375°F.—Gas Mark 4) for approximately 20-25 minutes.

## 32 Ginger cake (1)

6 oz. short crust pastry (Recipe 252)

*Cake mixture*
2 oz. margarine
1½ oz. soft brown sugar
1 egg
2 teaspoons syrup
2½ oz. self-raising flour
pinch salt

1 level teaspoon ground ginger
1 oz. crystallised ginger, chopped

*To decorate*
2-3 tablespoons glacé icing (Recipe 371)
crystallised ginger

Make pastry by usual method, roll out and line a 7-inch flan ring placed on a baking sheet, or sandwich tin. Spread 1 tablespoon syrup over pastry. Cream margarine and sugar together until light and fluffy. Lightly beat egg and add in tablespoons to mixture, beating in well after each addition. Stir in syrup. Sieve flour, salt, spice and ginger together and fold into mixture with chopped ginger. Put into pastry flan and smooth top. Bake in centre of a moderate oven 375°F.—Gas Mark 4) for about 40 minutes. Remove flan ring or turn out of tin and allow cake to cool on a wire tray. Decorate with white glacé icing and small pieces of crystallised ginger.

*Ginger cake*

## 33 Grasmere gingerbread or Grasmere shortcake

8 oz. plain flour
¼ teaspoon bicarbonate of soda
4 oz. margarine *or* butter
4 oz. brown sugar
½ teaspoon ground ginger

*Filling*
4 oz. icing sugar
2 oz. butter
¼ teaspoon ground ginger *or* little preserved ginger, chopped

Sieve flour and bicarbonate of soda together. Rub in margarine, add sugar and ginger. Line shallow tin with greased greaseproof paper and shake in crumbly mixture. Press firmly together, then bake in centre of a moderate oven (375°F.—Gas Mark 4) for about 25-30 minutes until slightly brown. Wait a few minutes then turn out carefully. Split through middle while hot and spread on filling when quite cold. Sandwich the two halves together. To make filling cream ingredients together.
**Note**
You can make this shortcake without any filling, in which case you may like to slightly increase the amount of ginger.

## 34 Ginger cake (2)

3-6 oz. preserved ginger
6 oz. margarine
6 oz. sugar
3 eggs

8 oz. flour (with plain flour
use 1 teaspoon baking
powder)*

* This gives best result with this cake

Drain ginger well and cut into small pieces. Cream margarine and sugar, add eggs, flour sifted with baking powder, if used, and chopped ginger. Bake in a 7-inch greased and floured cake tin for 1¼-1½ hours in centre of very moderate oven (350°F.—Gas Mark 3). If wished, ice with a ginger icing made by moistening icing sugar with some of the ginger syrup.

**Variation**
About 4 oz. sultanas could be added to preserved ginger. For colourful topping—without icing—decorate with sliced preserved ginger and a dessert apple.

## 35 Yorkshire parkin

1 heaped teaspoon ground
  ginger
1 teaspoon mixed spice
8 oz. flour
1½ lb. medium oatmeal

8 oz. margarine or butter or
  margarine and lard mixed
1 lb. black treacle
8 oz. brown sugar

Sieve all the dry ingredients, except oatmeal, into a bowl, add oatmeal and mix well. Melt the margarine, treacle and sugar and pour on to the oatmeal mixture, beating thoroughly. Pour into a well greased and lined tin—8 or 9 inches square and bake for about 1½-2 hours in the centre of a very moderate oven (350°F.—Gas Mark 3). Keep for a day or two before cutting.

## 36 Saffron cakes

For saffron flavour: use either 1 good teaspoon powdered saffron, 1 small teaspoon liquid saffron or about 3d. worth of saffron (put in a cup of hot water, left in warm place overnight then strained off) to each 8 oz. flour. Saffron is becoming increasingly difficult to get. You will need to ask at a good chemist.

## 37 Plain saffron cake

6 oz. margarine
6 oz. sugar
saffron flavouring
2 eggs

8 oz. flour (with plain flour
use 2 level teaspoons
baking powder)
little milk

Cream margarine and sugar until soft. Add saffron flavouring (see Recipe 36) and beat well, then add the beaten eggs and flour sifted with baking powder, if used, alternately to the margarine mixture. Lastly put in enough milk to make a soft consistency. Put into 7-inch greased and floured tin and bake for nearly 2 hours in centre of oven at 375°F.—Gas Mark 4 for first hour, then at 350°F.—Gas Mark 3 for the rest of the time.

## 38 Fruit saffron cake

4 oz. margarine
4 oz. sugar*
saffron flavouring (see Recipe
  36)
1 egg
8 oz. flour (with plain flour

use 1½ level teaspoons
  baking powder)
3 oz. sultanas
2 oz. peel
8 oz. currants
milk to mix

* Use brown sugar if possible

Method as Recipe 37 adding fruit and peel last. Bake in greased and floured 8-inch cake tin for 2 hours in centre of very moderate oven (350°F.—Gas Mark 3).

## 39 Wakes cake

8 oz. plain flour
6 oz. butter
6 oz. castor sugar

1 oz. currants
1 egg

Rub flour and butter together, add sugar and currants, mix to a stiff dough with the beaten egg, knead a little, roll out, cut into rounds about ¼-inch thick and bake in a moderate oven (375°F.—Gas Mark 4) for approximately 15 minutes. The cakes should be a pale golden brown and the size of a saucer.

## 40 Rice cake

4 oz. butter
grated rind ½ lemon
8 oz. castor sugar

4 eggs
8 oz. ground rice

Cream butter with lemon rind until soft, add sugar and continue beating until light. Separate eggs and beat yolks into batter, one at a time. Whisk whites until stiff but not dry, then fold into mixture with ground rice. Pour into a greased 7-inch prepared cake tin and bake about 1 hour in centre of moderate oven (375°F.—Gas Mark 4).

## 41 Goosnargh cakes

12 oz. butter or margarine
1 lb. flour
2 oz. castor sugar

a few caraway and ground
  coriander seeds

Tip butter into flour and mix well without adding any moisture. Roll out to about ¼-inch thick and cut into round shapes. Coat thickly with sugar and seeds and bake just above centre of a moderate oven (375°F.—Gas Mark 3). They are better if the dough is made the day before baking. Dust with more sugar after baking.

## 42 Lightning lemon cake

6 oz. self-raising flour with 2
  level teaspoons baking
  powder or 6 oz. plain flour
  with 4 level teaspoons
  baking powder

4 oz. fat
4 oz. castor sugar
2 eggs
grated rind 1 lemon
1 tablespoon lemon juice

Sieve flour and baking powder into a bowl. Add fat, sugar, eggs, lemon rind and lemon juice, and mixing all ingredients beat for 1 minute. Turn into a 6-inch cake tin lined with greaseproof paper and brushed with melted fat. Bake in the centre of a very moderate oven (350°F.—Gas Mark 3) for 1-1¼ hours. Cool on a wire rack.

## 43  *Almond cake*

10 oz. plain flour
3 level teaspoons baking
   powder
8 oz. margarine
8 oz. castor sugar
3 eggs

1 small teaspoon almond
   essence
few drops vanilla essence
4 oz. ground almonds
3 tablespoons milk

Sieve flour and baking powder. Cream together margarine and sugar till light and fluffy. Add eggs, one at a time, beating thoroughly after each addition, and essences. Mix in ground almonds and fold in flour lightly with a metal spoon. Then add milk. Turn mixture into a greased and paper-lined 8-inch round cake tin. Bake in middle of oven (350°F.—Gas Mark 3) for 2-2¼ hours. Cool slightly in tin then turn out on to a wire tray.

*Almond cake*

## 44  *Economical Madeira cake*

4 oz. margarine
4 oz. castor sugar
8 oz. flour (with plain flour
   use 2 level teaspoons
   baking powder)
2 eggs

1 teaspoon grated lemon rind
milk to mix
little sugar
pieces candied lemon peel for
   top of cake

Cream together margarine and sugar until soft and light. Sieve flour and baking powder, if used, together. Beat eggs. Add eggs and flour alternately to margarine mixture, with lemon rind and enough milk to make a soft consistency. Put into greased and floured 7-inch cake tin, sprinkling a little sugar on top and putting on pieces of lemon peel. Bake for 1¼ hours in middle of a moderate oven (375°F.—Gas Mark 4).

*Economical Madeira cake*

## 45  *Rich Madeira cake*

6 oz. butter
6 oz. castor sugar
8 oz. flour (with plain flour
   use 2 level teaspoons baking
   powder)

3 eggs and very little milk *or*
   4 eggs and no milk
little sugar
pieces candied lemon peel for
   top of cake

Method as for economical Madeira cake (Recipe 44) but bake for 1½-1¾ hours in centre of very moderate oven (350°F.—Gas Mark 3).

## 46 Diabetic Madeira cake
### 1 piece = 10 C. IP.F.
### 93 CALORIES

2 oz. margarine
2 oz. sugar
2 eggs

3 oz. self-raising flour
grated lemon *or* orange rind

Cream margarine and sugar. Beat in eggs one at a time. Stir in flour by degrees. Beat well adding little grated orange or lemon rind. Cook in centre of very moderate oven for about 45 minutes. Cut into 12 even-sized pieces.

---

## 47 Rich cherry cake

Ingredients and method of mixing as rich Madeira cake (Recipe 45) but use 1 level teaspoon baking powder and plain flour if possible, 3 eggs and NO MILK. Add about 6-8 oz. halved glacé cherries, which should be rolled in flour.
If you wish to be absolutely certain the cherries will stay evenly distributed, wash off the syrup, dry and flour.

---

## 48 Economical cherry cake

Ingredients and method of mixing as economical Madeira cake (Recipe 44) but add 4 oz. halved and floured glacé cherries.

---

## 49 Rich currant cake

Ingredients and method of mixing as rich Madeira cake (Recipe 45) but add about 8 oz. currants.

---

## 50 Economical currant cake

Ingredients and method of mixing as economical Madeira cake (Recipe 44) but add about 6-8 oz. currants.

---

## 51 Rich chocolate cake

Ingredients and method of mixing as rich Madeira cake (Recipe 45), but use 6 oz. flour, 2 oz. chocolate powder instead of 8 oz. flour.

---

## 52 Economical chocolate cake

Ingredients and method of mixing as economical Madeira cake (Recipe 44) but use 7 oz. flour, 1 oz. cocoa powder instead of 8 oz. flour. When creaming the margarine and sugar add 1 level tablespoon golden syrup.

---

## 53 Coffee cakes

Either the rich or the economical Madeira cakes (Recipes 44 or 45) can be used as a basis for coffee cakes. The coffee flavourings can be put in either as liquid coffee essence (do not dilute this), strong coffee or diluted soluble coffee powder. On the other hand soluble powder can be used dry, and sieved with the flour. If using soluble coffee powder dry, use 2-3 teaspoons and omit this amount of flour. If using liquid coffee in some form, use to mix instead of milk.

---

## 54 Lemon cakes

Either the rich or economical Madeira cakes (Recipes 44 or 45) can be used for a light lemon cake. Cream the finely grated rind of 1 or 2 lemons with the margarine and sugar and add lemon juice to blend instead of milk. A little crystallised lemon peel can be used in the cake is wished.

---

## 55 Orange cakes

Either the rich or economical Madeira cakes (Recipes 44 or 45) can be used for a light orange cake. Cream the finely grated rind of 2 or 3 oranges with the margarine and sugar and add orange juice to blend instead of milk. A little crystallised orange peel can be used in the cake is wished.

---

## 56 Seed cakes

Either the rich or economical Madeira cakes (Recipes 44 or 45) can be used for a seed cake. Add a dessertspoon caraway seeds with the flour. Sprinkle the top of the cake with sugar and a few seeds before baking.

---

## 57 Potato cake

4 oz. short crust pastry
  (Recipe 252)
little jam

*Filling*
3 oz. margarine
3 oz. sugar
few drops vanilla essence *or*
  lemon juice *or* almond
  essence

1 egg
8 oz. cooked potato, mashed
  without milk or margarine
1 oz. chopped candied peel
1 oz. flour
½ teaspoon baking powder
3 oz. mixed dried fruit

Roll out the pastry thinly, and line a deep plate or flan ring. Spread thinly with jam. Cream together margarine, sugar and essence, then work in other ingredients. Spread over jam and bake for 30 minutes in the centre of the oven, allowing 20 minutes in a hot oven (450°F.—Gas Mark 7), and the rest of the time at 400°F.—Gas Mark 5. The filling should be firm and the pastry crisp.
**Note**
If the potatoes have been mashed already with margarine and milk, omit some of the margarine and egg from the recipe.

## 58 Dorset apple cake

4 oz. margarine *or* margarine
and fat mixed
8 oz. flour (with plain flour
use 2 level teaspoons baking
powder)

4 oz. sugar
2 oz. currants
8 oz. chopped apple, fairly
sweet variety
little milk

Rub fat into the flour (which should first be sieved with baking powder, if used).
Add sugar and currants, then the chopped apple. Mix with enough milk to
make a stiff dough.
Grease a large flat sandwich tin and spread with the mixture. Put into centre of
moderately hot oven (400°F.—Gas Mark 5) for about an hour, lowering the
heat slightly after the first half hour if cake is becoming too brown. Turn out, cut
into fingers and serve with butter and brown sugar.

## 59 Potato apple cake

5 oz. butter
8 oz. self-raising flour
¼ teaspoon powdered
cinnamon
4 oz. castor sugar

4 oz. cooked sieved potato
2 large cooking apples
2 eggs
little milk

Rub the butter into the sifted flour and cinnamon. Stir in the sugar, potato
and very thinly sliced apples. Add the beaten eggs and mix to a fairly soft consistency. If necessary add a little cold milk. Place mixture in a greased loaf
or cake tin and bake in centre of moderate oven (375°F.—Gas Mark 4) for
1-1¼ hours. Dredge with icing or castor sugar.

*Potato scones; potato apple cake*

## 60 Cornflour cake

4 oz. cornflour
1 level teaspoon baking
powder
2 oz. margarine

3 oz. sugar
2 eggs
grated rind 1 lemon

Sift cornflour and baking powder together. Cream margarine and sugar well,
then gradually beat in the eggs, then the cornflour and lastly the lemon rind.
Put into a well greased and floured 7-inch tin and bake for approximately
30 minutes in the centre of a moderately hot oven (375-400°F.—Gas Mark 4-5).

2. Boiled fruit cake

3. Walnut cherry gâteau

# SPONGES AND EASY-TO-MAKE GÂTEAUX

Many people feel that sponge cakes are extremely difficult. As a matter of fact, when once you have achieved the 'art' or 'knack' they can be extremely simple.
Read the following instructions rather carefully, for the way you put the ingredients together is probably more important in a sponge cake than in any other.

## 61 *To make good sponge cakes*

Sieve flour well.
Be careful how you FOLD it into the egg and sugar or margarine and sugar mixture. Overhandling of the flour spoils more sponge cakes than anything else.

In the type of recipe that whisks eggs and sugar do make certain the mixture really IS thick before adding flour.
In the type of mixture where butter or margarine or cooking fat and sugar are creamed make certain they are really well creamed before adding eggs and flour.
Do NOT add the beaten egg too quickly, otherwise the mixture will curdle.
At the first sign of curdling FOLD in a little flour.
Test the cake carefully before taking from the oven—press gently but firmly in the centre of the cake to make certain it is firm.
With the light type of sponge allow to stand for a few minutes before turning out of the tin. With the extra light sponge, in which egg whites are stiffly beaten and added to the mixture, INVERT the cake tin over the wire rack and allow cake to drop out when ready.
Cool away from a draught.

## 62 *Successful whisked sponge cakes*

The true sponge cake, in which either the whole eggs are whisked with the sugar, or to give an even lighter result the egg yolks alone are whisked then the stiffly beaten whites put in at the end, needs careful handling.
Remember:
1 Beat the eggs until really thick and fluffy. An egg whisk is essential, an electric whisk ideal. If you do it over hot water by standing bowl above a saucepan of HOT (not boiling) water be very careful that the egg mixture does not get too hot, and always continue whisking after you remove from the heat.
2 The way in which you put the flour in is very important—this should be *folded* in with a metal spoon with a flick of your wrist. Make sure it is thoroughly absorbed by the egg mixture—but *never* over-beat.
3 DON'T keep this type of cake waiting before it is baked.

## 63 *Sponge Sandwich (whisking method)*

3 large eggs, at least day old
4 oz. castor sugar
3 oz. flour (½ level teaspoon baking powder can be added with plain flour)

1 tablespoon hot water
1 oz. melted butter *or* margarine—if cake is to be kept for day or two

Put the eggs and sugar into a basin and whisk hard until thick. You will get a lighter result if NOT whisked over hot water. FOLD in the well sieved flour with baking powder, if used, carefully and gently with a metal spoon. FOLD in water and margarine or butter. Grease and flour or grease and coat with equal quantities of flour and sugar two 7-inch sandwich tins. Divide the mixture between them and bake for 10-12 minutes near top of really hot oven—with gas it is a good idea to heat the oven on 8 then turn to 6 or 7 when cakes go in. With electricity heat to 450-475°F. then re-set oven to 425°F. when cakes go in. Test by pressing gently but firmly in the centre of the cakes. When firm they are cooked. Take out of oven, leave for a minute, tap tins sharply then turn on to a rack. COOL AWAY FROM A DRAUGHT. Sandwich together with jam, and dust on top with sieved icing sugar.

## 64 *Chocolate sponge*

As above, but omit ½ oz. flour and add ½ oz. cocoa powder, *or* omit 1 oz. flour and use 1½ oz. drinking chocolate powder instead. Fill with whipped cream, cover with icing sugar *or* chocolate icing (Recipe 372).

## 65 *Sponge cake*

Use Recipe 63, but instead of baking in 2 sandwich tins use a 7-inch cake tin, which should be prepared in the same way. Bake the cake in the centre of a moderate oven (375°F.—Gas Mark 4) for approximately 35 minutes. Test as described in Recipe 63, remove tin from oven, leave for a few minutes, then invert over a wire cake rack, allow to drop out. If cake sticks, shake tin very firmly before turning over rack again.

## 66 *Luxury sponge*

2 tablespoons butter
5 eggs
8 oz. castor sugar

6 oz. flour (with plain flour
use 1½ level teaspoons
baking powder)
vanilla essence

Melt butter, but allow to cool. Whisk egg yolks and sugar until thick and creamy. Fold in *very well sifted flour* with baking powder, if used, then the stiffly beaten egg whites, essence and melted butter. Pour into either two 9-inch buttered sandwich tins, which should be dusted also with equal quantities of flour and castor sugar; or one 8-inch cake tin. If using one tin, bake in the centre of a moderate oven for approximately 50-60 minutes (350-375°F.—Gas Mark 3-4). If using the two sandwich tins, bake just above the middle of the oven and make certain you have plenty of room in the tins, because this mixture rises. Allow approximately 25 minutes for the sandwich cakes in a moderate oven (375°F.—Gas Mark 4).

## 67 *Coffee sponge*

As Recipe 63, using 1 tablespoon coffee essence instead of hot water, or 1 teaspoon soluble coffee powder dissolved in 3 teaspoons water. Fill with whipped cream and cover top and sides with coffee icing (Recipe 373). Press flaked almonds into icing.

## 68 *Swiss roll*

*For a large Swiss roll tin (approximately 9 × 14 inches) use ingredients as Recipe 63*
*For a smaller Swiss roll tin (approximately 7 × 11 inches) use:*

2 large eggs
3 oz. castor sugar
2 oz. flour (just under ½
teaspoon baking powder
with plain flour)

1½ dessertspoons hot water
¾ oz. melted butter
warmed jam and castor sugar

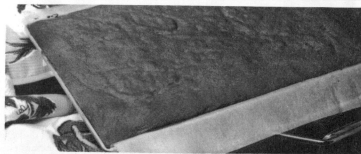

*Swiss roll 1 The mixture ready for rolling.*

Method of mixing is exactly the same as Recipe 63. Line the Swiss roll tin with well greased greaseproof paper. You will find it easier to get a flat surface if you grease the tin, under the paper, slightly. To obtain neat corners to the paper cut down these with scissors. Pour in the mixture, and bake near the top of a hot oven (425-450°F.—Gas Mark 6-7) for approximately 7-10 minutes. Some people find they obtain a better result if they bake at a very hot oven temperature (475°F.—Gas Mark 8). Test rather early during the cooking period for the first time you make this in your cooker, since the roll will tend to crack if over-baked.

While the cake is cooking WARM the jam; this must not be too hot.

Put a sheet of greaseproof paper ready, and sprinkle lavishly with castor sugar.

When the roll is ready, invert tin over the sugared paper. Remove the paper on the bottom of the cake. If this is at all difficult all you need to do is brush it with cold water (on a pastry brush). Cut off the crisp edges, spread with jam.

To facilitate easy rolling make a shallow cut in the roll about 1 inch from the end nearest you, then fold this over firmly. Use the paper to help in rolling firmly. Allow to cool away from a draught. IF THE ROLL IS A LITTLE OVER-BAKED roll on a damp tea cloth instead of sugared paper. Lift off the cloth and dredge with castor sugar. IF YOU WISH TO FILL WITH CREAM roll the paper inside the roll or use a second sheet of paper and place this on the sponge and roll. When cold gently unroll and fill with whipped cream; re-roll.

*Swiss roll 2 The mixture turned on to sugared greaseproof paper.*

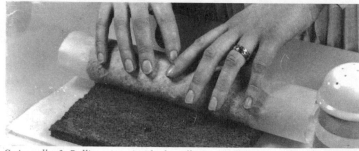

*Swiss roll 3 Rolling paper inside the roll.*

## 69 *Almond Swiss roll*

Ingredients as above, but add a little almond essence to the eggs and sugar when whisking. Put the mixture into the tin, and sprinkle LIGHTLY with very finely shredded almonds. Bake and roll as before. If the almonds have become rather crisp you may need to roll on a DAMP TEA CLOTH instead of on the paper.

## 70 *Chocolate Swiss roll*

3 eggs
3 oz. castor sugar
2½ oz. flour (with plain flour
use ½ teaspoon baking
powder)

1 tablespoon cocoa
fresh *or* butter cream (Recipe
387), for filling

Whisk eggs and sugar until thick, light and fluffy. Carefully fold in sieved flour with baking powder, if used, and cocoa. Pour into a greased and lined Swiss roll tin. Bake near top of hot oven (425-450°F.—Gas Mark 6-7) for about 10-12 minutes. When cooked turn at once on to a piece of sugared greaseproof paper. Trim edges with a sharp knife and carefully roll up so that greaseproof paper is rolled inside. Allow to cool and then gently unroll. Remove paper. Spread evenly with cream and roll up again. Sprinkle with castor sugar.
*(Illustrated in colour plate 4).*

## 71 Orange or lemon Swiss roll

Ingredients as Recipe 68, but use orange or lemon juice instead of hot water. This should be heated. To give a stronger flavour add a little VERY FINELY grated orange or lemon rind to the eggs and sugar. Fill with warmed lemon or orange marmalade or curd.

## 72 Coffee Swiss roll

Ingredients as Recipe 68, but use very strong coffee instead of water; this should be heated. Fill with warmed apricot jam or if you wish to fill with cream roll sponge with paper inside, then when cold un-roll, spread with whipped cream and re-roll.

In the chocolate Swiss roll it is suggested you roll with the sugared paper inside. Some people find this difficult, in which case put a second piece of greaseproof paper on top of cake and roll this inside the sponge.

## 73 Marzipan and cherry Swiss roll

Ingredients as Recipe 68, but when the cake is cooked spread with very soft marzipan (Recipe 385) mixed with chopped glacé cherries. To give the soft marzipan use the ordinary recipe, but add enough extra egg or milk to give the consistency of a very thick cream.

## 74 Frosted roll

3 oz. flour (with plain flour use ½ level teaspoon baking powder)
2 eggs
2 oz. castor sugar
1 tablespoon hot water
2 tablespoons warm jam

*To decorate*
lemon glacé icing made with 8 oz. sugar etc. (Recipe 374)
crystallised pineapple *or* ginger

Sieve together the flour and baking powder, if used. Whisk the eggs and sugar over a basin of hot water until the mixture is thick and will hold its shape. Add the hot water, then lightly fold in the sieved flour. Spread the mixture into a greaseproof paper lined Swiss roll tin and bake near top of a hot oven (425°F.—Gas Mark 6) for 8-12 minutes. Turn out on to greaseproof paper lightly dusted with castor sugar. Spread immediately with the warmed jam, trim away crisp edge and roll up firmly. When cold pour over the glacé icing and decorate, when half set, with small pieces of crystallised pineapple or crystallised ginger.

*Frosted roll*

## 75 Creaming method for sponges

Although the whisking method for making sponges is thought by many to produce the best type of cake, the creamed sponge is extremely popular. If correctly made it should be very light, have a sponge texture, and it does keep better.

As stressed in Number 61 it is essential to cream fat and sugar well—until they are light in colour and very soft. Do not melt the fat in this type of recipe, as that will exclude the air and the sponge will not be as good. The very best way to cream is to use your hands. This softens the mixture and will give the best opportunity to soften rather hard fat quickly. Beat the eggs in gradually, then add the sieved flour VERY GENTLY. A wooden spoon can be used for creaming (if you do not wish to use your hands) and adding the eggs, but a metal spoon is necessary when folding in the flour.

## 76 *Victoria sandwich*

8 oz. flour (with plain flour 2
level teaspoons baking
powder)
8 oz. margarine *or* butter
8 oz. castor sugar

4 medium-sized eggs (if the
eggs are unusually small,
use a dessertspoon water to
make up the extra liquid)

Quantities of ingredients are often written as the weight of eggs in fat, sugar and flour and if you wish you can still continue to weigh in this manner, putting the eggs—still in their shells—on the scales in place of weights. You are fairly safe, though, in assuming that the weight of an average egg is 2 oz., so that you would use the following ingredients to make an 8 to 9-inch sandwich cake. Use half quantities for 6-inch sandwich tins or 6 oz. flour, etc. for 7 to 7½-inch tins.

Sieve flour and baking powder, if used, together. Cream margarine and sugar until soft and white. Break eggs into a cup to ensure each one is good before beating thoroughly in a basin. Add a little of the beaten egg to the margarine mixture and stir carefully. Add a little flour and stir gently. Continue in this way, adding egg and flour alternately until thoroughly mixed. Grease and flour two 8-inch sandwich tins carefully and divide the mixture equally between them. Spread slightly away from the centre, so that the 2 halves will be flat. Bake for a good 20 minutes in a moderate oven (375-400°F.—Gas Mark 4-5). When using a gas oven either put the tins side by side on a shelf just about 2 rungs from the top of the oven, or put one under the other. With electric oven or solid fuel put one about the second rung from the top and one the second rung from the bottom, or have tins side by side on same shelf. Test by pressing gently but firmly on top and if no impression is left by the finger the cake is ready to come out of the oven. Turn out of the tins on to a wire rack. It is quite a good idea to give the tins a sharp tap on the table before attempting to turn out the cakes, so loosening the cake away from the sides and bottom of the tin.
When cold sandwich together with jam and sprinkle with icing sugar.

*Victoria sandwich*

## 77 *Coffee sandwich*

Ingredients as above, but instead of 8 oz. flour in the large sponge use 8½ oz. and add 1 tablespoon coffee essence or 3 teaspoons soluble coffee blended with 1 tablespoon water. It is a good idea to add this to the eggs to prevent curdling. Fill with jam, cream or coffee butter icing (Recipe 389) and cover with sieved icing sugar or coffee icing (Recipe 373).

## 78 *Chocolate sandwich*

Ingredients as above, but instead of 8 oz. flour in the large sponge use a good 7 oz. flour and a scant 1 oz. cocoa powder. Sieve together well. Fill with jam, cream or chocolate butter icing (Recipe 388) and cover with sieved icing sugar or chocolate butter icing (Recipe 388) or chocolate glacé icing (Recipe 372). A less usual result is obtained by filling and covering with coffee icing.

## 79 *Economical Victoria sandwich*

8 oz. flour (with plain flour 2
level teaspoons baking
powder)
4-5 oz. margarine *or* butter

4-5 oz. sugar
2-3 eggs
water to mix

Method as Victoria sandwich, Recipe 76, but when the flour has been added fold in enough water to give a soft creamy consistency. As this is a less rich mixture it should be baked at the higher temperature given in Recipe 76.

## 80 *Lemon or orange sandwich*

Ingredients as Victoria sandwich, but add grated rind of 1 or 2 lemons or oranges when creaming fat and sugar. Omit 1 egg in the large sized sponge and add 2-3 tablespoons fruit juice. Use 3 medium-sized eggs in the sponge using 6 oz. flour etc., and add 1 good tablespoon fruit juice; use 2 really small or 1 large and 1 small egg in the sponge using 4 oz. flour and add a small tablespoon fruit juice. Fill with jam, curd or fruit flavoured butter icing (Recipes 390, 391) and cover with fruit flavoured glacé icing (Recipes 374, 375).

## 81 *Coconut sponge*

Use Recipe 76. Omit 2 oz. flour in the large cake and use 2 oz. desiccated coconut, or omit 1½ oz. flour in the cake using 6 oz. flour etc., and use the same amount of coconut. In the smallest sponge omit 1 oz. flour and use this amount of desiccated coconut. Fill with cream or apricot jam, sieved icing sugar or coconut to cover.

## 82 *Wonder sponge*

4 oz. margarine
4 oz. castor sugar
1 dessertspoon honey
2 eggs, unbeaten

5 oz. self-raising flour and
½ level teaspoon baking
powder
3 tablespoons milk

Slice up the margarine and put it into a slightly warm mixing bowl together with all the remaining ingredients. Beat with a wooden spoon for ½-1 minute until smooth. Spread the mixture in a greased and floured deep 7-inch cake tin. Bake in the centre of a moderate oven (375°F.—Gas Mark 4) for 35-40 minutes.

## 83 Swiss roll with fat

2 oz. margarine
2 oz. castor sugar
2 medium eggs

3 oz. flour (with plain flour
¾ teaspoon baking powder)
jam
castor sugar to sprinkle

Cream the margarine and sugar well, gradually beat in the eggs then fold in the sieved flour with baking powder, if used. Test the mixture for consistency and it should flow easily from the spoon. If it does not do this then fold in a little WARM water. Pour into a 7 × 11 inch Swiss roll tin, and bake for about 10 minutes near the top of a moderately hot oven (400°F.—Gas Mark 5). Warm the jam and when the cake is cooked turn on to well sugared paper, or a damp cloth. Spread with the jam and roll firmly.

For various hints on rolling, and for variations in flavour, see Recipes 68-73. This type of Swiss roll is not as easy to roll for the first time, but of course keeps better as there is a higher proportion of fat in it.

*Swiss roll with fat*

## 84 Mandarin cream sponge

ingredients as for Victoria
sandwich (Recipe 76)

mandarin orange segments
whipped cream

When cold sandwich together, and cover top with well drained mandarin orange segments and whipped cream.

## 85 Using Genoese pastry

Many people are surprised to find that Genoese pastry is really a type of sponge cake, but made richer and firmer by adding a high percentage of butter. The method of mixing is as described in Recipe 62 for the whisking method of sponge cakes. It is an ideal cake for small fancies or *petits fours*, being firm to ice with an excellent texture.

## 86 Genoese pastry

3 large eggs
4 oz. castor sugar
3 oz. flour (with plain flour
use ½ teaspoon baking
powder)

4 oz. melted butter, allowed
to cool

Put eggs and sugar into a basin and stand over a saucepan of hot water. Whisk together until thick. Take basin off heat and continue to whisk until egg mixture is cold. *Fold* in flour—which should be sieved with baking powder, if used—then melted butter. This is a case where the use of butter is well justified, for if making this mixture a day or so before decorating it keeps so much better. For *petits fours* line a tin measuring approximately 10 × 8 inches with greased and floured greaseproof paper and bake near top of a moderately hot oven (400°F—Gas Mark 5) for approximately 14 minutes until firm and pale golden in colour. Turn out of tin straight away. Alternatively, bake in 2 sandwich tins. When cold cut into small shapes and ice as wished.

## 87 Chocolate custard sponge

5 oz. self-raising flour
1 oz. vanilla flavoured custard powder
1 oz. cocoa powder

6 oz. margarine
6 oz. castor sugar
3 eggs
1 tablespoon milk

Sieve the flour, custard powder and cocoa powder twice. Cream margarine and sugar together till light and fluffy then add the eggs, one at a time, beating thoroughly after each addition. Fold in half the flour mixture with a metal spoon, stir in the milk then fold in remaining flour mixture. Place the mixture in two 8-inch greased sandwich tins and bake at 375°F.—Gas Mark 5 for 25-30 minutes, till well risen and springy to the touch. Turn out on to a wire tray. When cold sandwich together with chocolate butter cream (Recipe 88), and dust the top with sieved icing sugar.

Sieving the flour, custard powder and cocoa.

Beating in the eggs.

Folding in the sieved flour mixture.

The cakes sandwiched together with chocolate butter cream.

## 88 Chocolate butter cream

3 oz. icing sugar
1 dessertspoon cocoa powder
2 oz. butter

1 dessertspoon hot water
few drops vanilla essence

Sift icing sugar and cocoa together then cream with the butter till light in texture and paler in colour. Add the water and essence and beat in thoroughly.

## 89 Golden sponge cakes

5 oz. margarine
4-5 oz. sugar
3 level dessertspoons golden syrup
10 oz. plain flour (with 4

level teaspoons baking powder; with self-raising flour use 1 teaspoon)
1 egg
milk to mix

Cream margarine, sugar and syrup. Sieve flour and baking powder. Beat egg well, add to margarine. Next stir in flour and milk alternately. Put into tin 8 × 12 inches lined with greased greaseproof paper, then bake for approximately 25 minutes near top of hot oven (450°F.—Gas Mark 7). Cut into required shapes.
*To decorate*
Use water icing (Recipe 371) on some cakes, jam then coconut on others, butter icing (Recipe 387) on the rest. The sponge is thick enough to split and put jam through the middle.

## 90 Pineapple and cherry cream basket

6 oz. margarine *or* butter
6 oz. castor sugar
3 eggs
vanilla essence
6 oz. flour (with plain flour use 1½ level teaspoons baking powder)

1 tablespoon cocoa powder

*To decorate*
cream
pineapple
cherries

Grease three 7-inch sandwich tins. Cream butter and sugar until fluffy. Beat in whisked eggs. Add vanilla essence. Fold in sieved flour, warm water to form a soft dropping consistency. Spread one-third into one sandwich tin. Into the remaining mixture fold sieved cocoa adding more warm water to keep the required consistency. Divide between other two sandwich tins. Bake in moderate oven (375°F.—Gas Mark 4) for about 20 minutes.
Whip cream until thick. Use half cream to sandwich chocolate and vanilla sponge, latter being placed on top. Spread remaining cream over this. Cut second chocolate sponge into half and place one half flat on top of cream. Arrange pineapple and cherries on uncovered cream. Add the other chocolate sponge half to form the open basket lid.

Add more cherries and pineapple to lower layer of cream. Sprinkle with sieved icing sugar.

## 91 *Sponge fingers*

2 large eggs
3 oz. castor sugar
2 oz. flour (with plain flour

use ½ teaspoon baking
powder)
little extra sugar

Put the eggs and sugar into a basin and whisk until thick and creamy. For further details on whisking method see Number 62. Fold in the sieved flour. Either pipe the mixture on to flat well greased baking tins (using a cloth or nylon bag and a large plain éclair pipe) or put into sponge finger tins. These should be well greased and floured. Shake castor sugar on top of the cakes, and bake for approximately 7-10 minutes near the top of a moderately hot oven (400°F. —Gas Mark 5).

## 92 *Savoys*

Ingredients as Recipe 91, and method of mixing the same, but instead of making finger shapes either pipe into small rounds or put teaspoons of the mixture on to the trays. When cooked sandwich together with jam or cream.

## 93 *Small sponge cakes*

Ingredients and method of mixing as Recipe 91 but put the mixture into proper small oblong sponge cake tins, which should be well greased and dusted with a mixture of flour and sugar. As these are slightly deeper you will find the cakes will take a little longer to bake so put in the oven just above the centre. Dredge rather lavishly with sugar before baking and allow approximately 12-14 minutes cooking.

## 94 *Raspberry baskets*

Ingredients and method of mixing as Recipe 91, but bake in small well greased and floured patty tins. Turn out and when cold top with whipped cream, frozen, canned or fresh raspberries. Make handles of moistened angelica.

## 95 *Dream sponge*

4 oz. margarine
6 oz. castor sugar
3 egg yolks
6 oz. flour (with plain flour
use 1½ level teaspoons
baking powder)
4 egg whites

little milk to mix (sour if
possible)

*Filling*
whipped cream
jam
sieved icing sugar

Cream together the margarine and sugar; this is a little harder than usual, as you have a higher proportion of sugar. Gradually beat in the egg yolks, the sieved flour, and lastly fold in the stiffly beaten egg whites. Add enough milk to give a really soft consistency. Divide between two 7-inch greased and floured sandwich tins, and bake just above the centre of a moderate oven (375°F.—Gas Mark 4). Sandwich together with whipped cream and jam, and cover the top with sieved icing sugar.

## 96 *Lady Baltimore cake*

ingredients as for dream sponge (Recipe 95)

*Filling*
American frosting made with
12 oz. sugar etc. (Recipe
(396)

3 oz. seedless raisins
3 oz. walnuts, chopped
2 oz. figs, finely chopped
1 oz. whole walnuts

Mix half frosting with raisins, chopped walnuts and figs. Sandwich cake with this. Cover top of cake with rest of frosting and decorate with whole walnuts.

## 97 *Cream star cake*

ingredients as for dream sponge (Recipe 95)

*Filling*
4 tablespoons redcurrant jelly
4 tablespoons whipped cream

*Icing and Decoration*
4 tablespoons redcurrant jelly
1 level teaspoon cornflour
2 tablespoons water
whipped cream

Make the dream sponge and when cold sandwich together with the 4 tablespoons redcurrant jelly and cream. Put the redcurrant jelly and cornflour blended with the water into a saucepan, bring to the boil and cook, stirring all the time, until thick and clear. Cool slightly, then spread over the top of the cake. When quite firm stand a star shaped cutter in the centre of the cake and fill this shape with piped whipped cream.

## 98 *Banana cream sponge*

ingredients as for dream sponge (Recipe 95)

*Filling*
2 *or* 3 bananas, mashed
icing sugar

few drops lemon juice
whipped cream

Make the dream sponge, and when cold sandwich together with the bananas, mashed with a little icing sugar and lemon juice and whipped cream. Cover the top of the cake with sieved icing sugar.

## 99  Raspberry gâteau

ingredients as for dream sponge (Recipe 95)

*Filling*
fresh raspberries or raspberry
  jam
whipped cream

*Icing and decoration*
1 level teaspoon cornflour
1 tablespoon water
4 tablespoons raspberry jam
whipped cream

Sandwich cooked dream sponge together with jam or crushed fruit and cream. Blend the cornflour with the water, put into a saucepan with 4 tablespoons jam and boil together until thick and clear. Spread on top of the cake and decorate with piped whipped cream.

## 100  Fiesta cream gâteau

4 oz. plain flour
2 level teaspoons baking
  powder
3 eggs
4 oz. castor sugar
4 tablespoons milk
2 oz. butter *or* margarine

*Filling and topping*
1 lemon, orange *or*
  strawberry jelly
½ pint boiling water
3 tablespoons evaporated
  milk

Sift flour with baking powder three times. Whisk eggs till creamy, add sugar then re-whisk (with the bowl over hot water) till the mixture is pale in colour and thick enough in consistency to hold its own weight. Lightly fold in flour and baking powder with a metal spoon then quickly stir in milk, heated to boiling point with the butter. Divide equally between two 8-inch sandwich tins, each well-greased and lined at the bottom with a round of greaseproof paper. Place near the top of a moderately hot oven (400°F.—Gas Mark 5) and bake for approximately 17 minutes. Turn out and cool on a wire tray.
Dissolve jelly in the boiling water, then divide equally in half. Leave in a cool place. When one half has thickened whisk briskly till frothy. Add evaporated milk to this and re-whisk till almost set. Sandwich cake together with two-thirds of the whisked milk jelly, then pile rest of this in the *centre* of the top of the cake. Decorate edges with the second half of jelly. This should be chopped, when set, with a knife on damp greaseproof paper.

## 101  Ginger sponge sandwich

4 oz. margarine *or* butter
4 oz. castor sugar
2 large eggs
4 oz. self-raising flour (with
  plain flour use 1 teaspoon
  baking powder)
1 level teaspoon ground
  ginger
good pinch mixed spice
grated rind 1 lemon

*Filling*
2 oz. butter
3 oz. icing sugar
½ teaspoon lemon rind, grated
½ teaspoon ground ginger
2 oz. crystallised ginger

Cream together margarine or butter and sugar until soft and light. Add beaten eggs and sieved dry ingredients alternately, taking care not to overbeat. Lastly add lemon rind. Put into two 6-inch greased and floured tins and bake for about 17 minutes near top of a moderately hot oven (375-400°F.—Gas Mark 4-5). Turn out and cool on a wire rack.

*Filling*
Cream together butter and sieved icing sugar. Add grated lemon rind and ground ginger. Chop crystallised ginger and mix into half the filling. Spread between cakes and then swirl rest of plain butter icing on top. Decorate with pieces of ginger.

## 102  Honey sponge

4 oz. flour (with plain flour
  use 1½ level teaspoons
  baking powder)
½ level teaspoon
  bicarbonate soda
pinch cinnamon *or* mixed
  spice

3 oz. margarine
3 level tablespoons honey
2 eggs
3 tablespoons water

Sieve dry ingredients. Cream margarine, honey and add eggs and flour alternately. Lastly stir in water. Put into two 6-inch well greased sandwich tins and bake near top of moderately hot oven (400°F.—Gas Mark 5) for approximately 20 minutes.

## 103  Mocha Shell Cake

*Sponge cake*
4 oz. luxury margarine
4 oz. castor sugar
1 dessertspoon honey
2 eggs, unbeaten
5 oz. self-raising flour
½ level teaspoon baking powder
3 tablespoons milk
2 teaspoons coffee essence

*Filling*
1 tablespoon honey
2 oz. plain chocolate
2 oz. margarine
3-4 drops vanilla essence

*Icing*
6 oz. icing sugar
2 oz. margarine
1 dessertspoon honey
1 tablespoon milk
2 teaspoons coffee essence

Slice the margarine and put it into a slightly warmed mixing bowl together with the remaining ingredients for the sponge. Beat well with a wooden spoon for about one minute until smooth. Spread the mixture into two greased and floured 7-inch sandwich tins and bake in a moderately hot oven (400°F.—Gas Mark 5) for approximately 20 minutes. Remove from tin and cool.

*Filling*
Melt the honey and chocolate together in a basin over a pan of hot water. Cool slightly then add, a spoonful at a time, to the well beaten margarine. Add flavouring. Cool to a spreading consistency and use to sandwich the two sponges together.

*Icing*
Sift the icing sugar into a bowl. Put the margarine into a small pan with the remaining ingredients. Stir over gentle heat until the margarine has melted. Pour into the icing sugar and stir with a wooden spoon until smooth. Coat the cake with icing. Ridge the top by drawing the tip of a table knife from side to side across the cake. With the back of the knife draw the tip down across the ridges so that all the lines meet at one point, making a shell design.

*(Illustrated in colour plate 23.)*

## 104 *Orange and chocolate gâteau*

4 oz. flour (with plain flour
   use 1 level teaspoon
   baking powder)
4 oz. margarine *or* butter
4 oz. castor sugar
2 eggs
finely grated rind 1 orange

*Filling and decoration*
4 oz. margarine *or* butter
6 oz. icing sugar
2 level dessertspoons cocoa
1 dessertspoon milk
1 can mandarin oranges
few drops vanilla essence
chocolate vermicelli

Sieve flour. Cream together margarine and sugar till light in colour and fluffy. Add the eggs, one at a time, beating thoroughly after each addition; beat in the orange rind. Gently fold in the flour with a metal spoon, then turn the mixture into two well greased 7-inch sandwich tins. Bake side by side on third shelf from the top of a moderate oven (375°F.—Gas Mark 4) for approximately 25 minutes. Turn out on to a wire tray to cool.

*For filling and decoration*
Cream together the margarine, sieved icing sugar and cocoa until light, fluffy and smooth. Add the milk and essence and beat in thoroughly.
Spread one of the cakes with half the chocolate cream, cover with half well drained mandarin orange sections, then top with the other sandwich cake. Spread top and sides with cream, press chocolate vermicelli round the sides and finally decorate with rosettes, using remaining chocolate cream, round the edges and with mandarin orange sections placed attractively on the top. Chill slightly before serving.

*Orange and chocolate gâteau*

## 105 *Orange and lemon sponge*

6 oz. margarine
6 oz. castor sugar
grated rind 1 orange
grated rind 1 lemon
2 large eggs
6 oz. flour (with plain flour
   use 1½ teaspoons baking
   powder)

1 tablespoon orange juice
1 tablespoon lemon juice

*Filling and decoration*
lemon curd
icing sugar
lemon *or* orange slices

Cream margarine, sugar and fruit rinds very well. Gradually beat in eggs, then sieved flour, and finally add fruit juices. Put into two greased and floured 7-inch or 8-inch sandwich tins and bake for approximately 25 minutes in a moderate oven (375°F.—Gas Mark 4). Turn out and cool; sandwich together with lemon curd. Dust the top of cake with icing sugar and decorate with lemon or orange slices.

## 106 *Harlequin cake*

Most plain sponge mixtures can be turned into a delightfully variegated or Harlequin cake. Choose your favourite sponge (see recipes in this chapter) and when the mixture is prepared, divide it into three or even four portions. Leave one portion plain, tint another pink with cochineal, a third green with apple or sap green colouring. If you have four portions, the fourth can be coloured and flavoured with a little coffee or chocolate. Arrange blobs of the cake mixture into one large tin or sandwich tins and bake according to times and temperatures given in the specific recipe. One cake can be covered with butter icing (Recipe 387). For sandwich cakes, fill with cream or butter icing and then decorate on top as liked.

## 107 *First birthday cake*

You will find the sponge recipes in this section ideal for making a baby's birthday cake, particularly those with little fat, i.e. Recipe 63 onwards.
To give a very fine texture omit 1 oz. flour and use 1 oz. cornflour instead; this gives an ideal texture for small children.

*For other birthday cakes see Recipes 153, 154, 180.*

# CAKES FROM OTHER COUNTRIES

In this section I have collected some of the interesting types of cakes to be found in other countries.

America, with its tradition of light fluffy cakes, provides chiffon cakes, upside-down cakes which make a good sweet as well as a delicious recipe for tea, and shortcakes that can be used throughout the year with various fruits.

Australia is famous for its use of meringues and you will find Pavlova cake and other meringue recipes.

As well as these, some of the delicious cakes from Europe have been included.

## 108 *American fruit cake*

3 oz. cooking fat
4 oz. castor sugar
3 eggs
½ teaspoon vanilla essence
4 oz. plain flour
½ level teaspoon baking powder
½ level teaspoon salt

4 oz. walnut halves
8 oz. stoned dates
3 oz. whole seedless raisins
4 oz. chopped candied peel
3 oz. red maraschino cherries
3 oz. green maraschino cherries (use red if green not available)

Cream cooking fat and sugar together until light and fluffy. Add eggs one at a time, beating each in thoroughly. If mixture shows any signs of curdling beat in a little of the sieved flour. Beat in the vanilla essence. Fold in the sieved flour, baking powder and salt. Mix the walnut halves, whole dates, whole raisins, mixed peel and whole cherries and fold into the cake mixture. Place in a cake tin about 8 × 6 inches, lined with grease-proof paper and brushed with melted cooking fat. Bake in a slow oven (300°F.—Gas Mark 2) in the middle of the oven for 2¼-2½ hours. Allow to cool slightly in the tin, then turn out and finish cooling on a cake rack. Decorate top if liked.

*American fruit cake*

## 109 *American apple cake*

10 oz. flour
1 oz. castor sugar
3 level teaspoons baking powder*
¾ teaspoon salt
4 oz. butter *or* margarine

2 oz. grated cheese
about ¼ pint milk
4 eating apples
2-3 oz. brown sugar
½ teaspoon cinnamon
1 tablespoon melted butter

* *With self-raising flour use 1 level teaspoon baking powder*

Sift flour, castor sugar, baking powder and salt together. Rub in butter or margarine and then mix in cheese. Add sufficient milk to make a soft but not sticky dough. Turn out on floured board and knead lightly. Pat out dough in an ungreased Swiss roll tin, approximately 7 × 10 inches. Pare and core apples and slice thinly. Arrange in rows across dough. Sprinkle with brown sugar and cinnamon mixed together. Brush over with melted butter. Bake just above centre of a hot oven (425°F.—Gas Mark 6) for 25 minutes till golden brown. (*Illustrated in colour plate 5*).

This cake is excellent with morning coffee.

## 110 *American bride's cake*

At weddings in America it is usual to make a sponge, like a Victoria sandwich (generally called a butter sponge), to cut at the wedding and to send pieces of rich fruit cake after the wedding—this is often known as the bridegroom's cake.

The coloured plate 15 illustrates a typical American bride's cake.

For a 3-tier cake you will need Victoria sandwich mixture using 1 lb. 4 oz. butter or margarine, see Recipe 76 and butter icing using 2 lb. butter etc., see Recipe 387 and a little cochineal, if liked.

Make and bake the Victoria sandwich mixture in 10-inch, 8-inch and 6-inch cake tins. When cold, coat each cake with half the butter icing tinted with a few drops of cochineal to give a pale pink colour. Put one cake on top of the other in a pyramid, then pipe with coloured butter icing. If preferred the cakes can be coated with American frosting, then piped with butter icing.

(*Illustrated in colour plate 6.*)

## 111 Devil's food cake

6 oz. flour (with plain flour
  1¼ level teaspoons baking
  powder)
½ teaspoon salt
2 oz. butter
8 oz. sugar
2 eggs
4 tablespoons sour milk *or*
  carton yoghourt
6 full tablespoons boiling
  black coffee

2 oz. plain melted chocolate
1 level teaspoon bicarbonate
  of soda
1 teaspoon vanilla essence
seven-minute icing
  (Recipe 404)
chocolate glacé icing
  (Recipe 372)

Sift flour, baking powder, if used, and salt. Cream butter and sugar. Beat until light. Beat in eggs a little at a time. Add a little flour and sour milk alternately and end by adding flour. Pour boiling coffee on to melted chocolate and add bicarbonate of soda. Cool slightly and add to mixture. Stir in vanilla essence. Bake in two well greased 9-inch sandwich tins just above centre of moderate oven (375°F. —Gas Mark 4) for about 25 minutes. When cool fill and frost with seven-minute icing. Complete decoration by running a thin trail of chocolate glacé icing across the top.

## 112 Mocha Devil's food cake

Ingredients as above, but replace 1 teaspoon flour with 1 teaspoon instant coffee powder. When cake is cooked cover with coffee butter icing (Recipe 389) decorate with grated chocolate.

## 113 Coconut devil's food cake

Ingredients as above, but omit 2 oz. flour and use 2 oz. desiccated coconut instead. Make chocolate butter icing (Recipe 388) but add 1 oz. coconut to this. Decorate with a little desiccated coconut on top.

## 114 Walnut devil's food cake

Ingredients as above, but use 2 oz. finely chopped walnuts in place of 2 oz. flour. Decorate as before, arranging halved walnuts on top of cake.

## 115 Almond devil's food cake

Ingredients as above, but use 2 oz. ground almonds in place of 2 oz. flour. Decorate as before, but arrange blanched almonds on top of the cake.

## 116 Peach and cherry upside-down cake

*Cake mixture*
6 oz. flour (with plain flour
  use 1½ teaspoons baking
  powder)
2 oz. fine semolina
4 oz. butter *or* margarine
4 oz. castor sugar
¼ teaspoon vanilla essence
2 eggs

3 dessertspoons milk

*Topping*
1 oz. melted butter *or*
  margarine
peach slices and canned red
  cherries, well drained
1 oz. brown sugar

*For topping*
Melt butter or margarine and pour into an 8-inch square cake tin. Arrange peach slices and cherries attractively in the bottom of the tin; sprinkle with brown sugar.

*For cake*
Sieve flour with baking powder, if used, and semolina into a basin. Cream fat and sugar together until light and fluffy. Add essence. Beat in half the eggs thoroughly, then fold in flour and semolina alternately with remaining eggs and milk. Spread mixture evenly over fruit and sugar.
Bake at 400°F.—Gas Mark 5 for 15 minutes and at 335°F.—Gas Mark 3 for 45 minutes. Turn out and cool on a wire tray.

*Arranging peaches and cherries in the bottom of the tin*

*Placing the cake mixture on top of the fruit and sugar*

*The cooked Peach and cherry upside-down cake*

**117** *Apple upside-down cake*

Apples are an excellent choice in an upside-down cake.
Slice the apples, peeling if liked and place in the bottom of the tin. Put over the topping as above, adding cherries, dates for extra colour. Use either a plain cake mixture or Gingerbread (Recipe 20 or 29). Bake at temperatures and for time given in these recipes.
(*Illustrated on the frontispiece*).

**118** *Apricot upside-down cake*

As Recipe 116, using apricots instead of peaches. A little grated lemon rind and lemon juice instead of milk can be added to the cake mixture.

**119** *Banana upside-down cake*

Cut 4 bananas into fairly thick slices, sprinkle with lemon juice. Use 2 oz. brown sugar and 2 oz. butter for the topping.

**120** *Chocolate pear upside-down cake*

Arrange either canned pears or dessert pears at the bottom of the tin. If using dessert pears a little extra sugar can be used, and the pears sprinkled with lemon juice to keep them a good colour. Omit 1 oz. flour and use 1 oz. cocoa powder in the cake recipe.

**121** *Coffee upside-down cake*

Any fruit can be used at the bottom of the tin, but pears or apricots with a few chopped walnuts or glacé cherries are particularly good. Mix with 3 dessertspoons very strong coffee instead of milk.

**122** *Spiced upside-down cake*

Any fruit can be used at the bottom of the tin, but apples or pears are particularly suitable; add a few raisins to apples. Sieve 1 teaspoon mixed spice, and ½ teaspoon cinnamon or nutmeg with the flour in the cake. A few sultanas or raisins can also be used in the cake mixture.

**123** *Angel cake*

6-8 egg whites
4 oz. flour
½ teaspoon cream of tartar

6 oz. castor sugar
few drops vanilla essence

Beat egg whites until very stiff. Sieve flour and cream of tartar. Fold first sugar, then flour, into egg whites, lastly folding in vanilla essence. Butter an angel tin, i.e. a ring mould, 8 to 9-inches in diameter and put in mixture. Bake for just 1 hour in a low oven (300°F.—Gas Mark 2). Do not turn cake out of tin straight away but turn it upside down over a wire sieve, and it should drop from tin when cold.
**Note**
If egg whites are very fresh and therefore whip up to a very dry mixture, it is advisable to fold 1 tablespoon water into mixture at the end. This gives a softer texture. When cake is quite cold cover with water icing (Recipe 371) and decorate with cherries.

**124** *Chocolate angel cake (1)*

Ingredients as above, but use 2 oz. chocolate powder instead of same amount of flour. Sieve flour, chocolate powder and cream of tartar at least twice to make certain mixture is smooth. Ice with coffee or chocolate flavoured icing (Recipe 373 or 372).

**125** *Chocolate angel cake (2)*

Ingredients as Angel Cake but omit 1 oz. flour and use 1 oz. cocoa powder instead. Sieve cocoa with flour very carefully. Cover cake when baked and cool with white glacé icing (Recipe 371) and if liked melt about 2 oz. chocolate and trickle this over top of icing.

**126** *Lemon angel cake*

Ingredients as Angel Cake but mix very finely grated rind of 2 lemons with sugar and add 1 tablespoon lemon juice to mixture instead of water. Dust with sieved icing sugar or coat with lemon glacé icing (Recipe 374).

**127** *Coffee angel cake*

Ingredients as Angel Cake but take out 2 teaspoons of flour, and add 2 teaspoons instant coffee instead. When cake is cool, cover with coffee glacé icing (Recipe 373) and decorate with nuts.

**128** *Chiffon cake*

7 oz. flour (with plain flour use 1½ level teaspoons baking powder)
pinch salt
1 level teaspoon baking powder

½ level teaspoon cream of tartar
5 oz. cooking fat
5 oz. castor sugar
3 egg whites
3 tablespoons milk
white fudge icing (Recipe 407)

Sieve flour, salt, baking powder and cream of tartar together. Cream fat and sugar in a bowl until light and fluffy. Add whites of egg one at a time and beat thoroughly. Fold in flour and milk. Divide mixture between two 7-inch sandwich tins lined with greased paper, and smooth over tops. Bake in middle of moderately hot oven (400°F.—Gas Mark 5) for 30-35 minutes. Turn out to cool on a cake rack.
When cool sandwich together with icing, cover top and sides with remaining icing.

*Chiffon cake*

## 129  Chocolate chiffon cake

Use ingredients as above, but use 1 oz. cocoa powder instead of 1 oz. flour or use 2 oz. chocolate powder instead of 1½ oz. flour. Decorate with white or chocolate fudge icing (Recipes 407 or 408).

## 130  Coffee chiffon cake

Use ingredients as above, but mix with strong coffee instead of milk. Diluted instant coffee is excellent for this. Decorate with white or chocolate or coffee fudge icing (Recipes 407, 408, 409).

## 131  Lemon chiffon cake

Use ingredients as above, but add finely grated rind of 1 or 2 lemons and mix with lemon juice instead of milk. Decorate with white or lemon fudge icing (Recipes 407 or 410).

## 132  Orange chiffon cake

Use ingredients as above, but add finely grated rind of 2 oranges and mix with orange juice instead of milk. Decorate with white or orange fudge icing (Recipes 407 or 410).

## 133  Banana chiffon cake

9 oz. flour (with plain flour
  2 level teaspoons of baking
  powder)
12 oz. castor sugar
½ teaspoon salt
8 tablespoons olive *or*
  corn oil

5 medium-sized egg yolks
2-3 bananas, mashed
1 dessertspoon fresh lemon
  juice
½ level teaspoon cream of
  tartar
7 egg whites

Sift together flour with baking powder, if used, sugar, and salt into mixing bowl. Make a well in dry ingredients and add oil, egg yolks, bananas and lemon juice. Beat until smooth. Add cream of tartar to egg whites. Beat egg whites in a large mixing bowl until they form very stiff peaks. DO NOT UNDERBEAT. Gradually and gently fold banana mixture into egg whites, until just blended. DO NOT STIR. Pour into ungreased, 10-inch ring tin, 4-inches deep. Bake in a very moderate oven (325-350°F.—Gas Mark 3) about 1 hour 5 minutes. Immediately turn pan upside down, placing the tube part over a small necked bottle or funnel so that the pan is elevated about 1 inch above surface of table. Let cake hang until cold. Loosen cake from sides and tube of pan with spatula. Turn pan over and tap edge sharply to loosen cake. Spread top and sides of cake with frosting (Recipe 396) if liked.

## 134 Cherry merry-go-round

4 oz. self-raising flour
2 level teaspoons cinnamon
4 oz. margarine
4 oz. castor sugar
2 eggs
1 tablespoon milk

*Filling and topping*
black cherry jam
whipped fresh cream *or*
  butter cream
fresh cherries

Sift flour with cinnamon. Cream fat and sugar together till light
and fluffy, then add eggs, one at a time, beating thoroughly after
each addition. Fold in half quantity of flour, add milk then fold
in rest of flour. Turn mixture into a 7-inch round cake tin, well
greased and lined with greaseproof paper. Bake in centre of
moderate oven (375°F.—Gas Mark 4) for 40-45 minutes. Turn
out on to a wire tray. When cool, cut through the centre and
sandwich together with jam. Spread cream thickly over top and
decorate with rings of stoned cherries.

*Cherry merry-go-round*

## 135 Golden shortcake

5 oz. flour (with plain flour
  use 2 level teaspoons
  baking powder)
1 oz. custard powder
4 oz. margarine

4 oz. castor sugar
2 eggs
1 small can pears
canned *or* fresh strawberries
whipped cream

Sieve flour and custard powder together with baking powder, if used. Rub in
margarine, add sugar and beaten eggs. DO NOT ADD ANY MORE
MOISTURE. Divide mixture between two 7-inch greased and floured sandwich
tins and bake for about 20 minutes just above centre of moderately hot oven
(400-425°F.—Gas Mark 5-6). Turn out very carefully, as this is very short when
hot; when cold sandwich together with a mixture of pears and strawberries.
Smooth whipped cream over the top and decorate with whole strawberries.
*(Illustrated in colour plate 7)*.

## 136 Strawberry shortcake

3 oz. plain flour
1½ oz. cornflour
2 level teaspoons baking
  powder
4 oz. margarine
2 oz. castor sugar
1 egg

*Filling and topping*
1 small punnet fresh
  strawberries
¼ pint double cream
1 egg white

Sieve flour, cornflour and baking powder. Cream together margarine and sugar until light and fluffy. Add egg and beat in
thoroughly. Add sieved flour, cornflour and baking powder and
fold in lightly with a metal spoon. Grease a 7-inch sandwich tin
and line bottom with a round of greased greaseproof paper.
Place mixture in tin, smooth flat on top and bake on second shelf
from top of moderate oven (400°F.—Gas Mark 5) for 25-30
minutes. Cool on a wire tray. Cut shortcake through centre.
Prepare strawberries. Keep back about 8 of the best to decorate
top and slice remainder. Place double cream in a bowl, whisk
until stiff. Whisk egg white until stiff. Fold egg white into cream.
Mix half cream with sliced strawberries. Spread on to half of
shortcake. Place other half on top. Pile remaining cream on top
and decorate with a circle of strawberries.

*Strawberry shortcake*

## 137 Pavlova cake

3 egg whites
8-12 oz. castor sugar
6 oz. can pure cream or
½ pint fresh double cream

1 small can fruit or
8 oz. fresh fruit

Draw on a greaseproof paper an oval or round, 8-inches in diameter, place on a greased tray. Whisk egg whites and castor sugar until very stiff. Colour to suit taste. Place in a forcing bag fitted with a vegetable star pipe. Pipe round pencil shape and over entire centre. Pipe round edge building it up to form a wall. Bake in a very slow oven (200°F.—Gas Mark 0-¼) for 2-3 hours until dry and crisp. Lift off the tray and paper whilst still warm. Cool, and store in airtight tin. When required to serve, open the tin of cream without shaking, pour off the whey and fill the meringue case with thick cream in layers with the fruit. If fresh cream is used whip it until thick.

## 138 Chocolate meringue gâteau

*Meringue*
2 egg whites
cochineal
4 oz. castor sugar

*Cake mixture*
6 oz. margarine
6 oz. castor sugar
2 whole eggs
2 egg yolks (from meringues)

8 oz. flour (with plain flour
  use 2 level teaspoons
  baking powder)
1 tablespoon cocoa powder

*To decorate*
fresh *or* butter cream
sliced canned peaches
meringues

Whisk egg whites until very stiff. Whisk in cochineal and half sugar. Fold in remaining sugar. Pile or pipe on to a greased, floured baking tray and allow to dry off in very cool oven (200-250°F.—Gas Mark 0-¼). When cooked these may be stored in an air-tight tin until required.
Cream fat and sugar until light and fluffy. Beat in gradually, lightly whisked eggs. Fold in sieved flour with baking powder, if used, and cocoa, adding sufficient water to form soft dropping consistency. Put one-third of mixture into prepared 6-inch sandwich tin. Bake near top of oven (375°F.—Gas Mark 4) for 20 minutes. Turn remaining mixture into prepared 8 to 8½-inch sandwich tin and bake in same oven for about 40 minutes. Allow to cool.
Spread cream over centre of large sponge, and stand smaller one on it. Arrange sliced peaches in centre and around uncovered edge of bottom layer. Pipe cream around sides of smaller sponge and complete decoration with meringues and cream.
(*Illustrated in colour on the jacket.*)

## 139 Summer party delight

*Meringue*
3 egg whites
6 oz. castor sugar
3 teaspoons cocoa powder

*Decoration*
fresh cream *or* ice cream
apricots
canned *or* glacé cherries
angelica

Put egg whites into bowl, and whisk until very stiff. Whisk in sieved cocoa and half sugar. Fold in remaining sugar. Make meringue base by using a ½-inch plain vegetable piping tube, and piping on to a well oiled baking tray. Cover with greaseproof paper after 30 minutes. Put into very cool oven (200-250°F.— Gas Mark 0-¼) and allow to dry out until firm. This takes about 3 hours at least. store in tin until required.
**To decorate**
Whip cream until just thick. Pile or pipe on to meringue base. Decorate with canned apricots, cherries and angelica.

## 140 Australian meringue cake

3 oz. seeded raisins
2 tablespoons sherry
2 oz. margarine
2 oz. castor sugar
2 egg yolks
4 oz. flour (with plain flour
  1 level teaspoon baking
  powder)

pinch salt
2 tablespoons milk

*For meringue*
2 egg whites
3 oz. castor sugar
! oz. blanched almonds,
  chopped

Cut up raisins and soak in sherry for about 30 minutes. Cream together margarine and sugar until light and fluffy, and beat in egg yolks. Sieve flour with baking powder, if used, and salt and mix in alternately with milk. Drain raisins and add half to cake mixture together with any sherry left from soaking. Put mixture into a greased 7-inch sandwich tin and sprinkle over remaining raisins. Bake just about centre of a moderate oven (375°F.—Gas Mark 4) for 20 minutes, and meanwhile prepare meringue topping.
Whisk egg whites stiffly and gradually whisk in sugar and fold in almonds. Pipe the meringue mixture on top of the cake and continue to cook for a further 35-40 minutes, lowering heat to 275-300°F.—Gas Mark 1-2. Remove carefully from tin on to a tea towel, and then on to a cake rack. Serve cold cut into slices.

*Australian meringue cake*

## 141 Maori kisses (from New Zealand)

3 oz. margarine
3 oz. castor sugar
4 oz. plain flour
1 level tablespoon cocoa
   powder
1 level teaspoon baking
   powder

pinch salt
1 oz. walnuts, chopped
6 oz. dates, chopped
1 tablespoon milk
vanilla butter icing
   (Recipe 387)

Cream together margarine and sugar until light and fluffy. Work
in sieved flour, cocoa, baking powder and salt. Add walnuts,
dates and milk, and mix well together. Place in teaspoonfuls on
a greased baking sheet and cook in a moderate oven (375°F.—
Gas Mark 4) for 15-20 minutes. Sandwich together with vanilla
butter icing when cold.

*Maori kisses*

## 142 Koeksisters (from South Africa) (pronounced Cooksisters)

1 oz. margarine
8 oz. plain flour
pinch salt
2 level teaspoons baking
   powder
1 egg

4-5 tablespoons milk

*Syrup*
1 lb. granulated sugar
½ pint water
1 stick cinnamon

Rub margarine into sieved flour and salt. Add baking powder,
well-beaten egg and sufficient milk to form a rolling dough.
Roll out to a 12-inch rectangle, ¼-inch thick and from this cut
strips 3 × 1 inch. Cut each strip into 3 lengthways, not completely
cutting through to end and plait, pinching together at end. Fry
a few at a time in oil heated to approximately 375°F. until a
golden brown. Drain and dip at once into cold syrup. Lift out
and put on cake rack. To make syrup put ingredients into a
strong pan and stir over gentle heat until sugar dissolves. Boil
rapidly for 1 minute. The stick of cinnamon can be removed
from the syrup, rinsed, dried and used again. Koeksisters keep
well but must be kept apart in the tin.

*Koeksisters*

## 143 Chinese rice cakes

4 oz. plain flour
1 oz. ground rice
½ oz. cornflour
3 oz. sugar
pinch salt
¼ level teaspoon baking
   powder

3 oz. lard
½ egg
1 tablespoon water
¼ teaspoon almond essence
few shelled almonds

Sift flour, ground rice, cornflour, sugar, salt and baking powder together into a
mixing bowl. Rub in lard until mixture resembles fine breadcrumbs then mix
to a smooth dough with ½ egg, water and almond essence. Form dough into
small balls and place on a greased baking tray. Place an almond on top of each
cake and brush with egg. Bake 15-20 minutes in centre of moderately hot oven
(400°F.—Gas Mark 5).

4. Chocolate swiss roll

5. American apple cake

# 144 Gâteau St. Honoré

4 oz. flaky pastry (Recipe 257)
1 dessertspoon castor sugar

*Choux pastry*
¼ pint water
2 oz. margarine
4 oz. plain flour
3 eggs

*Filling for buns*
¼ pint double cream
1 good teaspoon sugar

*Decoration for buns*
syrup made with 2 tablespoons
  sugar and 1 tablespoon
  water
chopped pistachio nuts

*Filling for Gâteau*
½ pint milk
little lemon rind *or*
  vanilla essence
2 eggs
1 oz. sugar
1 oz. powdered gelatine
¼ pint double cream

*Decoration for gâteau*
glacé cherries
angelica

Roll the flaky pastry into a round, measuring 10-inches in diameter. Prick with fork and sprinkle with castor sugar. Transfer to a baking tray and leave aside whilst preparing the choux pastry.

**Choux pastry**

Bring water and margarine to boil in pan. Add flour and mix thoroughly. Allow to cool and gradually work in whisked eggs. Put portion into piping bag with ¼-inch plain tube, and pipe two circles round the edge of the pastry. Bake in a hot oven (450°F.—Gas Mark 7) for 15-20 minutes. Cool on a wire tray. Fill a second piping bag, fitted with a ½-inch plain tube and pipe small rounds the size of a penny on to a greased baking tray. Cover with a roasting pan and bake at 450°F.—Gas Mark 7 for 15-20 minutes. Allow to cool and fill each bun with whipped sweetened cream. Dip top of each bun in the syrup made by boiling sugar and water together and sprinkle with chopped pistachio nuts. Dip the base of each bun in the syrup and place in position on top of the choux pastry rings circling the flaky pastry base.

**Filling**

Bring milk and flavouring to the boil and pour over well beaten eggs. Strain, add sugar, and stir over a gentle heat till thick. Allow to cool. Allow gelatine to soften in 2 tablespoons cold water and then allow to dissolve in a pan over a gentle heat. Add the dissolved gelatine to the cooling egg mixture. When almost set add the unsweetened whipped cream. Fill pastry ring. For added decoration place a glacé cherry and two 'leaves' of angelica between each bun on top of cake.

*Gâteau St. Honore*

## 145 Linzer Torte

4 oz. plain flour
(preferably plain)
1 level teaspoon cinnamon
3 oz. butter *or* margarine
2 oz. castor sugar

3 oz. ground almonds
1 egg yolk
4 oz. raspberry jam
egg for brushing

Sieve together flour and cinnamon, then rub in butter or margarine. Add sugar and almonds and sufficient beaten egg yolk to form a pliable paste. Chill for at least an hour, roll out three-quarters fairly thickly and line a well-greased 7-inch plain flan ring. Fill with raspberry jam and arrange strips of remaining pastry in a trellis pattern over the top. Mark all round edge with a fork then brush pastry with beaten egg. Bake in centre of moderately hot oven (400°F. —Gas Mark 5) for 30-40 minutes. Leave to cool before cutting and, if liked, coat top of torte thickly with sieved icing sugar before serving.

*Linzer Torte*

## 146 Sachertorte

scant 5 oz. flour
6 eggs
5 oz. chocolate
5 oz. butter
5 oz. icing sugar

*To decorate*
apricot jam
chocolate icing (Recipe 147)

Sift flour twice. Separate egg yolks and whites. Break chocolate into small pieces, add a tablespoon water and put in a warm place to melt. Cream butter with 4 oz. sugar, add egg yolks gradually. Add the melted chocolate (which must be soft but not hot) and stir well. Whisk egg whites until stiff, whisk in remaining 1 oz. sugar. Fold stiffly beaten egg whites into butter/chocolate mixture alternately with the flour. Bake in greased and floured 9-inch cake tin in centre of moderate oven (375°F.—Gas Mark 4) for 50-60 minutes. When cold spread with warmed apricot jam and chocolate icing (Recipe 147). This gâteau should not be very high and the thickness of the icing should about equal that of the apricot jam.

## 147 Chocolate icing

Break 6 oz. plain chocolate into small pieces, put to melt over hot water with 1 tablespoon water. Add a drop of olive oil. Stir constantly until mixture has thickened sufficiently to spread over gâteau.

## 148 Orange torte

4 oz. luxury margarine
3 oz. castor sugar
3 eggs
2 tablespoons orange juice
grated rind 1 orange
4 oz. self-raising flour ⎫ sieved
1 oz. cornflour ⎬ together
3 oz. ground almonds

*Orange icing*
3 oz. icing sugar
1 tablespoon water
2 egg yolks
grated rind 1 orange
¼ pint whipped double cream

Cream the margarine and sugar together until light and fluffy. Beat in the eggs one at a time, adding a little of the sieved flour with the second and third eggs. Beat in the orange juice and rind. Fold in flour and ground almonds. Divide the mixture into three and place in three 7-inch sandwich tins, previously brushed with melted margarine and lined with greaseproof paper. Bake in a very moderate oven (350°F.—Gas Mark 3) for 25-30 minutes. Remove and cool on a wire tray.

**To make the icing**

Place the icing sugar and water in a saucepan and dissolve over a gentle heat; continue heating until it clears completely. Leave to cool then add egg yolks and orange rind. Pour onto the cream and beat until thick and will hold its own shape. Sandwich the layers of torte together wich icing and cover the top. Smooth the top with the blade of a knife.

*Orange torte*

## 149 Swiss apple sponge
### An unusual dessert cake

1 oz. butter
about 2 oz. fine breadcrumbs
  *or* semi-sweet biscuit crumbs
4 small dessert apples
2 oz. blanched almonds
½ pint milk
1½ oz. semolina

4 oz. butter *or* margarine
4 oz. sugar
3 eggs
1 rounded teaspoon cinnamon
few blanched almonds to
  decorate
2 oz. raisins (optional)

Butter a small loose-bottomed cake tin (or better still a spring-form 8-inch cake tin) and coat with crumbs. Peel, core and slice apples. Chop almonds. Heat milk, stir in semolina, cook gently 3 minutes, stirring. Set aside to cool. Cream butter and sugar. Beat in egg yolks and cinnamon. Add almonds and raisins and stir in semolina mixture. Fold stiffly whisked egg whites in and then apple slices. Pour into prepared cake tin and bake in centre of a very moderate oven (350°F.—Gas Mark 4) for 1 hour 15 minutes. Serve hot or cold. Decorate with a few blanched almonds.

*Swiss apple sponge*

## 150 Rum gâteau

¼ oz. yeast
1 teaspoon sugar
4 tablespoons tepid milk
4 oz. plain flour
1 oz. currants (optional)
2 oz. margarine
2 eggs

*Syrup*
2-3 oz. golden syrup *or* sugar
¼ pint water
juice ½ lemon
1½-2 tablespoons rum

*To decorate*
cream
angelica

Cream the yeast with a teaspoon of sugar. Add the tepid milk and a sprinkling of flour. Put into a warm place for 20 minutes. Work in the rest of the flour, currants, the melted margarine and the beaten eggs. Grease a large tin and coat lightly with flour. Half fill with the mixture and put into a warm place to prove for 20-25 minutes, then bake for 30 minutes in the centre of a hot oven (450°F.—Gas Mark 7). Turn out of tin and prick with a knitting needle.

Boil sugar or syrup with water and lemon juice to a clear syrup. Add 1½-2 tablespoons rum. Pour over gâteau; decorate with cream and angelica.

## 151 *Rum baba*

Ingredients as Rum gâteau (Recipe 150), but instead of baking in 1 large tin, half fill warmed greased patty tins, or proper Baba tins. Prove for approximately 20 minutes, then bake near top of very hot oven (475°F.—Gas Mark 8) for a good 10 minutes. Turn out, prick with a knitting needle or skewer and soak in the syrup. Decorate with whipped cream when cold, cherries or nuts and angelica.

**Variations**

**Baba with fruit**

Use 2 oz. currants in the recipe and top with very thick apple purée and cream.

**Savarin**

Bake in a warmed ring tin for approximately 25 minutes in centre of hot oven (450°F.—Gas Mark 7).

**Savarin with fruit**

When baked fill the centre with fruit.

## 152 *Italian fritter cakes*
### *Dessert cakes*

| *Dessert cakes* | oil *or* fat for frying |
|---|---|
| 1 pint milk | 4 tablespoons apricot jam |
| ¼ teaspoon salt | 1 tablespoon water |
| 4 tablespoons semolina | 1 oz. blanched almonds, chopped |
| 2 tablespoons sugar | |
| 1 egg | 1 oz. glacé cherries |
| fine browned breadcrumbs | |

Warm the milk. Add salt and sprinkle in the semolina and sugar. Stir until the mixture comes to the boil and thickens. Pour while still hot into a shallow baking tray, rinsed with cold water. Allow to get quite cold and set. Turn out carefully and cut into small squares. Coat with beaten egg and breadcrumbs. Fry until golden brown. If shallow frying turn to brown both sides. Drain on crumpled kitchen paper.

The jam for the sauce can be sieved or left chunky. Heat it with the water. Remove from heat and add the sliced almonds and cherries. Pile the hot fritters on a serving dish and pour the hot sauce over them; serve at once. For extra creaminess beat an egg yolk into the cooked semolina and fold in the stiffly whisked egg white.

A similar Hungarian recipe has a sauce of hot raspberry jam. These cakes are delicious too if dusted with sugar and cinnamon as soon as they are fried, and served with or without butter.

To vary this recipe add chopped dates, raisins or currants. For extra flavour grated orange or lemon rind or vanilla essence can be added. Less sugar may be used.

# CAKES FOR SPECIAL OCCASIONS

In this section you will find cakes for every special occasion—from the traditional wedding and Christmas cake to more unusual shortcakes, etc. to serve when fruit is plentiful.

It is advisable to try out a cake, if possible, before the particular occasion, so that you are sure that it will be popular with your family and you are familiar with the method of making, baking and decorating.

## 153 *Happy birthday cakes*

| | |
|---|---|
| 8 oz. flour (with plain flour 2 teaspoons baking powder) | *Filling* 3 level tablespoons raspberry jam |
| 2 oz. fine semolina | |
| 8 oz. butter *or* margarine | |
| 8 oz. castor sugar | *Raspberry marshmallow frosting* |
| 4 eggs | 3 rounded tablespoons raspberry jam |
| ½ teaspoon vanilla essence | |
| 2 tablespoons milk | 1 egg white |

Sift flour and semolina into a basin. Cream fat and sugar together till light and fluffy, then add eggs, one at a time, beating thoroughly after each addition. (1 tablespoon of flour and semolina mixture added with each egg helps to prevent curdling.) Add essence, then lightly fold in flour alternately with milk. Transfer mixture to a greased and paper-lined 12 × 8 inches Swiss roll tin and bake in centre of moderate oven (400°F.—Gas Mark 5) for 35 minutes, until well-risen and firm to touch. Turn out on to a wire tray, remove paper and leave until cold. Cut cake into 5 rounds (keep remaining pieces for a party trifle) with a 3½-inch biscuit cutter. Split each in half then sandwich together with raspberry jam.

**Frosting**

Heat raspberry jam slowly, strain, return to pan and reheat gently. Whisk egg white till stiff and peaky then pour in hot jam. Re-whisk till frosting is cold and stiff enough for spreading. Spread over the cakes and top each one with a candle in a holder.

## 154 *Anniversary cake*

| | |
|---|---|
| 4 oz. butter *or* margarine | *Uncooked frosting* |
| 4 oz. castor sugar | 10 oz. icing sugar, sieved |
| grated rind 1 orange | 5 oz. butter |
| 3 eggs | 1 dessertspoon milk *or* mandarin orange syrup |
| 4 oz. flour (with plain flour 1 teaspoon baking powder) | *To decorate* |
| 4 oz. fine semolina | 1 small can mandarin oranges |
| 2 tablespoons strained orange juice | |

Cream butter or margarine and sugar and orange rind till light and fluffy. Beat in eggs one at a time. Stir in sifted flour with baking powder, if used, and semolina and then the orange juice. Turn into a well greased cake tin (about 7 × 3 inches deep) and bake in centre of a moderate oven (375°F.—Gas Mark 4) for 1-1¼ hours. To make the frosting, cream together icing sugar and butter until very light and fluffy. Beat in the milk. When cold cover top and sides smoothly with a layer of frosting. Pipe with remainder of frosting, using a large nozzle, or whirl it with a fork. Decorate with canned mandarin slices and place the required number of candles in a circle in centre of cake.

*Many of the other cakes, i.e. the rich Christmas cakes, Dundee cakes or sponge cakes can be used for birthday celebrations. See also Recipe 107 for first birthday cake.*

## 155 *Christening cake*

12 oz. plain flour
4 oz. fine semolina
12 oz. butter *or* margarine
12 oz. castor sugar
6 eggs
12 oz. each cleaned currants
  and sultanas
8 oz. chopped candied peel
6 oz. glacé cherries,
  quartered
4 oz. almonds, blanched and
  finely chopped

3 dessertspoons brandy,
  sherry or rose water

*To decorate*
almond paste made with
  12 oz. ground almonds
  (Recipe 385)
royal icing made with 2-2½ lb.
  icing sugar etc. (Recipe 382)

Sift flour and semolina. Cream fat and sugar till light and fluffy. Beat in eggs, one at a time, sifting in one rounded tablespoon flour and semolina with each egg to prevent curdling. Add fruit, peel, cherries, almonds and brandy and mix thoroughly. Lastly, stir in remaining flour and semolina. Transfer to a 10-inch round cake tin, well greased and lined with a double thickness of greaseproof paper and tie a thick band of newspaper round outside of tin. Bake in centre of slow oven (300°F.—Gas Mark 2) for 2 hours then reduce heat to very slow (275°F.—Gas Mark 1) for a further 2½-3 hours. If top of cake appears to be browning too rapidly, cover with brown paper. Leave at least 15 minutes before turning out of tin. Cool on a wire tray. Wrap in greaseproof paper or aluminium foil and store in an airtight tin for at least a week before decorating.

**To decorate**
Brush top and sides of cake with melted golden syrup, egg white or with 2 rounded tablespoons apricot jam, melted and sieved. Cover neatly with almond paste. See Number 383 for directions on coating with almond paste.
Spread icing thickly over top and sides of cake, smoothing with a palette knife dipped from time to time in hot water and shaken dry. Leave for a few days for icing to harden before decorating; if you wish to keep royal icing soft, cover with damp cloth (see Number 383).

**For piping**
Put a deep frill of fine lace or net round edge of a 12-inch cake board, securing with transparent adhesive tape, then stand cake on the board. Put selected ornament centrally on top of cake (fixing it with a little prepared icing) and decorate its base with one or two rows of piped shells or rosettes. Continue decoration along top and lower edges of cake, using a larger pipe for a bolder effect.
Scatter artificial rosebuds on frill. See Number 384 for directions on decorating and piping.

**Note**
You need approximately 1½-1¾ lb. icing sugar etc. for coating cake and 12 oz. for piping.

## 156 *Mincemeat upside-down cake*

2 oz. self-raising flour and
  ¾ level teaspoon baking
  powder *or* 2 oz. plain flour
  and 1¼ level teaspoons
  baking powder
1 level teaspoon mixed spice
2 oz. castor sugar
1½ oz. cooking fat

1 egg
1-2 teaspoons cold water
3-4 rounded tablespoons
  mincemeat

*To decorate*
roasted sliced almonds
glacé cherries

Sieve flour, baking powder, mixed spice and sugar into a bowl. Add fat, egg and water and beat for about 1 minute until all ingredients are well mixed. Brush a star-shape tin (or 7-inch square tin) with melted fat and place mincemeat evenly over bottom. Place cake mixture on top and smooth over. Bake in moderately hot oven (400°F.—Gas Mark 5, in middle of oven) for 25-30 minutes. Turn on to a warm dish and decorate with almonds and cherries.

## 157 *Scotch bun*

*Pastry*
12 oz. flour
¾ teaspoon baking powder
6 oz. whipped-up cooking fat
1 oz. sugar
pinch salt
egg to glaze

*Filling*
3-4 lb. dried fruit

4 oz. orange peel, chopped
8 oz. almonds, chopped
1 lb. flour
8 oz. sugar
1½ oz. mixed spice
½ oz. cream of tartar
½ oz. bicarbonate of soda
2 eggs
little milk

This should be made several weeks at least before it is to be eaten (by tradition at Hogmanay festival). Grease a 9-inch baking tin. Make pastry first: sieve flour with baking powder and rub in fat. Add sugar and salt, work into a stiff paste with water and roll out thinly. Line tin with paste, reserving enough to cover top. Prepare ingredients for filling, put into a large bowl and use just enough fresh milk to moisten, mixing with the hands. Put mixture into lined tin, damp edges of pastry, and cover with rest of pastry, prick all over with a fork and brush with beaten egg. Bake for 2 hours in a very moderate oven (350°F.—Gas Mark 3) then for 1-2 hours at 300°F.—Gas Mark 2. For half quantities use a 7-inch tin and bake for approximately 2¼-2½ hours.

*Scotch bun*

## 158 *Economical Christmas cake*

A traditional Christmas cake is a rich cake, but if your family prefers a less 'fruity' mixture use either of the Dundee cake recipes—Numbers 13 and 15. These cakes will not keep as well as a rich fruit cake so should not be made too long before Christmas. For a light type of cake, i.e. not dark and spiced, try White Christmas cake, Recipe 166.

## 159 *Christmas cake (1)*

8 oz. margarine
8 oz. brown sugar
1 teaspoon vanilla essence
1 teaspoon almond essence
2 tablespoons orange marmalade
4 eggs
8 oz. plain flour
2 oz. fine semolina
2-4 level teaspoons mixed spice
¼ level teaspoon salt
1 level teaspoon bicarbonate of soda
8 oz. raisins

8 oz. sultanas
8 oz. currants
8 oz. dates
4 oz. cherries
4 oz. figs
4 oz. chopped candied peel
4 oz. crystallised ginger
4 oz. chopped almonds (optional)
4 tablespoons brandy, sherry *or* strong black coffee

*To decorate*
marzipan (Recipe 385)
royal icing (Recipe 382)

Prepare cake tin with 3 linings of paper at bottom and sides and a band of brown paper round outside. Beat margarine, sugar and essence to a smooth cream. Beat in marmalade. Beat in eggs one at a time. Stir in sifted flour, semolina, spice, salt and crushed bicarbonate of soda. Add prepared fruit (seeded and chopped), peel and almonds. Stir in liquid. Turn into prepared tin, smoothing down evenly. Place in centre of slow oven and cook slowly, for a soft-outside cover for first half of cooking time with two thicknesses of paper. This quantity is for a 9 to 10-inch tin and takes about 4 hours in a slow oven (300°F.— Gas Mark 2). Double the above quantity is sufficient for a 12-inch tin and takes 5½-6 hours in a very slow oven (275°F.— Gas Mark 1). Half the above quantity is sufficient for a tin 5-6 inches in diameter and takes about 2½ hours in a very moderate oven (325-350°F.—Gas Mark 2-3). Test carefully to see if cooked (see Number 176). Leave in the tin for 30 minutes, turn out and cool on a wire tray.
Cover with marzipan and rough ice as shown in the photograph. Decorate with sprigs of holly and stars.

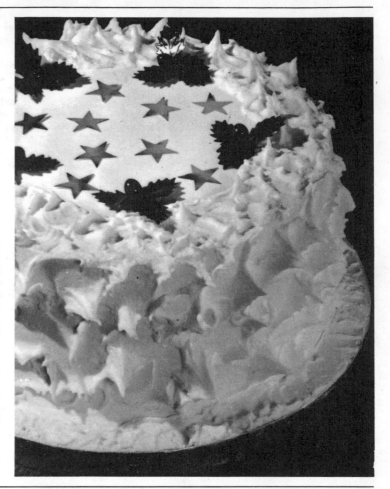

*Christmas cake*

## 160 *Christmas parcel cake*

6 oz. cooking fat
6 oz. soft brown sugar
4 eggs
2 rounded tablespoons treacle
grated rind 1 lemon
8 oz. plain flour
1 level teaspoon mixed spice
½ level teaspoon cinnamon
½ level teaspoon nutmeg
pinch salt
1 lb. currants
8 oz. sultanas

4 oz. raisins, stoned and chopped
3 oz. glacé cherries, chopped
3 oz. chopped candied peel
3 oz. almonds, chopped
2 oz. ground almonds
2 tablespoons brandy

*To decorate*
almond paste (Recipe 385)
royal icing (Recipe 382) *or* American frosting (Recipe 396)

Cream fat and sugar together until light and fluffy. Add eggs one at a time beating each in thoroughly before adding the next. Beat in treacle and lemon rind. Sieve flour, spices and salt together. Prepare and wash fruit, and fold in alternately with sieved flour and remainder of ingredients, lastly folding in brandy. Place in an oblong 10×8 inches tin brushed with melted fat and lined with greaseproof paper. Protect outside of tin with a double thickness of brown paper (or newspaper). Bake in the middle of a very slow oven (275°F.—Gas Mark 1) for about 3¾-4 hours. Test carefully (see Number 176).
Coat with almond paste and coloured royal icing (Recipe 382) or American frosting (Recipe 396). Decorate to make a parcel with fancy ribbon, almond paste label and a candle in a holder.

*Christmas parcel cake*

## 161 *Diabetic Christmas cake*
### *1 piece = 10 C. 3 P. 6F.*
### *106 CALORIES*

¼ oz. raisins
½ oz. currants
grated lemon rind
grated orange peel
little peel from sugarless
   marmalade
2 oz. margarine
1½ oz. sugar

3 oz. self-raising flour
1 oz. blanched almonds
½ wineglass brandy (optional)
2 eggs
pinch ground ginger *or*
   cinnamon
pinch mixed spice

Prepare fruit, cream margarine and sugar. Beat in eggs, one at a time. Stir in flour by degrees—add other ingredients and mix gently. Put into small greased cake tin and cook in centre of very moderate oven (350°F.—Gas Mark 3) for about 45 minutes to 1 hour. Turn out and cool on a wire rack. Cut into 12 even-sized pieces.

---

## 162 *Christmas Cake (2)*

*This makes 9-inch round or 8-inch square cake*

12 oz. flour, preferably plain
1 teaspoon cinnamon
1 teaspoon mixed spice
¼ teaspoon salt
4 oz. chopped candied peel
2 lb. dried fruit, preferably
   1 lb. currants, 8 oz. sultanas,
   8 oz. raisins
4 oz. cherries
4 oz. blanched almonds
finely grated rind 1 lemon

4 eggs
4 tablespoons milk *or* sherry
   *or* brandy
8 oz. margarine *or* butter
8 oz. sugar, preferably
   Demerara
1 tablespoon black treacle

*To decorate*
almond paste (Recipe 385)
royal icing (Recipe 382)

Sieve together all dry ingredients. Mix peel, fruit, cherries, lightly floured if very sticky, chopped almonds and lemon rind. Whisk eggs and brandy together. Cream margarine, sugar and black treacle until soft. Add flour and egg mixtures alternately to margarine—do not overbeat when mixing. Lastly, stir in fruit mixture. Put into an 8 to 9-inch tin lined with double thickness of greased greaseproof paper round sides, and with brown paper and greased greaseproof paper at bottom. Tie a double band of brown paper round outside of tin, standing well up above top of it. Put in middle of oven. Bake for 3¼-3½ hours at Gas Mark 3 for the first 1½ hours, then Gas Mark 2 for remainder of time. In electric oven put cake in at 300-350°F.—and after 1½ hours reduce heat to 275-300°F. See Number 176 for testing rich cakes. Cool in tin, then store in airtight tin. For a very moist cake, prick cold cake and pour over little sherry at intervals before icing. Make cake at least 3 weeks before Christmas. Cover with marzipan and royal icing a week before Christmas.
*(Illustrated in colour plate 8.)*

---

## 163 *Celebration cake*

12 oz. butter
8 oz. soft brown sugar
8 oz. black treacle
6 eggs
1 lb. 2 oz. self-raising flour or
   preferably plain flour and
   3 level teaspoons baking
   powder
finely grated rind of 2 large
   oranges
6 oz. quartered glacé cherries
6 oz. currants

*Orange Icing*
juice ½ orange (about 2
   tablespoons)
½ lb. sieved icing sugar

*For decoration*
1 6-inch orange candle
about 24 small pieces glacé
   orange and lemon slices
angelica

Well grease and line a 9-inch round cake tin and a 6-inch round cake tin. Cream together butter, sugar and treacle until soft and light. Gradually beat in eggs, then fold in sieved flour, with baking powder, if used, grated orange rind, cherries and currants. Put two-thirds of the mixture into the 9-inch tin and one-third into the 6-inch tin. Bake in the centre of a very moderate oven (350-375°F.—Gas Mark 3-4). Allow 1½ hours for the smaller cake and 2 hours for the larger. Lower the heat after 1 hour, if necessary. Turn out and cool. To make icing and decoration; gradually beat orange juice into sieved icing sugar until smooth and a coating consistency. Stand the larger cake upside down on cake stand. Spoon icing to within 2 inches of edge of cake allowing icing to trickle down sides. Place smaller cake upside down in centre of larger cake. Ice top of small cake and allow some of icing to trickle down sides. Place candle in centre of top cake, protected by a piece of foil. Take semi-circular orange and lemon glacé slices, snip along straight edge and turn into cones. Put thin strips of lemon slices in centre of cones to make 'stamens'. Place several cones around candle and bunches of cones on iced edge of bottom cake. Cut diamond shaped strips of angelica and place among cones.
*(Illustrated in colour plate 9.)*

## 164 Bûche de Noël (Yule Log)

2 oz. cooking fat
4 oz. castor sugar
2 eggs
4 oz. flour
  (with plain flour use level
  teaspoon baking powder)
1 tablespoon warm water

*Icing*
2 oz. cooking fat
6 oz. icing sugar, sieved
1-2 dessertspoons milk
2 oz. cocoa powder, sieved
2 oz. glacé fruits

Cream fat and half the sugar together, gradually add the remaining sugar. Beat until light and fluffy. Add eggs one at a time beating each in thoroughly. Fold in sieved flour and water. Place in a Swiss roll tin 12 × 8 inches lined with greaseproof paper brushed with melted fat. Bake near the top of a fairly hot oven (400°F.—Gas Mark 5) for 10-15 minutes. Turn out onto greaseproof paper, trim edges and roll up quickly with greaseproof paper and leave on a cake rack to cool. Cream the fat in a basin and gradually cream in icing sugar, adding a little milk to keep to a spreading consistency. Beat well until light and fluffy. Mix the glacé fruits into half the icing. Unroll the Swiss roll, spread with icing and re-roll. Beat the cocoa powder into the remaining icing and spread over the roll. Mark in lines with a fork. Decorate with sprigs of holly etc.

*Bûche de Noel*

## 165 Easy Christmas logs

A Christmas log cake is very popular, especially with the children. Recipe 164 has offered one suggestion for making this, but any Swiss roll (Recipe 68) can be used for the base. Fill with chocolate of coffee butter icing or try mixing grated chocolate into a whipped cream filling, or adding sieved chestnut purée to butter icing—which can be flavoured as desired.

When the cake is filled it should be iced with chocolate, coffee or some dark butter icing (Recipe 387 onwards); this should be marked to give the 'lines' on a tree trunk.

## 166 White Christmas cake

8 oz. margarine
8 oz. castor sugar
4 large eggs
12 oz. plain flour
1 level teaspoon baking
  powder
½ level teaspoon salt
8 oz. light coloured sultanas
8 oz. citron peel, chopped

4 oz. blanched almonds,
  chopped
4 oz. glacé cherries,
  quartered
2 oz. glacé pineapple,
  chopped
grated rind 1 lemon
1 tablespoon lemon juice
royal icing (Recipe 382)

Cream together margarine and castor sugar until light and fluffy. Beat in eggs thoroughly, adding one at a time. Sieve together flour, baking powder and salt, and fold into creamed mixture. Add prepared fruit, nuts, lemon rind and juice, and mix in evenly. Put mixture into a round 8-inch cake tin, double lined with greaseproof paper, and bake in centre of a very moderate oven (325°F.—Gas Mark 3) for 2½-3 hours. Cover with royal icing and decorate as wished. It is best to put on two layers of icing although this cake can be covered with marzipan if desired (Recipe 385) and iced afterwards.

*White Christmas cake*

## 167 Christmas biscuits

2 oz. margarine
2 oz. castor sugar
grated rind ½ lemon
½ beaten egg
1½ oz. ground almonds
4 oz. plain flour

*To decorate* (*optional*)
glacé cherries *or* angelica *or*
blanched almonds

Cream together margarine, sugar and lemon rind until light and fluffy. Beat in egg and ground almonds and lastly, mix in sieved flour. Form into a smooth ball and roll out to ½-inch thickness on a lightly floured pastry board. Cut into fancy shapes, brush with beaten egg or milk and decorate with glacé cherries, angelica or blanched almonds, if liked. Bake in centre of a moderate oven (375°F.—Gas Mark 4) to a very pale golden brown, about 15-20 minutes. Cool on a cake rack and store in an airtight tin.

*Christmas biscuits*

## 168 Vaniljekranse (Vanilla Rings)

3 oz. butter
4 oz. plain flour
1 small egg, or the yolk only
  of a large egg

3 oz. castor sugar
3 teaspoons vanilla essence
pinch salt

Rub butter into flour with fingertips until mixture is like fine breadcrumbs. Add beaten egg (do not whisk) or egg yolk, sugar, vanilla essence and salt. Mix dough with a wooden spoon. Knead lightly with fingers to make it smooth. Place soft dough in a forcing bag with a large nozzle and force out into rings 2 inches in diameter on a greased baking tray. Bake in centre of a very moderate oven (350°F.—Gas Mark 3) till light brown.

## 169 Fine ginger biscuits

1½ oz. butter
6 oz. plain flour
3 oz. castor sugar
½ teaspoon baking powder

1 tablespoon ground ginger
1 teaspoon cinnamon
1 small egg *or* ½ a large egg

Rub butter into flour until it is like fine breadcrumbs. Add rest of dry ingredients and mix to a dough with lightly beaten egg. Roll mixture into thin sausage shapes ½ inch in diameter and length of baking tray. Place these rolls about 1½ inches apart. Bake in centre of a moderate oven (375°F.—Gas Mark 4) until mixture turns a darker brown, approximately 8-10 minutes. When cooked cut into diamond-shaped pieces. Store in an airtight tin.

## 170 Jødekager (Jewish cake)

1 large egg, separated
4 oz. castor sugar
1¾ teaspoons cinnamon *or*
  cardamom

3 oz. butter
4 oz. plain flour
pinch salt
blanched almonds to decorate

Reserve white of egg, 1 oz. of sugar and 1 teaspoon of cinnamon or cardamom for glazing. Then rub butter into flour with fingertips till mixture is like fine breadcrumbs. Add egg yolk, sugar, salt and spice. Mix dough with a wooden spoon, kneading lightly with fingers to make it smooth. Roll out dough to ¼ inch thickness. Cut out biscuits using 1½-inch pastry cutter. Brush top of biscuits with egg white to which 1 oz. sugar and 1 teaspoon spice has been added. Place a blanched almond on each biscuit. Bake in a very moderate oven (350°F.—Gas Mark 3) for approximately 15 minutes.

## 171 Christmas cracker cake

2 oz. cooking fat
4 oz. castor sugar
2 eggs
3 oz. self-raising flour
1 oz. cocoa powder

1 tablespoon warm water
cream filling (Recipe 172)
marzipan made with 6 oz.
  ground almonds etc.
  (Recipe 385)
little jam

Cream fat and half sugar together, gradually adding remaining sugar until light and fluffy. Add eggs one at a time, beating each in thoroughly. Fold in sieved flour and cocoa, lastly adding water. Place in a Swiss roll tin 12 × 8 inches, lined with greaseproof paper and brushed with melted fat. Spread evenly and bake in a moderately hot oven (400°F.—Gas Mark 5 near top of oven) for 10-15 minutes. Turn out on to sugared greaseproof paper, trim edges and roll quickly. Leave until set and cold.
Make the cream filling. Carefully unroll cake, remove paper, spread with cream filling and re-roll. Make marzipan and knead well. Roll out to length and circumference of the cake. Brush cake first with a little boiled, sieved jam and cover with marzipan. Make paper ends to fit cake and decorate with holly.

## 172 Cream filling

1 rounded dessertspoon
cornflour
4 tablespoons milk
½ oz. cooking fat

1 rounded dessertspoon
castor sugar
vanilla essence

Mix cornflour to a smooth paste with a little cold milk. Boil remaining milk. Pour over blended cornflour. Return to saucepan and cook for 3 minutes, stirring continuously. Cover with damp greaseproof paper and leave to cool. Cream fat, sugar and vanilla essence together and whisk in cornflour mixture.

## 173 Kerstkrans (Dutch Ring)

4 oz. quick flaky pastry
(Recipe 258)

*Almond filling*
5 oz. ground almonds
5 oz. granulated sugar
1 small egg
grated rind 1 lemon

*Topping*
apricot jam
2 rounded tablespoons icing
sugar
1 tablespoon water
few drops lemon essence
glacé cherries
angelica

Make pastry. Mix ground almonds and sugar together then mix in egg and lemon rind. Knead well together. Roll into a long roll about 1 inch in diameter and 16-18 inches long.

Roll out pastry thinly to a strip one inch longer than almond filling and 4-inches wide. Place almond mixture on top of pastry, brush one edge of pastry with water and roll up loosely (making sure that seam comes underneath). Place roll on a baking sheet to form a ring. Join edges together carefully to make a secure seam. Brush over with egg or milk and prick with a fork. Bake near top of a hot oven (450°F.—Gas Mark 7) for 20-25 minutes.

Whilst still hot brush over top of cake with warmed apricot jam. Mix sieved icing and sugar with water and lemon essence to make a thin icing, and pour over jam. Allow to cool a little on baking sheet, then remove and cool on a cake rack. Decorate with halved cherries and angelica; if liked a sprig of holly or a red ribbon can be put on one side.

*Kerskrans (Dutch ring)*

## 174 Christmas clock cake

This attractive Christmas clock cake was originally made with ready-prepared cake mix but any of the cake recipes could be used instead if liked. Choose either a rich Christmas cake, or as it is an ideal cake for a children's party, one of the sponge cakes in that section (Recipe 63 onwards). The cake can be covered with marzipan or just coated with glacé or royal icing (see section on Icings, Number 370 onwards). Decorate with a piped border of butter icing in a contrasting colour and pipe greetings on top of the cake. The small watches make attractive gifts for young children. Cut pieces of greaseproof paper exactly the same shape as the outline of the watch, attach these to the watches with a little icing, then press against the sides of the cake.

*Christmas clock cake*

## 175 *Wedding cake*

*For 6-inch round or 5-inch square tier ; use a tin 3 inches in depth.*

| | |
|---|---|
| 6 oz. butter *or* margarine | ½ teaspoon mixed spice |
| 6 oz. sugar, preferably brown | 12 oz. currants |
| 1 teaspoon black treacle *or* gravy browning | 6 oz. raisins |
| | 6 oz. sultanas |
| 2 eggs | 2 oz. chopped candied peel |
| 3 dessertspoons brandy, sherry, rum *or* whisky | 2 oz. glacé cherries |
| | 2 oz. almonds, chopped |
| 6 oz. plain flour | 1 teaspoon grated lemon rind |

Cream together margarine or butter, sugar and treacle. Beat eggs well and add brandy. Sieve all dry ingredients together. Mix fruit, floured cherries, nuts and peel. Add egg and flour mixture alternately to butter mixture, stirring well but not over-beating. Lastly, mix in fruit. Put into prepared tin and bake in *centre* of a moderate oven for 3 hours (350°F.—Gas Mark 3 for first hour and 300°F.—Gas Mark 2 for rest of time). Allow to cool in tin. Store with paper on cake.

For an 8-inch round or 7-inch square cake use double ingredients and bake for 4½ hours—reduce heat after 2 hours. For a 10-inch round or 9-inch square cake use four times the ingredients and bake for 6 hours. For a 12-inch round or 11-inch square cake use 6 times the ingredients and bake for 7½-8 hours. For quantities of marzipan and royal icing see Recipes 385 and 382.

Cake tins

| | | |
|---|---|---|
| 8-inch round tin | = | 7-inch square |
| 9-inch round tin | = | 8-inch square |
| 10-inch round tin | = | 9-inch square |
| 11-inch round tin | = | 10-inch square, etc. |

*Wedding cake*

## 176 *Baking and testing wedding and other rich cakes*

A great deal of time and expensive ingredients go into making a wedding cake, or any rich fruit cake, and these can be wasted if care is not taken in baking and timing. It must be stressed that in every cake recipe the oven temperatures given are AVERAGE only, and as cookers vary quite appreciably it is important to check the baking temperature and suggested position in the oven against your own cooker instruction book or chart.

Line cake tins for rich fruit cakes most carefully; a round of brown paper and double thickness of greased greaseproof paper at the bottom of the tin protects the base of the cake. Cut a double band of greaseproof paper for the sides of the tin, making this about 2 inches deeper than the cake tin. Cut ½-inch 'slits' at the bottom of the band of paper—about ¾ inch apart. This makes sure it fits well at the bottom of the tin. If you grease the tin lightly before putting in the band of paper you have a better and flatter surface.

Tie a deep band of brown paper on the outside of the tin. The paper not only protects the cake during baking, it helps to keep it moist.

TO TEST the cake, look carefully when you think it is cooked. If it has shrunk away from the sides of the tin it is ready to come out, but test further by listening most carefully. If the cake is quite quiet it is cooked—if there is a faint 'humming' noise, it is not ready and should be returned to the oven. A further test for less rich cakes is to press very firmly on top, and to insert a warm skewer (use a very fine one) into the cake. If this comes out quite clean the cake is cooked, but if it is sticky then it is not ready. The difficulty with this method of testing with rich cakes is that they are so full of fruit the skewer can get sticky even when the cake IS cooked; that is why 'listening' is a better test.

To give a very rich moistness to wedding and other fruit cakes, they should be pricked with a steel skewer or with a knitting needle after cooling and sherry, brandy or rum poured steadily over the cake. This can be done every 7-14 days during storing.

## 177 More wedding cake recipes

Recipe 175 is for a very rich mixture, which must be kept some time to be perfect. If you have less time to make the cake use the Christmas cake recipe 162 for this is perfect if kept from 3 weeks onwards.

**Icing wedding cakes**

You will find all details on coating cakes and piping cakes given in the Icings section (Numbers 383 and 384) but when icing a wedding cake it is usual to cut a portion of the cake after coating with marzipan, then to insert a band of ribbon (protected from the greasiness of the cake by folded greaseproof paper or foil) with the ends of the ribbon left hanging outside. The cake is then iced in the usual way, but when the cake is cut at the wedding reception the first slice is easily removed as all the knife needs to cut through is the icing. This is important as a rich cake, heavily iced, can be difficult to cut.

The decorations on a wedding cake need not be elaborate at all—as you will see the piping etc. on the cake in the black and white photograph is very simple and all that remains is to complete the cake with an ornament and perhaps small sprays of white flowers, and silver horseshoes.

It is advisable NOT to stand the tiers of the cake on top of one another too long before the wedding. Store each cake in a box or better still airtight tin, and put together just before the wedding day.

## 178 Silver wedding cake

This can be exactly the same recipe as the wedding cake, Recipe 175, but when decorating it is usual to have all ornaments silver coloured and perhaps to have some reference in the piping on top or on the sides of the cake to the original wedding date.

## 179 Golden wedding cake

This too can be exactly the same recipe as the wedding cake, Recipe 175, but when decorating use gold coloured ornaments and flowers and gold coloured ribbon. If most of the guests are to be elderly it may be advisable to choose a less rich cake, even a good sponge mixture.

## 180 Twenty-first birthday cake

8 oz. margarine
8 oz. castor sugar
4 eggs
12 oz. plain flour
½ level teaspoon salt
1 level teaspoon baking powder
8 oz. light-coloured sultanas
9 oz. citron peel, chopped
4 oz. blanched almonds, chopped
4 oz. glacé cherries, quartered
2 oz. glacé pineapple, chopped

Cream margarine with sugar until light and fluffy. Add slightly whisked eggs in tablespoonfuls, beating well after each addition. Sieve together flour, salt and baking powder and fold into creamed mixture. Add prepared fruit, peel, almonds, cherries, pineapple, lemon rind and lemon juice. Mix in evenly. Put mixture into a round 8-inch cake tin, double-lined with greaseproof paper, and bake in a very moderate oven (350°F.—Gas Mark 3) for 2½-3 hours. It is advisable to lower heat to 275-300°F.—Gas Mark 2 after 1½ hours. Test carefully.

Make royal icing. Continue beating until the icing is smooth and glossy and of a stiff consistency. Ice the cake and a round of cardboard too. This should be iced on one side and when quite dry gently turned over and icing put over on the other side. Decorate as shown with 'dots' made by writing pipe No. 2 and rose pipe. Attach 'lid' to cake with line of icing and when firm put key, flower and ribbon in position.

*Twenty-first birthday cake*

## 181 Buttercup cake
### (using egg YOLKS only)

6 oz. margarine *or* butter
6 oz. sugar
little orange or lemon rind to
    flavour
4 egg yolks*

6 oz. flour (with plain flour 1½
    level teaspoons baking
    powder)
orange *or* lemon juice to
    moisten

*\* This is an ideal cake to make with yolks left from Angel cake*

Cream butter and sugar and orange or lemon rind until soft. Gradually stir in egg yolks, flour with baking powder, if used, and enough fruit juice to moisten. Put into a 7-inch tin, which should be well greased and floured and bake for about 1¼ hours in the centre of a moderate oven (375°F.—Gas Mark 4).

## 182 Buttercup layer cake

4 oz. butter
5 oz. castor sugar
2 tablespoons orange rind
yolks of 6 eggs *or* 3 whole
    eggs*
6 oz. flour (with plain flour
    use 2 level teaspoons baking
    powder)
2 tablespoons orange juice

*Orange butter icing*
4 oz. butter
6 oz. icing sugar
grated rind 1 orange

*Orange icing*
6 oz. icing sugar
1½ tablespoons orange juice

*\* This is an ideal cake to make with yolks left from Angel cake*

Cream butter, sugar and orange rind until soft and light. Gradually beat in egg yolks. If mixture shows signs of curdling fold in a small quantity of sieved flour. Fold in flour with baking powder, if used, and orange juice. Put mixture into two 7-inch greased and floured sandwich tins, and bake just above centre of a moderately hot oven (400°F.—Gas Mark 5) for about 20 minutes. Sandwich together with butter icing, and cover top with orange icing. Decorate with a spray of artificial buttercups or with piped flowers of butter icing and angelica. To make butter icing, cream butter and sieved icing sugar thoroughly then gradually add orange rind. To make icing, pour juice gradually on to sieved icing sugar.

## 183 Cherry layer cake

*Icing and decoration*
butter icing (Recipe 387)
1-2 oz. glacé cherries, finely
    chopped

glacé icing (Recipe 371)
angelica
glacé cherries

Ingredients as for Buttercup layer cake (Recipe 182) but use 2 tablespoons milk instead of same amount of orange juice, and add 3 oz. chopped and floured glacé cherries.
Sandwich the cake together with the butter icing and finely chopped glacé cherries. Cover top of cake with white glacé icing and sprays made from angelica and glacé cherries.

## 184 Pineapple layer cake

Ingredients as for Buttercup layer cake (Recipe 182) but use 2 tablespoons pineapple juice or pineapple essence diluted with water instead of orange juice. Add 3 oz. finely chopped crystallised pineapple. Decorate with glacé icing made by mixing 6 oz. sieved icing sugar with a little pineapple syrup (or add a few drops pineapple essence and warm water). Arrange pieces of glacé cherries and pineapple on top of the cake.

## 185 Catherine wheels

3½ oz. butter *or* margarine
3½ oz. castor sugar
1 egg
7 oz. plain flour

few drops vanilla essence
1 oz. cocoa powder
egg white for glazing

Cream together butter or margarine and sugar till light and fluffy. Beat in egg. Divide mixture into two portions. To one half add 4 oz. sieved flour and a few drops of vanilla essence and form into a semi-stiff paste. To remaining half add 3 oz. flour, sieved with 1 oz. cocoa. Turn both mixtures on to a lightly floured board, knead quickly and roll out into equal-sized oblongs. Brush one piece with lightly beaten egg white and cover with the other piece. Trim edges then brush top with egg white and roll up as for a Swiss roll. Cut into rounds, place on a greased baking tray and bake centre of moderately hot oven (400°F.—Gas Mark 5) for 15 minutes.

*Catherine wheels; Guy Fawkes cake; Rockets*

## 186 *Guy Fawkes cake*

4 oz. flour (with plain flour use ½ level teaspoon baking powder)
3 large eggs
3 oz. castor sugar
1 tablespoon boiling water
3 tablespoons jam

*Icing*
14 oz. icing sugar, sieved
3 tablespoons orange, lemon *or* grapefruit juice*
cochineal

\* *To make the icing blend icing sugar with fruit juice, adding few drops cochineal to the icing used for piping*

Sieve together flour and baking powder. Whisk eggs and castor sugar over a basin of hot water till they are very thick and double in volume (mixture should be able to hold its own weight). Stir in boiling water, then quickly and lightly cut and fold in sieved flour with baking powder, if used. Spread mixture evenly into a greased and paper lined tin 14 × 9 inches and bake near the top of a hot oven (450°F.—Gas Mark 7) for 7-8 minutes. Turn out on to a wire tray. When cold, cut in half across and sandwich together with jam. Cover with icing and leave to set. Using a forcing bag and No. 2 writing tube, pipe a jagged edge round top of cake to represent an explosion and write 'Guy Fawkes' in centre. The glacé icing for piping should be coloured bright pink.

## 187 *Rockets*

Ingredients and method as for Guy Fawkes cake (Recipe 186) but bake mixture in larger tin if possible to give thinner sponge. When cooked, turn on to a sheet of greaseproof paper lightly covered with castor sugar and placed upon a damp tea towel, and cut in half lengthwise thus making two large thin sponges. Trim away crusty edges, spread with warmed jam and roll the two pieces up as for a Swiss roll, starting with longer sides. Cut each long roll into 5 pieces, giving 10 miniature Swiss rolls. When thoroughly cold, coat with chocolate glacé icing (Recipe 188). Insert a spill or stick in one end of each 'rocket'.

## 188 *Chocolate glacé icing*

3 oz. plain chocolate
½ oz. butter
2 tablespoons water
6 oz. icing sugar, sieved

Melt chocolate, butter and water gently over low heat. Stir in icing sugar. Beat well to blend all ingredients.

## 189 *Jumping jacks*

4 oz. plain flour
2½ oz. butter *or* margarine
1 oz. desiccated coconut
2 oz. castor sugar
beaten egg to mix

*To decorate*
butter cream (Recipe 190)
angelica

Sieve flour and rub in fat till mixture is as fine as breadcrumbs. Add coconut and sugar and mix to a stiff paste with beaten egg. Turn out on to a lightly floured board, knead quickly and roll out thinly. Cut into oblongs 2 × 1½ inches. Put on greased trays and bake in centre of moderately hot oven (400°F.—Gas Mark 5) for 10-12 minutes or till biscuits are a light golden. Cool on baking tray. Using a forcing bag and star tube, decorate each biscuit with a continuous up-and-down line of butter cream. Band across with strips of angelica.

## 190 *Butter cream*

2 oz. unsalted butter
2½ oz. icing sugar, sieved
few drops vanilla essence

Beat together above ingredients till mixture is smooth and creamy.

## 191 *Jack's house*

4 oz. cooking fat
4 oz. soft brown sugar
2 eggs, lightly beaten
8 oz. treacle
½ teaspoon bicarbonate of soda
2 tablespoons milk
8 oz. plain flour
½ teaspoon ground ginger

6 oz. raisins
2 oz. stem ginger, finely chopped

*Icing*
1 lb. icing sugar
2 egg whites
1-2 tablespoons lemon juice

Cream fat and sugar until light and fluffy. Beat in eggs a little at a time. Beat in treacle and bicarbonate of soda dissolved in milk. Sieve flour and ground ginger and fold into creamed mixture. Stir in washed and dried raisins and ginger. Spread mixture evenly in a greased and lined oblong cake tin 8 × 10 inches. Bake in centre of a very moderate oven (350°F.—Gas Mark 3) for 50-55 minutes. Cool on rack.
Beat sieved icing sugar and egg whites together till smooth. Beat in sufficient lemon juice to give soft consistency. Spread over top and sides of gingerbread. When icing has set build house of cards on top of cake and arrange Christmas trees and toy animals in front of house.

*Jack's house*

## 192 Gingerbread house

¼ pint and 4 tablespoons water
¼ teaspoon cinnamon
pinch mixed spice
1 teaspoon ground ginger
8 oz. honey

8 oz. sugar
1 lb. plain flour
1 egg yolk
glacé or royal icing (Recipes 371 or 382)

Put water, spices, honey and sugar into a pan, bring to boil. Add flour, stir well and leave overnight. Next day beat in egg yolk, knead very well and roll out to about good ¼-inch in thickness. Cut into following shapes:
2 sides of house—cut out doors and windows
2 ends of house
2 roof sections
chimney pieces (unless using marzipan for this).
Carefully put pieces on to a greased and floured baking tin and bake for an hour in middle of a very moderate oven (350°F.—Gas Mark 3). When cold pieces should be firm, but not too hard. Make up small quantity of icing, glacé or royal, and use this to hold pieces together. Ice in windows or doors. Stand on cake board and put trees etc. round.

## 193 Drum cake

Victoria sandwich (Recipe 76)
apricot jam
marzipan made with 8 oz. ground almonds etc. (Recipe 385)

little red colouring
glacé icing, made with 10 oz. icing sugar etc. (Recipe 371)
2 sticks barley sugar

Bake Victoria sandwich as directed in Recipe 76 and when cold sandwich together with jam. Make marzipan, take out a small quantity, colour this rather bright pink, and roll on sugared paper or a board to two narrow bands the circumference of cake. Spread cake with sieved apricot jam, and roll out rest of marzipan to cover sides and top. For directions on doing this see Recipe 383. Cover cake with icing and when this is nearly firm, press two bands of pink marzipan into position. Pipe over this with glacé icing which will pipe quite well for a band like this. Decorate with sticks of barley sugar.

## 194 Humpty Dumpty cake

4 oz. margarine
4 oz. castor sugar
2 eggs
4 oz. self-raising flour
lemon curd
butter icing (Recipe 387)
7-inch square cake board

*To decorate*
1 oz. desiccated coconut
green colouring
1 oz. plain chocolate
1 large plain chocolate Easter egg
almond paste (Recipe 385) made with 8 oz. ground almonds, etc.

Cream the margarine and sugar until light and fluffy. Beat in the eggs thoroughly, one at a time. Fold in the sieved flour. Place the mixture in a prepared 12 × 8 inches Swiss roll tin. Bake in the centre of a moderate oven (375°F.—Gas Mark 4) for 20-25 minutes. Cool on a wire tray and remove the paper while the cake is still hot. Trim the edges with a sharp knife and cut into three equal pieces. Sandwich these together with lemon curd. Make the butter icing and tint it pale pink. Cover the top and sides of the cake with this and place on the cake board. Colour the coconut green. Spread a little lemon curd on the board and sprinkle on the coconut to represent grass.
Melt the chocolate in a small basin over hot water. Paint the melted chocolate on the icing with a small paint brush in a brick design. Mould one third of the almond paste into a shallow round and curve the centre in the shape of a dish. Spread with lemon curd and place the Easter egg on top. Cut out the eyes, nose and mouth from the almond paste, rolled thinly and coloured if wished. Make the arms, legs, hat and bow from the remaining almond paste. Secure Humpty Dumpty on the wall with a little icing.

*Humpty Dumpty cake*

## 195 Mayday cake

6 oz. cooking fat or butter
6 oz. castor sugar
4 eggs
7 oz. flour (with plain flour
  use 1½ teaspoons baking
  powder)
½ teaspoon vanilla essence
1 rounded tablespoon cocoa
  powder
4 oz. almonds, chopped

*Icing and decoration*
3 oz. cooking fat
8 oz. icing sugar
cocoa powder
few drops vanilla essence
2 dessertspoons milk
roasted flaked almonds
1 medium-sized can cherries
  for filling
striped drinking straw
wooden cocktail sticks
coloured ribbons
cherry

Cream cooking fat and sugar together until light and fluffy. Add the eggs and beat in thoroughly one at a time, beating in a little flour if the mixture shows signs of curdling. Beat in vanilla essence. Finally fold in sieved flour, with baking powder, if used, cocoa and the chopped almonds. Divide the mixture evenly between two greased 8-inch sandwich tins. Bake in centre of a moderate oven (375°F.—Gas Mark 4) for 30-35 minutes. Cool on a cake rack.

To make the icing, cream cooking fat with half the sieved icing sugar and cocoa until light and fluffy. Gradually beat in the remaining icing sugar, adding a little essence and enough milk to make icing of a spreading consistency. Drain and stone the cherries.

With one sandwich cake, ice round the edges and roll in roast flaked almonds. Place on a cake board or plate and lightly spread a layer of icing over the top. Place the stoned cherries all over the surface. With the second cake lightly spread icing over the bottom and sides, rolling the sides in roasted almonds. Place the iced side on top of the cherries to form a sandwich. Ice the top and sprinkle with flaked almonds.

Place a piece of striped drinking straw in the centre of the cake and coloured cocktail sticks evenly near the edge all round the top of the cake. Cut pieces of coloured ribbon long enough to pierce on a cocktail stick on the opposite side of the cake, as illustrated. When ribbon lengths are cut pierce the centres together with a cocktail stick leaving the ribbons half way up. Stick one end inside the top of the straw, then fasten the ribbons to appropriate sticks round the cake. Place a cherry on top of the stick.

*Mayday cake*

## 196 Hyacinth cake

4 oz. butter
4 oz. sugar
2 eggs
5 oz. plain flour
1 oz. cornflour
1½ level teaspoons baking
  powder

*Decoration*
apricot jam
marzipan made with 4 oz.
  ground almonds etc.
  (Recipe 385)

chocolate glacé icing
  (Recipe 372)
3 wooden skewers
green colouring
9 marshmallows
strawberry butter icing
  (Recipe 387)*
angelica

*\* Add few drops strawberry essence to butter icing*

Beat butter and sugar together until soft and creamy. Whisk the eggs. Sift flour, cornflour and baking powder together and add to creamed mixture, alternately with the beaten eggs. Add a little milk—blended mixture should just drop from a spoon. Put the mixture into a greased oblong tin (about 9 × 5 × 3 inches) and bake in centre of a moderate oven (375°F.—Gas Mark 4) for about 1 hour.

**To decorate**

Brush the sides of the cake with melted jam and cover with almond paste or marzipan, coloured green. Ice the top of the cake with melted chocolate or chocolate icing to represent the earth. Paint three wooden skewers with green colouring to make flower stems. Impale three marshmallows on each skewer, and pipe strawberry butter icing over the marshmallows to form the flowers. Place the flowers on the chocolate 'soil' and surround with green angelica leaves.

6. American bride's cake

7. Golden shortcake

## 197 Blossom cake

4 oz. margarine
4 oz. castor sugar
2 eggs
grated rind 1 orange
4 oz. self-raising flour and 1
level teaspoon baking
powder or 4 oz. plain flour
with 2 level teaspoons
baking powder, sieved
together

*Chocolate icing*
1 oz. margarine or butter
3 tablespoons cold water
2 oz. milk chocolate
6 oz. icing sugar, sieved

Place all the ingredients together in a mixing bowl, then beat well for 2 minutes with a wooden spoon. Grease an 8-inch round sandwich cake tin with melted margarine and line the bottom with a round of greaseproof paper. Place the mixture into the prepared tin. Bake just above centre of a moderate oven (375°F.—Gas Mark 4) for 30-35 minutes. Remove from the oven. Cool on a wire tray.

**To decorate**

Put the margarine, water and chocolate in a bowl and place over a saucepan of boiling water. Stir with a wooden spoon until the chocolate is dissolved and continue stirring until the mixture thickens. Remove the bowl, cool slightly, and beat in the icing sugar. Continue beating until the icing is of a coating consistency. Pour over the sandwich cake and leave to set. Remove from the wire tray, place on a cake board or a plate. Place a circle of blossom in the centre and tie a blue band of ribbon round the cake.

## 198 Simnel cake

8 oz. plain flour
pinch salt
3 rounded teaspoons mixed
spice
pinch bicarbonate of soda
6 oz. castor sugar
6 oz. cooking fat
6 oz. currants
4 oz. sultanas
2 oz. glacé cherries
1 oz. almonds, chopped
1 oz. chopped candied peel

3 eggs
2 tablespoons milk

*Decoration*
1 lb. almond paste (Recipe
385)
little apricot jam or purée
1 egg white
small amount glacé icing
(Recipe 371)
Easter decorations

Sieve flour, salt, spice, bicarbonate of soda and sugar together into a bowl. Add the cooking fat, fruit, chopped cherries, almonds, peel, eggs and milk. Mix thoroughly together for 1-2 minutes. Roll out half the almond paste to a 7-inch round. Place half the cake mixture in a 7-inch cake tin, lined with grease-proof paper and brushed with melted cooking fat. Smooth over, place on the round of almond paste, then remaining cake mixture, smoothing over evenly. Bake in a slow oven (300°F.—Gas Mark 2) on the middle shelf for 2¼-2½ hours. Cool on a cake rack.

When cold remove the paper and brush the top over with boiled apricot jam or purée. Roll out remaining almond paste and place on top of the cake, decorating with almond paste balls, eggs, etc. Brush over with egg white and place in the middle of a moderately hot oven (400°F.—Gas Mark 5) for 10-15 minutes to lightly brown the almond paste. Remove and cool, then ice the centre with glacé icing and decorate with Easter chicks etc.

*Simmel cake*

## 199 Traditional simnel cake

5 oz. margarine
1 oz. cooking fat
5-6 oz. sugar
1 dessertspoon golden syrup
or treacle
8 oz. flour (with plain flour
use 1½ level teaspoons
baking powder)
1 teaspoon mixed spice
1 teaspoon cinnamon
1 teaspoon grated lemon rind
1 lb. dried fruit

2 oz. chopped candied peel
2 eggs
3 tablespoons milk (sherry
could be used)

*Marzipan—for the top and
middle\**
8 oz. ground almonds
4 oz. castor sugar
4 oz. icing sugar
few drops almond essence
2 egg yolks

*\* (for the top only, use half the quantity of marzipan)*

Cream margarine, cooking fat, sugar and syrup. Sieve dry ingredients, mix fruit etc., beat eggs and milk together. Stir the flour and eggs alternately into margarine, then the fruit.

**To make the marzipan**

Mix the ingredients together, knead well and use half to form into round slightly smaller than the size of the cake tin.

Put half the cake mixture into a greased and floured 8-inch cake tin, then add the round of marzipan. Cover with the rest of the fruit cake mixture. Bake for approximately 2¾ hours in a very moderate oven—about 350°F.—Gas Mark 3. Cool slightly before turning out of tin. Brush top with melted jam or egg white and cover with marzipan, fluting the edges. Brown under a hot grill for a few minutes or return to a very low oven until the marzipan is quite golden brown and crisp.

## 200 *Easter biscuits*

4 oz. margarine *or* butter
4 oz. castor sugar
8 oz. flour, preferably plain, *or* 6 oz. flour for richer biscuits

2-4 oz. dried fruit
½-1 teaspoon mixed spice
little egg yolk *or* milk to mix

Cream margarine and sugar until soft. Work in flour, fruit and spice. Knead well, then add enough egg or milk to bind mixture. Roll out to ¼-inch thick, cut into large rounds, put on baking trays and bake for about 15 minutes in the centre of a moderate oven (375°F.—Gas Mark 4). Cool on tin.

## 201 *Butterscotch Easter cake*

6 oz. plain flour
¼ teaspoon bicarbonate soda
2 oz. castor sugar
4 oz. golden syrup
3 oz. butter
3 oz. plain cooking chocolate

1 egg
2 tablespoons evaporated milk
vanilla essence
butterscotch icing (Recipe 202)
Easter decorations

Sieve flour and bicarbonate of soda. Add castor sugar. Dissolve syrup, butter and chocolate in saucepan over a gentle heat. Make a well in centre of flour and add chocolate mixture. Add beaten egg, evaporated milk and a little vanilla essence. Mix until smooth. Pour into a 7-inch greased and floured tin and cook in centre of very moderate oven (350°F.—Gas Mark 3) for 1¼-1½ hours. When cake is quite cold, slice it across with a sharp knife into three rounds. Sandwich rounds with the butterscotch icing (Recipe 202) and put rest of icing on top and round sides of the cake. Mark in lines with a fork all over. Finally, decorate cake with sugar eggs and chocolate nests and place a chicken in centre.

*Butterscotch Easter cake*

## 202 *Butterscotch icing*

6 oz. butter
6 oz. soft brown sugar
6 tablespoons evaporated milk

1 lb. sifted icing sugar
vanilla essence

Cream butter and brown sugar. Add the evaporated milk and icing sugar alternately. Flavour with vanilla essence.

## 203 *Spiced simnel cake*

5 oz. butter
5 oz. brown sugar
5 oz. golden syrup (see Recipe 204)
8 oz. flour (with plain flour use 2 level teaspoons baking powder)
2 teaspoons mixed spice
½ level teaspoon bicarbonate soda

2 eggs
3 tablespoons milk

*To decorate*
apricot jam
marzipan made with 4 oz. ground almonds etc. (Recipe 385)

Put butter, sugar and syrup into a pan and heat gently until syrup has melted. Sieve flour, baking powder, if used, spice, bicarbonate of soda, and pour syrup mixture over it and beat very well. Add eggs and beat again. Heat milk in syrup saucepan, add with a final beating to mixture. Pour into a 7-inch cake tin lined with greased greaseproof paper. Bake for about 1¼ hours in centre of a very moderate oven (350°F.—Gas Mark 3) until firm. Cool for a few minutes before turning out. When cool, cover top with sieved apricot jam and marzipan. Decorate as Traditional simnel cake (Recipe 199).

## 204 *To weigh golden syrup*

Flour scale pan lightly and pour in syrup. You will find that it turns out of scale easily and DOES NOT STICK. Or see weights and measures at beginning of this book for spoon measures.

## 205 _Cherry fudge simnel cake_

6 oz. glacé cherries
8 oz. butter _or_ margarine
8 oz. castor sugar
5 eggs

10 oz. flour (with plain flour use 1 level teaspoon baking powder)
apricot jam
fudge icing (Recipe 206)

First rinse away sticky syrup from cherries, dry, and flour. Cream butter and sugar until soft and light, add the beaten eggs and flour with baking powder, if used, being careful not to overbeat the flour. Lastly, stir in the cherries. Put into a 7-inch or 8-inch cake tin lined with greased greaseproof paper and bake for approximately 1¾ hours for 7-inch tin or 1½ hours for 8-inch tin in centre of very moderate oven (350°F.—Gas Mark 3). When cold brush top with apricot jam and coat with fudge icing.

## 206 _Fudge icing_

8 oz. granulated sugar
4 tablespoons full cream condensed milk

1 tablespoon water
1 oz. butter
few drops vanilla essence

Put the sugar and condensed milk and water into saucepan, stir thoroughly until sugar has dissolved, add butter and vanilla essence, then boil steadily stirring from time to time to prevent burning, until mixture JUST forms a soft ball when tested in cold water—235°F. (i.e. a little softer than real fudge). Beat until mixture JUST begins to thicken then turn out of pan on to cake and spread with knife dipped in hot water. Decorate with chickens etc.
**Note**
A more economical fudge icing can be made with ordinary milk instead of condensed. If liked this can be used on the traditional Simnel cake instead of marzipan. For a round of fudge icing inside cake, double the ingredients. Split cake and spread centre with icing, sandwich together again and then cover top with fudge icing.

## 207 _Nut simnel ring_

6 oz. margarine _or_ cooking fat
6 oz. castor sugar
1 level tablespoon golden syrup
3 eggs
1 tablespoon milk
6 oz. flour (with plain flour use 1½ level teaspoons baking powder)*

2 oz. ground almonds
4 oz. nuts, chopped†
8 oz. icing sugar
few drops almond essence
8 oz. marzipan (Recipe 385)
pink and green _or_ chocolate colouring

Cream margarine, sugar and golden syrup. Gradually add beaten eggs and milk, stir in flour with baking powder, if used, ground almonds and chopped nuts. Put into a well greased and floured ring tin and bake for approximately 1 hour in centre of moderate oven (375°F.—Gas Mark 4). Turn out and when cool coat with almond glacé icing—to make this, blend icing sugar with warm water and almond essence. Colour half the marzipan pink and half green or chocolate. Roll out on sugared board and cut out rabbit or chicken shapes. Press round side of cake.

_* Or use 8 oz. flour instead of 6 oz. flour and 2 oz. ground almonds_
_† Any kind of nuts can be used_

## 208 _Valentine cake_

8 oz. margarine
8 oz. castor sugar
4 eggs
8 oz. flour (with plain flour use 2 level teaspoons baking powder)

_Icing_
1 lb. icing sugar, sieved
8 oz. margarine
lemon juice
yellow colouring

Cream margarine and sugar until light and fluffy. Beat eggs well and add a tablespoon to margarine and sugar. Continue beating mixture well before adding more egg. Fold in flour and mix thoroughly. Divide mixture evenly between two heart-shaped tins measuring approximately 9 × 8½ inches. Smooth mixture in tins and bake just above centre of a moderate oven (375°F.— Gas Mark 4) for 30-35 minutes. Turn out and cool on a wire tray. Cream margarine and sugar until light and fluffy. Add a good teaspoonful of lemon juice and colour pale yellow, adding colouring drop by drop. Sandwich the two cakes with icing and cover top and sides with icing. Finish neatly with a fork, or, if you prefer, smooth the icing, using a knife dipped in warm water. Decorate with flowers.

_Valentine cake_

## 209 _Chocolate valentines_

_Rich short crust pastry_
4 oz. margarine
2 oz. castor sugar
6 oz. flour, preferably plain
1 egg yolk
little water

_Filling_
2 oz. glacé cherries
2 oz. hazel nuts _or_ almonds
2 oz. raisins
4 oz. block of chocolate

_To decorate_
glacé cherries
nuts

Cream margarine and sugar, work in flour, knead well, then add egg yolk and enough water to bind. Roll out thinly and line heart-shaped patty tins. Put in a cool place for a short time before baking. Prick bottom of each pastry case and bake for about 10 minutes above centre of a moderately hot oven (425°F.—Gas Mark 6). Cool pastry cases for 1-2 minutes in tins before taking out. When tartlets are cooled, fill with cherries, nuts and raisins. Melt chocolate in a basin over hot water, taking care it does not get too hot, otherwise you lose the gloss. Cover fruit in pastry cases with chocolate, and decorate on top with cherries and nuts.

## 210 Cupid's bows

2 oz. fine semolina
8 oz. flour (with plain flour use 2 level teaspoons baking powder)
4 oz. sugar
8 oz. margarine
1 egg yolk
pink royal icing *or* water icing (Recipes 382, 371)
2 oz. plain chocolate

Sift semolina, flour, baking powder, if used, and sugar into basin. Rub in margarine. Add egg yolk and knead to a stiff dough. Flour pastry board well and roll out mixture ¼-inch thick. Cut into heart shapes and place on a greased baking tin. Bake just above centre of a moderate oven (375°F.—Gas Mark 4) for 15 minutes. Allow the biscuits to cool, then cover with pink royal or pink water icing and decorate with melted chocolate, which should be put into an icing syringe or paper bag and piped with No. 2 writing pipe.

*Cupid's bows*

## 211 Rich plain cake

10 oz. butter *or* margarine
10 oz. sugar
12 oz. flour (with plain flour use 3 level teaspoons baking powder)
2 oz. ground almonds
6 eggs

Cream together butter and sugar until soft and light. Sieve flour, baking powder, if used, and ground almonds together. Beat eggs well, then stir eggs and flour alternately into the butter mixture. Put into an 8-inch lined tin and bake for approximately 2½ hours (325-350°F.—Gas Mark 3). The heat can be reduced slightly if necessary after 1½ hours' cooking. You can add chopped cherries and any crystallised fruits to this mixture, but flour them well before stirring into the cake mixture. This cake keeps well, so is an excellent alternative to a Christmas cake.

## 212 Spring bonnet biscuits

3 oz. butter
3 oz. sugar
6 oz. plain flour
2 oz. cornflour
1 level teaspoon baking powder
1 egg, beaten
marshmallows
glacé icing (Recipe 371)

**To make 'bonnet brims'**
Beat the butter and sugar together until white and creamy. Sift together flour, cornflour and baking powder and add it to the creamed mixture alternately with the beaten egg. Knead lightly to make a smooth, firm dough and roll out thinly. Cut into rounds with a 3-inch biscuit cutter, making some plain and others with fluted edges. Bake some of the biscuits flat on a baking sheet and others on inverted patty tins, to make a curved 'brim'. Bake in centre of moderate oven (375°F.—Gas Mark 4) for about 20 minutes.

**To make 'bonnet crowns'**
Put ½ marshmallow in the centre of each biscuit for the crown and cover each 'hat' with glacé icing in various pastel colours and flavours. For the best results, the icing should be fairly stiff. When the icing is firm trim your hats as you like—sugar flowers, piped icing 'ribbons', marzipan fruit, hundreds and thousands— the gayer the better. A variety of coloured and flavoured icings can be very simply made by using flavoured cornflour with icing sugar, in the proportions of 1 teaspoon of flavoured cornflour to 8 oz. of icing sugar.

*Spring bonnet biscuits*

## 213 Cakes with wholemeal flour

Many of the cakes in this book can be made with wholemeal instead of white flour. Those particularly suitable are the family cakes and plainer fruit cakes, in the first section of the book, but even the richer Victoria sandwich cake or Christmas type cake can be made with this type of flour if wished. If using the very coarse wholemeal flour, however, a better result is obtained if it is mixed with some white flour.

Wholemeal flour absorbs slightly more liquid when preparing the cakes and in consequence it is quite likely that they will take longer to bake. Wholemeal flour can vary in texture so it is a good idea when making a cake mixture to reserve a little of the flour, then you can leave this out if you find the mixture is the correct consistency. This applies particularly when making sponges where little if any extra liquid is normally added. If you use 3 eggs to rather less than 6 oz. wholemeal flour in a Victoria sandwich you get a good result.

## 214 Sandtorte

8 oz. butter
8 oz. sugar
4 egg yolks

8 oz. potato flour or
   cornflour
1 liqueur glass rum or brandy
4 egg whites, stiffly beaten

Cream butter and sugar thoroughly and gradually beat in the egg yolks. Continue beating well until very smooth. Stir in the sieved flour and rum very carefully. Lastly fold in the egg whites. Pour the mixture into a deep round 8-inch greased cake tin and bake for approximately 1 hour in the centre of a moderate oven (350-375°F.—Gas Mark 3-4).

## 215 Peanut butter cake

5 oz. peanut butter
6 oz. sugar
grated rind and juice 1 lemon
2 eggs

8 oz. flour (with plain flour
   use 2 level teaspoons
   baking powder)
little milk
lemon glacé icing (Recipe 374)

Cream the peanut butter and sugar with lemon rind. Beat in eggs, add flour with baking powder, if used, and lemon juice and a few drops of milk. Bake in a 7-inch greased and floured cake tin for about 1¼-1½ hours in the centre of a very moderate oven (350°F.—Gas Mark 3).
Cover with lemon glacé icing (Recipe 374).

## 216 Five o'clock cake

4 oz. butter
4 oz. sugar
5 oz. plain flour
1 oz. cornflour
2 level teaspoons baking
   powder*
2 eggs
a little milk, if necessary

*To ice the clock face*
6 oz. icing sugar
1 teaspoon strawberry
   flavoured cornflour
little warm water to mix

*To ice the clock base*
8 oz. icing sugar
1 tablespoon coffee essence
little warm water to mix

* With self-raising flour use ½ teaspoon baking powder

Grease a 6-inch sandwich tin for the cake's clock face and a 7-inch square tin for its base. Beat the butter and sugar together until soft and creamy. Sift the flour, cornflour and baking powder together and add to the creamed mixture alternately with the beaten eggs and milk. Then divide the mixture between the two tins and bake just above centre of a moderately hot oven (400°F.—Gas Mark 5) for about 20 minutes.
Sieve 6 oz. of icing sugar and the strawberry flavoured cornflour together and mix with a little warm water to a soft dropping consistency. Mix 8 oz. of icing sugar with 1 tablespoon of coffee essence and a few drops of warm water in the same way. Ice the clock base (the square cake) with coffee icing and the face with pink icing and set clock face on the coffee-iced square. Reserve enough of the coffee icing for piping on clock hands and numerals.

*Five o'clock cake*

## 217 Banana meringue torte

4 egg whites
4 oz. castor sugar
4 oz. icing sugar, sieved
½ pint double cream

6 bananas
little lemon juice
little sugar
glacé cherries

Whisk egg whites until very stiff, fold in sugar. Cut 2 rounds of greaseproof paper about 8 inches in diameter, put these on oiled baking tins, and oil or butter well. Spread or pipe meringue over these rounds. Bake for 3-4 hours in a very cool oven (200-250°F.—Gas Mark 0-¼). To lift off paper dip a palette knife in hot water, and insert very gently under meringues. Cool, and when quite cold store in airtight tins until ready to use. Whip cream lightly, mash three bananas and mix with lemon juice, a little sugar and about a third of the cream. Sandwich meringue rounds with this. Decorate with rest of cream, sliced bananas (dipped in lemon juice to keep them white) and glacé cherries.

*Banana meringue torte*

## 218 *Fresh fruit buns*

8 oz. flour (with plain flour
   use 2 slightly rounded
   teaspoons baking powder)
pinch salt
3-4 oz. margarine
3-4 oz. sugar

1 egg
milk to mix
fresh fruit (stoned cherries,
   small plums *or* halved
   apricots)

Sieve flour, baking powder, if used, and salt together. Rub in margarine and add all sugar except 1 oz. Add egg and enough milk to make a sticky consistency. Put into small heaps on a greased tin. Using the handle of a spoon, hollow out mixture to form a deep hole in centre of each bun. Put fruit in this, sprinkling it with sugar. Push cake mixture over fruit again and give a light dusting with sugar. Bake near top of a very hot oven (475°F.—Gas Mark 8) for 10 minutes.

## 219 *Strawberry vanilla shortcake*

4 oz. margarine *or* butter
4 oz. sugar
2 eggs
4 oz. flour (with plain flour
   use 1 level teaspoon baking
   powder)

*Filling*
1 level teaspoon powdered
   gelatine
1 tablespoon water
1 small can evaporated milk
1 dessertspoon castor sugar
vanilla essence
1 lb. strawberries
little angelica

Cream margarine with sugar. Add beaten eggs slowly and then beat in flour. If mixture is too dry add a little evaporated milk. Bake in two 6-inch sandwich tins for 20-25 minutes above centre of a moderately hot oven (375°F.—Gas Mark 4). Dissolve gelatine in tablespoon of cold water—this is done by standing basin over a gentle heat or over boiling water. Open can of evaporated milk, well chilled, and pour into a basin. Add dissolved gelatine. Sweeten with castor sugar and flavour with a few drops of vanilla essence. When mixture is beginning to set, whip until stiff. Spread half cake with half vanilla mixture and cover with sliced strawberries. Place other cake on top and spread with rest of filling. Decorate with whole strawberries and angelica.

*Other shortcakes will be found in Recipes 134-136.*

*Strawberry vanilla shortcake*

## 220 *Peach gâteau*

8 oz. luxury margarine
8 oz. castor sugar
4 eggs
8 oz. self-raising flour, sieved

*Filling and decoration*
1 small can peach halves
½ pint double cream, whipped
glacé cherry
angelica leaves
icing sugar

Cream the margarine and sugar together until light and fluffy. Beat in the eggs one at a time, adding a little of the sieved flour with every egg after the first. Using a metal tablespoon gently fold in the remaining flour. Place the mixture in two 8-inch sandwich tins, brushed with melted margarine and bottom lined with a round of greaseproof paper. Bake in the centre of a moderate oven (350°F. —Gas Mark 3) for 25-30 minutes. Turn out and cool on a wire tray. Sandwich together with most of the peaches and double cream. Place remaining cream on top and decorate with remaining peaches, a glacé cherry and angelica leaves. Dust with icing sugar.

*Peach gâteau.*

The following recipes are combinations of flavourings and new ideas which you will thoroughly enjoy trying.

Although new and original, they have been well tested, so you can follow them with every confidence.

## 221 *Fruit mallow cake*

4 oz. castor sugar
4 oz. butter *or* margarine
grated rind 1 lemon
1 tablespoon lemon juice
3 eggs
4 oz. plain flour
3 level teaspoons baking
   powder*
4 oz. semolina

*Topping*
1 small can red cherries
1 medium-sized can apricot
   halves
2 tablespoons granulated
   sugar
1 dessertspoon lemon juice *or*
   a dash or two of liqueur
1 banana
6 oz. marshmallows
1 oz. nuts, chopped

*\* With self-raising flour use 1½ level teaspoons baking powder*

Beat sugar, fat, lemon rind and 1 tablespoon lemon juice to a light, smooth cream. Beat in eggs one at a time. Stir in sieved flour, baking powder and semolina. Bake in a well-greased 8-inch square cake tin in centre of moderate oven (375°F.—Gas Mark 4) for 30-40 minutes, until firm, golden and well risen. Turn out when cool and allow to get cold.

Strain juice from cherries and apricots and boil ¼ pint of juice with 2 tablespoons of sugar for a minute or two. Add lemon juice or liqueur and pour over well drained fruit, including sliced banana. Stand 30 minutes. Add 2 tablespoons of remaining juice to marshmallows and melt over very low heat, removing just as soon as mallows lose their shape. Cut cake in two layers and spread bottom layer with half marshmallow. Strain fruit, reserving 9 apricots for top of cake, and arrange on marshmallow. Top with second cake layer and spread with remaining marshmallow. Arrange apricots on top and sprinkle with chopped nuts.

If preferred topping can be omitted and cake covered with lemon glacé icing (Recipe No. 374).

*Fruit mallow cake*

## 222 *Almond layer cake*

3 eggs
3 oz. castor sugar
almond essence
2½ oz. flour (with plain flour use
   ¾ teaspoon baking powder)
½ oz. cocoa powder
1 tablespoon ground almonds

*Decoration*
4 oz. butter
2 tablespoons ground almonds
almond essence
2 tablespoons cold water
icing sugar
green colouring
flaked almonds

Whisk eggs and sugar until thick and fluffy. Add almond essence. Carefully fold in sieved flour, baking powder, if used, cocoa and ground almonds. Pour into a greased and lined Swiss roll tin. Bake for about 15 minutes near top of moderately hot oven (400°F.—Gas Mark 5). Cool on a wire tray.

Put butter and ground almonds into a basin and cream to soft consistency. Add almond essence. Beat in cold water and sufficient sieved icing sugar to form a spreading consistency. Divide and colour one half pale green. Cut cake into three equal pieces and sandwich together with almond cream. Spread cream evenly around sides and dip into flaked almonds. Using a star-shaped and a plain piping tube, use remaining cream to decorate the cake.

## 223 *Strawberry cake*

4 oz. butter *or* margarine
4 oz. castor sugar
2 eggs
4½ oz. plain flour
1 packet strawberry flavoured
   cornflour

2 level teaspoons baking
   powder
4 dessertspoons milk
whipped cream
frosting (Recipe 396) *or*
   butter icing (Recipe 387)

Cream butter and sugar, add beaten eggs gradually. Sift plain flour, flavoured cornflour and baking powder together into a bowl. Stir into the egg mixture, then add milk. Divide equally between two greased 7-inch sandwich tins and bake about 20 minutes towards top of a moderately hot oven (400°F.—Gas Mark 5). When cold sandwich with cream and ice with the frosting (flavoured with a few drops of strawberry essence) or with butter icing, coloured pink with a little cochineal.

## 224 *Chocolate almond gâteau*

3 oz. chocolate
2 large eggs
3 oz. sugar
4 oz. ground almonds
3 oz. margarine, melted
chocolate butter icing
  (Recipe 388)

vanilla butter icing
  (Recipe 393)
1-2 oz. chocolate vermicelli *or*
  grated chocolate

Put grated or chopped chocolate into a basin and stand this over a saucepan of boiling water. Heat gently until chocolate has melted. Add egg yolks and sugar and beat well for about 5 minutes until thick and creamy. Take basin away from heat and continue beating until mixture is thick and clear. Fold ground almonds, together with melted margarine, into chocolate mixture, and lastly fold in stiffly beaten egg whites. Line a 7-inch cake tin with greased and floured paper. Put in mixture and bake for about 1¼ hours in centre of a moderate oven (375°F.—Gas Mark 4). When cake is quite cold, coat outside with piped chocolate and vanilla butter icings and shake a little chocolate vermicelli or grated chocolate over top.

**Note**

For a lighter cake use half flour (with plain flour use ½ teaspoon baking powder) and half ground almonds.

## 225 *Chocolate pompadour*

4 oz. cooking fat
4 oz. castor sugar
2 eggs
4 oz. flour (with plain flour
  use 1 teaspoon baking
  powder)
1 oz. cocoa powder
1 tablespoon warm water
2 tablespoons sherry
  (optional)

1 tablespoon orange squash
  (optional)

*Chocolate cream*
¼ pint double cream
2 oz. milk chocolate
1 oz. sliced almonds to
  decorate

Cream cooking fat and sugar together until light and fluffy. Add eggs one at a time beating in each one thoroughly before adding the next. Fold in sieved flour and cocoa, lastly adding the warm water. Divide equally between two 7-inch sandwich tins lined with paper and brushed with melted cooking fat. Bake in the middle of a moderate oven (375°F.—Gas Mark 4) for 20-25 minutes. Cool on a cake rack.

If liked turn cakes upside down when cold and mix the orange squash and sherry together. Spoon over the liquid until absorbed by the two cakes.

Whisk the cream until thick. Melt the chocolate in a basin over slowly boiling water, then mix into the cream. Sandwich the cakes together with half the chocolate cream and place remaining cream on top. Make about five swirls on top in half circles from the centre, and sprinkle the sliced almonds down each circle. Serve with morning coffee or afternoon tea, or as a luncheon sweet.

*Chocolate pompadour*

## 226 *Flake bar gâteau*

4 oz. margarine
4 oz. castor sugar
2 eggs
6 oz. flour (with plain flour
  use 1½ level teaspoons
  baking powder)

*Icing and decoration*
6 oz. icing sugar, sieved
3 oz. margarine *or* butter
chocolate vermicelli
3 small chocolate flake bars
1 chocolate button

Cream fat and sugar together until light and fluffy. Gradually beat in whisked eggs. Fold in sieved flour, with baking powder, if used, adding sufficient warm water to form a soft dropping consistency. Turn into 2 prepared 7-inch sandwich tins. Bake just above centre of moderate oven (375°F.—Gas Mark 4) for about 20 minutes.

Make butter cream by creaming together icing sugar and margarine. Add a little cold water if necessary to form a piping consistency. Use part of this to sandwich together the two sponges. Spread a thin layer around edge of sponge and roll into chocolate vermicelli. Arrange halved flake bars in a circle with chocolate button in the centre, and pipe stars of butter cream over top to complete decoration.

## 227 *Coffee refrigerator gâteau*

sponge fingers
Victoria sandwich cake, using
  half quantity ingredients
  (Recipe 76)
3 oz. butter
4 oz. castor sugar
2 egg yolks
¼ pint cold, double-strength
  black coffee

*To decorate*
¼ pint double cream
little egg white, beaten
walnuts, glacé cherries and
  angelica

Lightly grease the inside of an oblong ice-tray or similar dish with corn oil or melted butter. Line the inside with sponge fingers, cutting to size as necessary. Line the base with thin slices of sandwich cake. Cream the butter and sugar thoroughly, then beat in the egg yolks. Gradually beat in the black coffee. Pour the mixture into the prepared tray. Completely cover the top with slices of cake and place a heavy dish on top to press the contents. Leave for several hours in a refrigerator or cool place. Turn on to a serving dish; cover the sides with whipped cream to which a little beaten egg white has been added. Decorate the top with walnuts, glacé cherries and angelica.

**Note**

This is a very rich gâteau so only small servings are necessary.

8. Christmas cake

9. Celebration cake

10. Danish layer cake

11. Apple strudel

## 228  Chocolate pear delight

4 oz. margarine *or* butter
4 oz. sugar
2 eggs
6 oz. flour (with plain flour
   use 1½ level teaspoons
   baking powder)

1 tablespoon cocoa powder
1 can pears
cherries
whipped cream

Cream butter and sugar until light and fluffy. Beat in lightly whisked eggs. Carefully fold in sieved flour with baking powder, if used, and cocoa, adding sufficient warm water to form a soft dropping consistency. Turn into a greased and lined 8½-inch sandwich tin. Bake in centre of moderate oven (375°F.—Gas Mark 4) for 30-40 minutes. Cool on a wire tray. Strain a little fruit juice over sponge. Decorate as illustrated using pears, cherries and whipped cream.

*Chocolate pear delight*

## 229  Coffee butterscotch sandwich

4 oz. self-raising flour and
   1½ level teaspoons baking
   powder *or* 4 oz. plain flour
   and 2½ level teaspoons
   baking powder
4 oz. castor sugar
3 oz. cooking fat
2 eggs
1 tablespoon coffee essence

**Butterscotch frosting**
2 oz. cooking fat *or* butter
6 oz. brown sugar
5 tablespoons warm milk
6 oz. icing sugar

*To decorate (optional)*
cherries, walnuts

Sieve flour, baking powder and sugar into a bowl. Add fat, eggs and coffee essence, and mixing all ingredients beat for 1 minute. Turn into two 7-inch sandwich tins, brushed with melted fat, and bottom-lined. Bake in the middle of a moderately hot oven (375-400°F.—Gas Mark 5) for 20-25 minutes. Cool on a cake rack.

Melt the fat, add the brown sugar and stir well together. Add the warmed milk. Simmer very gently for 5 minutes. Cool a little. Beat in sieved icing sugar, continue beating until icing is thick enough to spread. Thin down with cream if necessary or re-beat over hot water. Put cakes together with a layer of frosting, then frost over the top of the cake, marking with a knife. Decorate if liked with cherries, walnuts, etc.

## 230  Coffee nut layer gâteau

4 oz. plain flour
¼ level teaspoon baking
   powder
3 large eggs

3 oz. castor sugar
coffee nut filling (Recipe 231)
few black grapes, to decorate

Sift flour and baking powder. Whisk eggs and sugar over a basin of hot water until mixture is very light in colour and thick enough to hold its own weight. Lightly fold in flour and baking powder with a metal spoon, then pour mixture into shallow tin, approximately 9 × 12 inches, well greased and lined with greaseproof paper. Smooth quickly with a knife, then bake towards the top of a moderately hot oven (400°F.—Gas Mark 5) for approximately 15 minutes. Turn out on to a wire tray, remove paper and cool.

Make the filling. Remove crisp edges from the sponge cake with a sharp knife, then cut into 3 strips approximately 8½ × 3½ inches. Sandwich together with some of the filling; use the remainder to coat the top and sides of the Gâteau. Decorate with a line of halved black grapes. Chill before serving.

*Coffee nut layer gâteau*

### 231 Coffee nut filling and frosting

4 oz. peanut butter
3 oz. butter *or* margarine
10 oz. icing sugar

1 dessertspoon strong black coffee
3 tablespoons milk

Cream peanut butter and butter or margarine with half the amount of sieved icing sugar. Add coffee and milk alternately with the rest of sieved icing sugar then beat until frosting is light in texture, smooth and fluffy.

### 232 Chocolate ginger dessert cake

6 oz. self-raising flour
3 rounded teaspoons powdered ginger
6 oz. butter *or* margarine
5 oz. soft brown sugar
3 eggs

*Filling*
5 tablespoons double cream, whipped, *or* mock cream (Recipe 416) *or* thick custard

*Icing and decoration*
3 oz. plain chocolate
2 oz. crystallised ginger
2 scant tablespoons water
small knob butter *or* margarine
8 oz. icing sugar, sieved
few drops vanilla essence

Sift together flour and ginger. Cream fat and sugar till light and fluffy, then add the eggs, one at a time, beating thoroughly after each addition. Fold in the flour, then divide mixture equally between two 8-inch greased sandwich tins. Bake at 375°F.—Gas Mark 4 for 25-30 minutes. Leave to cool on a wire tray then sandwich together with cream, mock cream or thick custard. Break chocolate into pieces, and cut the ginger. Put chocolate, water and butter into a basin over gently boiling water and stir till chocolate melts. Remove bowl from the pan then gradually add icing sugar. Beat till icing is smooth and shiny and flavour to taste with vanilla essence. Pour icing over cake so that top and sides are covered and smooth quickly with a palette knife. Leave icing to set slightly then decorate edge of cake with pieces of ginger.

*Chocolate ginger dessert cake*

### 233 Chestnut gâteau

4 oz. butter
4 oz. sugar
few drops vanilla essence
3 eggs
4 oz. flour (with plain flour use 1 teaspoon baking powder)
3 oz. cooked and sieved chestnuts

*Filling and topping*
4 oz. butter
4 oz. icing sugar
4 oz. cooked and sieved chestnuts
few drops vanilla essence
1 egg white, stiffly beaten

*To decorate*
grated chocolate

Cream butter, sugar and vanilla essence together until soft and white. Beat eggs well. Sieve flour, baking powder, if used, and already sieved chestnuts again. Stir eggs and flour mixture alternatively into butter. Line bottoms of two 7-inch sandwich tins with greased and floured paper and put in mixture. Bake for 20 minutes near top of a moderately hot oven (400°F.—Gas Mark 5). Cream butter and sugar together. Add chestnuts, vanilla essence, and lastly beaten egg white. Mix thoroughly before using. When cake is quite cold sandwich together with a third of the filling, then coat outside with same mixture. Pipe remainder of filling over the top. Decorate with grated chocolate.

### 234 Lagkage (Danish layer cake)

8 oz. fresh butter
8 oz. castor sugar
4 eggs

8 oz. plain flour
vanilla cream (Recipe 414)
glacé icing (Recipe 371)

Cream butter and sugar. Beat eggs and add gradually to butter and sugar. Then slowly mix in flour; consistency should be that of a sponge cake mixture. Grease three sandwich tins, 7 inches in diameter, and pour a third of mixture in each. Bake just above centre of moderate oven (375°F.—Gas Mark 4) for about 15 minutes. Each layer, when cooked, should be ½-inch thick.
The layers are sandwiched together alternately with vanilla cream (Recipe 414) and some kind of soft fruit (raspberries, strawberries, redcurrants etc.) in summer, and canned fruit (apricots, peaches etc.) in winter. Top of cake is decorated with glacé icing and pieces of fruit as used inside cake.

*(Illustrated in colour plate 10).*

### 235 Butterscotch cake

4 oz. butter
2 oz. sugar, preferably Demerara
2 oz. syrup

2 eggs
4 oz. flour (with plain flour add 2 level teaspoons baking powder)

Cream together the butter, sugar and syrup. Add the well beaten eggs and flour with baking powder, if used, alternately to the mixture. Pour into a greased and floured 6-inch cake tin and bake in centre of very moderate oven (350°F.—Gas Mark 3) for 1¼ hours *or* bake in small paper cases for about 15 minutes in a moderate oven (375°F.—Gas Mark 4).

## 236 *Orange sandwich cake*

4 oz. margarine
4 oz. castor sugar
2 eggs, unbeaten
finely grated rind ½ large
    orange
4 oz. self-raising flour and
    1 level teaspoon baking
    powder *or* 4 oz. plain
    flour and 2 level
    teaspoons baking powder

*Icing*
4 oz. margarine
8 oz. icing sugar
finely grated rind ½ large
    orange
1 tablespoon orange juice

*To decorate*
chocolate drops

Beat all ingredients together for about 1 minute or until well mixed. Place in either one 8-inch tin or two 7-inch sandwich tins. Smooth top. Bake on middle shelf of a moderate oven (375°F.—Gas Mark 4) for the one 8-inch cake for 30-35 minutes, or allow 20-25 minutes for two 7-inch cakes.
Beat all ingredients together until light and fluffy. Fill sandwich cake with a thin layer of icing and top with remainder. Decorate with chocolate drops.

*Orange sandwich cake*

## 237 *Battenburg cake*

6 oz. margarine
6 oz. sugar
8 oz. flour (with plain flour
    use 2 teaspoons baking
    powder)
2 eggs
little water to mix
cochineal
jam

*Marzipan*
8 oz. ground almonds
4 oz. icing sugar, sieved
4 oz. castor sugar
1 large egg *or* 2 egg yolks
few drops almond essence
castor sugar

Cream margarine and sugar together until quite soft. Sieve flour and baking powder, if used, and beat eggs. Add eggs and flour alternately to margarine, then just enough water to make soft consistency. Line a deep baking (Swiss roll) tin with greased and floured greaseproof paper, then fill half of tin with mixture. Colour rest of mixture pink, then put this into other half of cake tin. If by chance you have long tins you may like to bake different colours separately. Bake for about 25 minutes above centre in a moderately hot oven (400°F.—Gas Mark 5). When cool, cut cake into fingers. You should have two long white fingers and two long pink fingers. Cover sides with jam and put together so that you have at the bottom one white and one pink finger, then on top of white a pink finger, and on top of pink a white finger.
Mix all the ingredients for the marzipan together with the egg to make a smooth mixture. Roll out on a sugared board until large enough to wrap round the cake. Brush with jam and cover with marzipan making a seam underneath; flute the edges and mark the top in a criss-cross design with a knife, sprinkle with castor sugar.
For a chocolate cream Battenburg, make the cake mixture as above, colouring half pink and adding a little sieved cocoa to the remaining mixture. As the cocoa makes this rather stiffer, add a few drops of milk to moisten. Continue as above.
*(Illustrated in colour plate 21.)*

## 238 *Orange and chocolate sandwich*

4 oz. self-raising flour*
1½ level teaspoons baking
    powder *or* 4 oz. plain flour*
    2½ level teaspoons baking
    powder
4 oz. castor sugar
pinch salt
4 oz. cooking fat
2 eggs
½ teaspoon vanilla essence
1 dessertspoon milk

*Orange icing*
3 oz. cooking fat
8 oz. icing sugar
grated rind 1 orange
1 tablespoon orange juice
1 tablespoon milk

Sieve flour, cocoa, baking powder, sugar and salt into a basin. Add fat, eggs, vanilla and milk. Beat together about 1 minute until ingredients are well mixed. Turn into two 7-inch sandwich tins, brushed with melted fat and lined with greaseproof paper. Bake in moderately hot oven (400°F.—Gas Mark 5), for 20-25 minutes. Cool on a cake rack.
Cream fat with half sieved icing sugar, adding orange rind and orange juice. Beat well, gradually adding remaining sugar and milk. Sandwich cakes together with a layer of icing in middle. Frost over top and sides of cake with remaining icing, marking with a knife.

* *Before sieving, replace 1 heaped dessertspoon flour by 1 heaped*
  *dessertspoon cocoa*

## 239 Fruit cheese cake

½ oz. semi-sweet biscuit crumbs
12 oz.-1 lb. cottage cheese
2 oz. butter
4 oz. castor sugar
4 eggs

2 tablespoons stiffly whipped cream
2 level tablespoons cornflour
2 tablespoons lemon juice
1 teaspoon finely grated lemon rind

Prepare a 8 × 3-inches loose-bottomed cake tin by greasing well with butter and dust quickly with finely crushed biscuits. Sieve cottage cheese. Cream butter with sugar, then beat in egg yolks. Add cream, cornflour, lemon juice and rind and sieved cheese. Mix thoroughly to blend all ingredients. Lastly, fold in stiffly beaten egg whites. Turn into prepared tin and bake about 1½ hours in a very moderate oven (350°F.—Gas Mark 3). Leave to cool slightly in oven before removing from tin.
Serve cold with fruit and whipped cream.

## 240 Berry cheese shortcakes

4 oz. flour
½ teaspoon cream of tartar
¼ teaspoon bicarbonate of soda
1 oz. butter

1 egg
8 oz. cottage cheese
8 oz. strawberries or packet frozen strawberries
little sugar

Sieve flour and dry ingredients together, rub in butter, add egg and if necessary enough milk to give a rolling consistency. Roll out to about 1-inch thick and cut into rounds. Bake just above centre of hot oven (450°F.—Gas Mark 7) for about 15 minutes. Split shortcakes, sandwich together with cottage cheese and strawberries; top with a little cottage cheese and a strawberry. Dust lightly with sugar.

*Berry cheese shortcakes*

## 241 Cherry biscuit gâteau

6 oz. plain flour
2 oz. fine semolina
1 level teaspoon cinnamon
4 oz. butter or margarine
1 oz. ground almonds (optional)
3 oz. castor sugar
1 egg

*Filling and topping*
8 oz. cherries
1 rounded tablespoon icing sugar, sieved
1 egg white, stiffly whisked
¼ pint cream, whipped

Sieve flour, semolina and cinnamon into a bowl. Rub in butter, add almonds and castor sugar then bind with beaten egg. Knead quickly till smooth. Divide in two and put each into a 7-inch greased sandwich tin. Press out with knuckles till mixture covers base of each tin. Smooth tops with a palette knife then prick thoroughly. Mark edges attractively with either prongs of a fork or rounded end of a knife then bake in moderate oven (375°F.—Gas Mark 4) for 20 minutes. Allow to cool for a few minutes, then carefully remove biscuit rounds from tins and cool on a wire tray.
Reserve a few pairs of cherries for decorating. Cut remaining cherries in half and remove stones. Fold sugar and egg white into whipped cream. Mix two-thirds of cream with cherries and put between biscuit layers. Pile remaining cream on top of cake then decorate with whole cherries.

## 242 Apricot syrup cake

6 oz. butter or margarine
6 oz. golden syrup jelly
4 eggs
8 oz. self-raising flour
3 teaspoons grated orange rind

*Filling*
2 oz. butter

2 oz. golden syrup jelly
1 teaspoon grated orange rind

*Decoration*
4 oz. golden syrup jelly
2 oz. flaked almonds, browned
1 small can apricot halves

Cream the butter and golden syrup jelly together until light and fluffy, beat in eggs and fold in flour and orange rind. Turn into two 7-inch sandwich tins, greased and lightly floured, and bake in a moderate oven (375°F.—Gas Mark 4) for about 25 minutes. Turn out onto a wire tray and cool.
To make the cream filling, cream butter and golden syrup jelly together until light and fluffy then fold in orange rind. Use this to sandwich the two cakes together.
Brush the top and sides of the cake with golden syrup jelly, press three quarters of the nuts around the sides, arrange apricot halves round the top edge of the cake and sprinkle remaining nuts in the centre.

*Cherry biscuit gâteau*

*Apricot syrup cake*

## 243 Ginger crispies

2 oz. margarine
2 tablespoons golden syrup
2 oz. ready cooked oat cereal
½ teaspoon mixed spice
½ teaspoon ground ginger
1 oz. Demerara sugar

Melt margarine and syrup over low heat. Mix together remaining ingredients in a bowl, and stir in melted syrup and margarine. Mix carefully to avoid crushing cereal. Place dessertspoonfuls in very well greased bun or patty tins, and bake in moderate oven (375°F.—Gas Mark 4) for 10-15 minutes.

**Important**
Remove cookies from tins immediately by running a round-ended knife right round tins.

*Ginger crispies*

## 244 Macaroon rosettes

1 egg white
2½ oz. castor sugar
2½ oz. ground almonds
few drops almond essence
1 dessertspoon cornflour
rice paper

1½ oz. margarine

*To decorate*
2 oz. glacé cherries
2 oz. blanched almonds
1 tablespoon jam *or* jelly
1 tablespoon water

*Icing*
2 oz. icing sugar

Whisk egg white lightly, then stir in sugar, ground almonds, almond essence and cornflour. The mixture should be firm enough to roll out and if using a very large egg white you may need a little more cornflour. Roll out dough on a lightly sugared pastry board and cut into rounds about ¼-inch thick. Put on rice paper on a baking tray or on a lightly greased baking tray. Bake for 15 minutes in centre of a moderate oven (375°F.—Gas Mark 4). Let biscuits cool on tin, then cut or tear rice paper round them.
To make icing, cream margarine and icing sugar until soft. Spread liberally on top of biscuits, arrange nuts and cherries over this. Heat jam or jelly and water together, allow to cool, then brush over top to give a glaze.

## 245 Nutty fruit butterflies

8 oz. plain *or* self-raising flour
pinch salt
4 oz. cooking fat *or* butter
2 oz. almonds, chopped
1 rounded teaspoon castor sugar

1 egg yolk
1 tablespoon water
4 apricots, halved
whipped cream

Sieve flour and salt. Rub in cooking fat until mixture resembles fine breadcrumbs. Stir in chopped nuts and sugar. Mix to a smooth dough with egg yolk and water. Roll out ⅛-inch thick and cut into rounds with a 3-inch fluted cutter. Before baking cut half the rounds across centres to form half circles. Bake near top of a moderately hot oven (400°F.—Gas Mark 5) for 15-20 minutes. Cool on a cake rack.
When cold, cut apricot halves, place two pieces on each whole round of pastry, set two half rounds over top to form 'butterfly wings' and pipe cream down centre and at each end of apricots, as shown in the photograph.

*Nutty fruit butterflies*

## 246 Apple sauce cookies

8 oz. flour (with plain flour use 2 level teaspoons baking powder)
¼ level teaspoon bicarbonate of soda
1 teaspoon cinnamon
4 oz. margarine *or* butter

4 oz. brown sugar
1 small can apple sauce *or* ¼ pint thick apple purée
4 oz. currants *or* dates
1-2 oz. peanuts (optional)
1 egg

Sieve flour, baking powder, if used, soda and spice. Rub in margarine. Add sugar, apple sauce, currants, peanuts, beaten egg, mixing to a light consistency that holds its shape. Cook in spoonfuls on greased oven trays, or in patty cases near top of a hot oven (425°F.—Gas Mark 6) for 15-20 minutes.

### 247 Caramel nut cake

4 oz. margarine
4 oz. soft brown sugar
2 large eggs
4 oz. flour (with plain flour
  use 1 level teaspoon
  baking powder)

1 tablespoon hot water

*Filling and decoration*
caramel icing (Recipe 394)
nut brittle
hazel nuts

Beat together margarine and sugar until light and well blended.
Add eggs one at a time, beating thoroughly after each addition.
Fold half sieved flour, with baking powder, if used, into
mixture, then hot water, and lastly rest of flour. Divide mixture
between two greased 7-inch sandwich tins and bake near top of
a moderate oven (375°F.—Gas Mark 4) for 20-25 minutes.
Turn out and cool on a cake rack. Sandwich cake together
with some of the caramel icing. Spread top and sides with a
layer of caramel icing and finish sides with finely broken nut
brittle; top with rosettes of caramel icing and hazel nuts.

*Caramel nut cake*

### 248 Glazed apple gâteau

4 eggs
6 oz. castor sugar
grated rind ½ lemon
4 oz. flour (with plain flour
  use 1 level teaspoon baking
  powder)

*Apple mixture*
8 oz. sugar
½ pint water
juice 1 lemon
4 tablespoons redcurrant jelly

few drops red and yellow
  colouring
1 teaspoon cornflour
6-8 peeled, cored and sliced
  eating apples

*Rich butter cream*
6 oz. butter
12 oz. icing sugar
3 egg yolks
little grated chocolate

Break eggs into a basin, add sugar and beat until thick (see sponge Recipe 62).
Add lemon rind and fold in sifted flour. Pour mixture into two 8-inch greased
and floured sandwich tins and bake in a very moderate oven (350°F.—Gas
Mark 3) for 20-25 minutes. Turn out and cool.
Make a syrup with sugar, nearly all the water, lemon juice and redcurrant
jelly. Add few drops colouring and cornflour blended with rest of water and
cook until thickened. Poach apple slices in this until done, but do not allow the
apple slices to lose shape. Cool. Make rich butter cream by beating butter, sugar
and egg yolks until soft and light. Sandwich cakes together with very little
cream, half apple slices in thick glaze. Coat sides of cake with butter cream and
grated chocolate and decorate top with piped border of cream and neatly
arranged apple slices in their thick glaze.

### 249 Coconut cinnamon cake

4 oz. butter *or* margarine
4 oz. castor sugar
2 eggs
2 oz. desiccated coconut

6 oz. flour (with plain flour
  use 1½ level teaspoons
  baking powder)
2 tablespoons milk
cinnamon cream (Recipe 250)

Cream butter or margarine and sugar until light and fluffy, then add eggs, one
at a time, beating thoroughly after each addition. Add coconut, then lightly
fold in flour with baking powder, if used, alternately with the milk. Transfer
mixture to a well greased and floured 7-inch plain or fancy cake tin and bake in
centre of a very moderate oven (350°F.—Gas Mark 3) for 1-1¼ hours. Cool on a
wire tray. When cold, slice into 3 layers and sandwich together with cinnamon
cream (Recipe 250). Dust top with sieved icing sugar. For an interesting effect,
place a wire cooling tray or doyley over the top of the cake and sprinkle generously
with sieved icing sugar.

### 250 Cinnamon cream

6 oz. icing sugar sieved with
  1 rounded teaspoon
  cinnamon

3 oz. butter *or* margarine
1 dessertspoon milk

Cream icing sugar and cinnamon with butter or margarine till light and fluffy.
Beat in the milk.

### 251 Mocha gâteau

6 oz. butter
8 oz. soft brown sugar
2 eggs
2 egg yolks
6 oz. plain flour
2 packets chocolate flavoured
  cornflour
2 level teaspoons baking
  powder

4 fluid oz. strong coffee
  (6½ tablespoons)

*Filling and decoration*
chocolate butter icing using
  8 oz. butter etc. (Recipe 388)
4 oz. almonds, coarsely
  chopped

Beat butter and sugar till creamy, then beat in eggs and egg
yolks. Fold in sifted dry ingredients alternately with coffee.
Turn into two greased 8-inch sandwich tins. Bake for 40-50
minutes in centre of very moderate oven (350°F.—Gas Mark 3).
Spread just under half butter icing over one sandwich cake,
sprinkle with few almonds. Put cakes together. Spread some
icing round sides and roll in remaining almonds. Smooth icing
over top of gâteau and mark in sections with a knife. Pipe
remaining icing round top edge.

*Mocha gâteau*

# PASTRIES AND CAKES

Good pastry can form the basis of a number of delicious cakes for tea. It is, however, important to realise that where you combine cake ingredients with pastry you must be very certain that you are baking carefully, to give a good crisp pastry as well as a well cooked filling.

Generally speaking tarts with moist fillings are better baked in the centre of the oven, so that they do not become over-brown on top before the pastry is ready.

## 252 *Short crust pastry*

8 oz. flour
good pinch salt
4 oz. fat*

about 2 tablespoons cold
    water to mix

*\* There are many fats and combinations of fats that give a first class short crust pastry. Choose between:*

Modern whipped light fat. Use 3½ oz. only as it is very rich, *or*
Pure cooking fat or lard, *or*
Margarine—for best results use a table margarine, a superfine or luxury margarine, *or*
Butter, *or*
Perhaps the favourite of all—2 oz. margarine and 2 oz. cooking fat.

Sieve flour and salt and rub in fat until mixture looks like fine breadcrumbs. Using first a knife and then the fingertips to feel the pastry, gradually add enough cold water to make the dough of a rolling consistency. Lightly flour the rolling pin and pastry board. If a great deal of flour is necessary to roll out the pastry then you have undoubtedly made it too wet. Roll pastry to required thickness and shape, lifting and turning it to keep it light. Exact cooking times for pastry are given in the recipes but as a general rule it should be cooked in a hot oven (425-450°F.—Gas Mark 6-7).

## 253 *Simple-whip pastry*

3½ oz. cooking fat
3 tablespoons cold water

8 oz. flour
½ level teaspoon salt

Place the cooking fat in one piece with the water in a basin. Add 2 rounded tablespoons of flour and salt sieved together. Whisk together with a fork about half a minute until well mixed and fluffy. Add remaining flour, and stirring, form into a firm dough. Very lightly knead with the fingertips on a lightly floured board, moulding to a smooth ball. A little kneading does *not* harm the dough.

**Note**

For specially rich pastry use 4 oz. cooking fat and only 2 tablespoons water.

## 254 *Strawberry tarts*

8 oz. simple-whip *or* short crust pastry (Recipes 253, 252)
1 lb. strawberries

1 rounded teaspoon arrowroot
¼ pint water
1 oz. sugar
red colouring

Roll out pastry dough on a lightly floured board. Cut into 12-14 rounds with a 3-inch fluted cutter. Line bun tins with rounds. Prick all over with a fork. Bake near top of moderately hot oven (400°F.—Gas Mark 5) for 15-20 minutes. Cool on a wire tray. Hull, wash and dry strawberries and fill tarts. Blend arrowroot with 1 tablespoon water; boil remainder, add to arrowroot mixture and sugar; return to saucepan and boil for 3 minutes, stirring constantly. Add a few drops of colouring. When cool use as a glaze to cover fruit.

*Strawberry tarts; Coconut meringue slices; Open apple fingers*

## 255 Coconut-meringue slices

8 oz. simple-whip or
short crust pastry
(Recipes 253, 252)
raspberry jam

2 egg whites
4 oz. castor sugar
4 oz. desiccated coconut

Roll out pastry dough on a lightly floured board into an oblong large enough to line a 12 × 8 inches Swiss roll tin. Prick all over with a fork. Bake near top of moderately hot oven (400°F.—Gas Mark 6) for 20-25 minutes. Cool, spread bottom with raspberry jam. Whisk whites of egg until light and frothy. Add half sugar and whisk until very stiff. Fold in remaining sugar gradually, and 3 oz. coconut. Lightly spread it over jam. Sprinkle with remaining coconut. Bake near top of a moderate oven (375°F.—Gas Mark 4) for 10 minutes. Cut into fingers.

## 256 Open apple fingers

8 oz. simple-whip or
short crust pastry
(Recipes 253, 252)

1½ lb. cooking apples
2 tablespoons apricot jam
1 oz. almonds, chopped

Roll out pastry dough on a lightly floured board into an oblong large enough to line a 12 × 8 inches Swiss roll tin. Prick all over with a fork. Peel, core and slice apples; overlap them to fill pastry case. Carefully spread jam over apples. Sprinkle with almonds. Bake near top of moderately hot oven (400°F.—Gas Mark 5) for 40-45 minutes. When cold cut into fingers.

## 257 Flaky pastry (1)

8 oz. plain flour
pinch salt

5-6 oz. fat*
water to mix

* *Use All Butter or*
*All table margarine or superfine or luxury margarine or two-thirds table margarine and one-third modern whipped-up light fat or pure cooking fat*

Sieve flour with salt. Divide fat into three. Rub one portion into flour in usual way and mix to rolling consistency with cold water. Roll out to oblong shape. Now take the second portion of fat, divide it into small pieces and lay them on surface of two-thirds of dough. Leave remaining third without fat. Take its two corners and fold back over second third so that dough looks like an envelope with its flap open. Fold over top end of pastry, so closing the 'envelope'. Turn pastry at right angles, seal open ends of pastry and 'rib' it. This means depressing it with the rolling pin at intervals, so giving a corrugated effect and equalising the pressure of air. This makes it certain that the pastry will rise evenly. Repeat the process again using the remaining fat and turning pastry in same way. Roll out pastry once more, but should it begin to feel very soft and sticky put it into a cold place for 30 minutes to become firm before rolling out. Fold pastry as before, turn it, seal edges and 'rib' it. Altogether pastry should have three foldings and three rollings. It is then ready to stand in a cold place for a little while before baking, since the contrast between the cold and the heat of the oven makes the pastry rise better. To bake, use a very hot oven (475°F.—Gas Mark 8) for the first 15 minutes. After this lower the Gas Mark to 5 or 6, or turn the electric oven off to finish cooking for remaining time at a lower temperature.

## 258 Quick flaky pastry

4 oz. plain flour
pinch salt
2½ oz. cooking fat

2½-3 tablespoons cold water
½ teaspoon lemon juice
(optional)

Sieve flour and salt into a basin. Divide cooking fat into four portions and rub one portion into flour. Add the water and lemon, mixing with a knife to a smooth non-sticky dough. If the dough is too stiff, or there is some flour unabsorbed, add an extra teaspoon of water and mix until dough is smooth. Sprinkle with flour, form into an oblong shape with the fingers and turn out on to a floured board. Sprinkle with flour and leave to rest in a cool place for 30 minutes, covering with a damp cloth. Roll out to an oblong 6 × 3 inches. Dab small pieces of second portion of cooking fat evenly on the top two-thirds of the dough, leaving a margin of ½ inch all round. Fold the bottom third of the pastry upwards and the top third down to cover it. Brush off surplus flour. Seal the three open edges with a rolling pin and give the pastry a half turn to the left. Roll out again to a strip 6 × 3 inches. Add the third portion of cooking fat, dabbing it on in small pieces as before. Fold the pastry in three, seal, give a half turn and roll again. Repeat once more with the remaining portion of cooking fat. Roll out for the last time without cooking fat. Leave the pastry to rest for 30 minutes in a cool place as before.

## 259 Poinsettias

2 oz. icing sugar
2 oz. almonds, finely chopped

4 oz. quick flaky pastry
(Recipe 258)
few glacé cherries

Sprinkle the pastry board with a mixture of icing sugar and the very finely chopped almonds. Roll the pastry out on this to ½-inch thickness. Cut into 2½-inch squares. Place the squares on a baking sheet and cut 1 inch in from each corner towards the centre. Fold alternate corners into the centre in pinwheel fashion. Press gently in the centre. Decorate with a small piece of glacé cherry. Bake near the top of a hot oven (450°F.—Gas Mark 7) for 10-15 minutes. Serve as a biscuit with fruit.

*Poinsettias*

12. Banana chocolate flan

13. Chocolate gâteau

## 260 Fleur or flan pastry or biscuit crust
### (for sweet flans and fruit tarts)

4-5 oz. fat*
2 dessertspoons sugar
8 oz. flour

pinch salt
cold water or
1 egg yolk, to bind

* Table margarine **or** butter **or** the whipped-up light fat (vegetable shortening) is excellent. Use 3½ oz. only of latter.

Cream fat and sugar together until light in colour. Sieve flour and salt together and add creamed fat, mixing with a knife. Gradually add enough water or egg and water to make a firm rolling consistency. Use fingertips to feel the pastry (see short crust, Recipe 252). When dough rolls into a ball without undue pressure it is the right consistency. Bake in a moderately hot to hot oven (400-425°F.—Gas Mark 5-6). To line flan, put pastry over case and press down base and sides firmly then roll over top with rolling pin for a good edge.

## 261 Cream horns

8 oz. quick flaky pastry
  (Recipe 258)
  or flaky pastry
  (Recipe 257)

milk
raspberry jam
whipped cream

Make the pastry, then lightly brush the outsides of 12 cream horn tins with melted cooking fat. Roll out the pastry about ¼ inch thick, cut into strips about 1 inch wide by 12 inches long. Dampen along the edge of each strip with water. Beginning at the pointed end of each cone, wind the pastry round, each round overlapping the dampened edge of the previous one by ¼ inch. Place, a little apart, on the baking sheet, with the top-end joins underneath. Lightly brush the tops with milk. Bake near the top of a hot oven (450°F.—Gas Mark 7) for 15-20 minutes. Gently remove horn tins and cool on cake rack. Fill horns with ½ teaspoon raspberry jam in the base and pipe in whipped cream.

## 262 Puff pastry

8 oz. plain flour
good pinch salt
cold water to mix

few drops lemon juice
7-8 oz. fat*

* You have a good choice of fats here. Use:
Butter—the economical New Zealand butter is excellent **or** table **or** luxury margarine **or**
Two-thirds table margarine and one-third modern whipped-up light fat

Sieve flour and salt together. Mix to rolling consistency with cold water and lemon juice. Roll to oblong shape. Make fat into neat block and place in centre of pastry and fold over it first the bottom section of pastry and then the top section, so that the fat is quite covered. Turn the dough at right angles, seal edges and 'rib' carefully (see Recipe 257 for flaky pastry) and roll out. Fold dough into envelope, turn it, seal edges, 'rib' and roll again. Repeat five times, so making seven rollings and seven foldings in all. Put the pastry to rest in cold place once or twice between rollings to prevent it becoming sticky and soft. Always put it to rest before rolling it for the last time, and before baking. Bake in very hot oven (to make it rise, and keep in the fat). Bake for the first 10-15 minutes at 475-500°F.—Gas Mark 8-9, then lower to Gas Mark 5-6 or turn electric oven right off or re-set to 400°F. to finish cooking at lower temperature. Puff pastry should rise to four or five times its original thickness. When making cases it may be necessary to remove a little soft dough and return to oven to dry out.

## 263 Palmiers glacés

Make flaky or puff pastry (Recipes 257, 262) as usual, but on the last 2 rollings sprinkle the pastry board very lavishly with SUGAR, not flour. Roll out the pastry to a large oblong shape, then roll one long side as though you were rolling a Swiss roll, but stop at the centre. Roll the other side in just the same way so that rolls meet in the middle. Cut into slices about ⅓ inch thick, and bake on ungreased baking trays, in a very hot oven (475°F.—Gas Mark 8) for about 12 minutes. Turn over during cooking, so that both sides are a golden caramel colour. If wished sandwich together with jam or cream.

## 264 Jam puffs

8 oz. puff pastry
  (Recipe 262)
jam

egg white
castor sugar

Roll out the pastry until wafer thin. Cut into large squares. Put a little jam on half the square, dividing it diagonally. Damp the edges of the plain pastry and fold over so that it nearly meets the edges on the other side. Turn in the edges left. This means the join is just coming away from the edge of the now triangular shape. Put the puffs on to baking trays, turning them as you do so to keep the join on the under side. Brush with either water or egg white and dust liberally with castor sugar. Bake for a good 10 minutes near the top of a very hot oven (475°F.—Gas Mark 8).

## 265 Mille-feuilles
### (or Vanilla slices)

8 oz. puff pastry
  (Recipe 262)
jam

cream or confectioner's
  custard (Recipe 414)
chopped nuts
glacé icing (Recipe 371)

The puff pastry can either be cut into fingers or baked whole as one cake. If baking as a whole cake put the 2 rounds of pastry, each about ½ inch thick, into the centre of a very hot oven. Bake at 475°F.—Gas Mark 8 for a good 10 minutes, then lower to just a moderately hot oven until firm and pale brown in colour. Let the pastry get quite cold, then sandwich the 2 layers together with jam and sweetened cream or confectioner's custard. Coat the outside with more cream, and cover with chopped nuts. Cover the top with icing and nuts. For individual slices cut into fingers and bake for approximately 13 minutes. Decorate as large cake.

## 266  Eccles cakes

8 oz. puff pastry *or* flaky pastry
  (Recipes 262, 257)
2 oz. margarine
2 oz. sugar
2 oz. sultanas

2 oz. currants
2 oz. chopped candied peel
  grated rind and juice 1 lemon
  good pinch mixed spice

Roll the pastry out until it is about the thickness of a penny. Cut into large round shapes. Cream the margarine and sugar together, then work in all the ingredients. Put a spoonful of this mixture on one half of the pastry. Fold over, then press the edges very firmly together. If necessary, brush with a little milk or water to seal them. Shape with a rolling pin and your fingers until you have rounds. Make 2 or 3 splits on the top of each cake. Brush lightly with milk and castor sugar. Bake in the centre of a hot oven (450°F.—Gas Mark 7) for about 20 minutes. After 15 minutes the heat can be reduced if cakes are becoming too brown.

## 267  Banbury cakes

8 oz. puff *or* flaky pastry
  (Recipes 262, 257)
filling as for Eccles cakes
  (Recipe 266)

2 oz. cake crumbs *or*
  macaroon biscuit crumbs
castor sugar

Roll out the pastry to thickness of a penny. Cut into large oval shapes. Cream margarine and sugar together, then work in rest of filling with cake crumbs. Put a spoonful on to half the pastry, fold over and press the edges very firmly together. If necessary brush with a little milk or water to seal them. Shape with a rolling pin and your fingers into neat oval shapes. Make 2 or 3 slits on top of each cake. Brush tops with water and sprinkle with castor sugar. Bake in the centre of a hot oven (450°F.—Gas Mark 7) for about 20 minutes, reducing the heat if necessary after 15 minutes.

## 268  Shropshire mint cakes

1 oz. crystallised peel
2 oz. castor sugar
6 oz. currants
1 oz. butter

1 tablespoon freshly
  chopped mint
8 oz. flaky pastry
  (Recipe 257)

Mix all the ingredients for the filling together. Roll out flaky pastry and proceed as for Eccles cakes (Recipe 266).

## 269  Maids of honour

curds from 1 pint sour milk*
3 oz. margarine *or* butter
2 oz. sugar
1 dessertspoon brandy *or*
  sherry

1 oz. almonds, chopped
grated rind 1 lemon
pinch cinnamon
1 egg
8 oz. flaky *or* puff pastry
  (Recipes 257, 262)

*\* To speed souring milk warm to blood heat then stir in 1 teaspoon rennet*

To obtain curds, put milk through a muslin bag and allow it to drip overnight or for several hours. Cream margarine and sugar. Add curds, brandy, nuts, lemon rind and cinnamon. Beat egg well and work it in gradually. Put spoonfuls of mixture into patty tins, which should be lined with pastry. Bake for 20-25 minutes in middle of oven. Set heat at 475°F.—Gas Mark 8 for 10 minutes, then lower heat to 400°F.—Gas Mark 5 for remainder of time.

## 270  Mock maids of honour

4 oz. short crust *or* flaky pastry
  (Recipes 252, 257)
jam
1½ oz. butter
1½ oz. sugar

1 egg
6 oz. stale cake crumbs*
1 oz. ground almonds
glacé icing (Recipe 371)
glacé cherries

*\* If using plain cake crumbs a few sultanas can be added*

Line patty tins with thin pastry, and spread with a very little jam. Cream butter and sugar, add the egg, cake crumbs and ground almonds. Put spoonfuls of this mixture on top of the jam and bake the cakes just above the centre of a moderately hot oven (400-425°F.—Gas Mark 5-6) until the filling is firm and the pastry crisp and golden brown. When cold cover with a thick layer of glacé icing and a glacé cherry.

## 271  Choux pastry

¼ pint water
1 oz. margarine *or* butter
pinch sugar

3 oz. plain *or*
  self-raising flour
2 whole eggs and yolk of 1 egg
  or 3 small eggs

Put water, margarine or butter and sugar into a saucepan. Heat gently till fat has melted. Remove from heat. Stir in flour. Return pan to low heat and cook very gently but thoroughly, stirring all the time, until mixture is dry enough to form a ball and leave pan clean. Once again remove pan from heat and gradually add well beaten eggs. Do this slowly to produce a perfectly smooth mixture. Allow to cool, then use for cream buns and éclairs.

## 272  Cream buns

choux pastry (Recipe 271)
cream

either icing sugar *or* flavoured
  water icing to cover

There are several ways of making the shape of cream buns. The most simple is to grease and flour individual patty tins and put in a spoonful of the mixture. Or pile some of the mixture on to well-greased and floured baking trays. The correct method, however, is to put the mixture into piping bags and force through large plain pipes on to the floured and greased baking trays. If you have a deep tin which can be put right over the cakes while in the oven, use this, for it helps to give a far better shape to them. The tin should be light in weight and allow several inches in height, for buns will rise considerably as they cook. It is, however, quite possible to bake buns without the tin. Put the tray of cakes into the centre of a hot oven (450°F.—Gas Mark 7) for 35 minutes. Allow a good 5 minutes extra cooking time if they are covered. For the last 20 minutes reduce the heat to 400°F.—Gas Mark 5. At the end of this time the buns should be pale golden in colour, and feel very firm and crisp. Cool them gradually and away from a draught. You may sometimes find when you split the buns there is a little uncooked pastry left in the centre. This should be taken out carefully, and if you feel it necessary, the buns returned for a few minutes to a cool oven to dry.

When you are quite sure the buns are cold split them and fill with cream. Cover with sieved icing sugar or chocolate or coffee flavoured water icing (Recipe 372 or 373).

**Variation**
**Chocolate cream buns**
As above, but when cold split and fill with ice cream. Top with chocolate sauce and serve at once.

*Chocolate cream buns*

## 273 *Éclairs*

choux pastry (Recipe 271)          cream

Pipe mixture into finger shapes on well greased and floured baking trays, or put into greased and floured finger tins. Bake as Cream Buns (Recipes 272) without covering for 25 minutes. When cooked, split, fill with cream and cover with chocolate or coffee icing (Recipes 372, 373).

## 274 *Profiteroles*

Name given to tiny cream buns filled with cream and served with chocolate sauce as a sweet or covered with melted chocolate icing (Recipe 395).

## 275 *Choux swans*

Choux pastry lends itself to other types of cakes. For a special occasion it is possible to make swan shapes, which look most interesting, but are very simple. Put the choux pastry (Recipe 271) into a piping bag with a rather small plain rose pipe. Pipe firstly into oval shapes, as shown, on to well greased baking tins, then into the shape of the neck and head of the swan (see diagram).

It is a good idea to pipe the 'bodies' on one tin and the 'heads' on another, since the latter are more quickly baked. Cook the 'bodies' as cream buns, i.e. for a longer period, and the 'heads' as éclairs. When cooked and cold dust the base with sieved icing sugar, after filling with cream, and press the 'heads' into position.

The choux pastry can also be piped into ring shapes, the top covered with thinly shredded almonds, then baked as éclairs. When cooked and cold split each ring carefully and fill with cream and decorate with icing or icing sugar. The correct name of ring éclairs is Gâteaux Paris Brest.

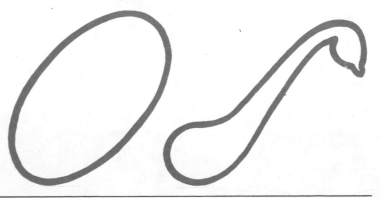

*Choux swans*

## 276 *Almond slices*

*Pastry*
8 oz. plain flour
pinch salt
4 oz. margarine
1 egg yolk
1 tablespoon water
raspberry *or* apricot jam

*Macaroon topping*
4 oz. castor sugar
4 oz. icing sugar
4 oz. ground almonds
2 oz. semolina
1 whole egg and 1 egg white
few drops almond essence
split blanched almonds to
  decorate

Sieve flour and salt into a basin. Rub in margarine until mixture resembles fine breadcrumbs. Mix to a stiff dough with the egg yolk and water. Knead lightly until smooth. Roll out and cut into two strips approximately 10 × 3 inches. Transfer to a greased baking tray. Pinch up long edges to form a thick band along both sides of each strip. Spread base thinly with raspberry or apricot jam.

**To make macaroon topping**
Mix the dry ingredients together. Stir in eggs and essence. Top strips of pastry with this mixture. Decorate with blanched almonds. Bake on the second shelf from the top of a fairly hot oven (400°F.—Gas Mark 5) for 25-30 minutes. Cool on a wire tray. When cold cut into fingers.

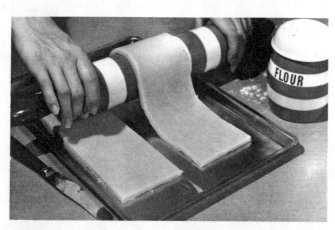

*Placing the strips of dough on a greased baking tray*

*Pinching the edges of the dough*

*Spreading over the macaroon topping*

*Cooled and cut into fingers*

## 277 *Macaroon tarts*

6 oz. short crust pastry
  (Recipe 252)
little jam
2 egg whites

few drops almond essence
4 oz. ground almonds
4 oz. castor sugar

Roll out the pastry, cut into rounds and line patty tins with this. Spread with a small amount of jam. Whisk the egg whites and add the almond essence, ground almonds and sugar. Spread this mixture into the patty cases, lined with pastry, being careful not to make them too full. If any pastry remains roll out very thinly indeed, cut into very narrow strips and make crosses of these on each tart. Bake for approximately 15-20 minutes in the centre of a hot oven (425-450°F.—Gas Mark 6-7).

**Variations:**
For economy use ½ ground almonds and ½ semolina or cake crumbs, or use 3 oz. ground almonds and 1 oz. cocoa powder.

## 278 *Coconut macaroon tarts*

5 oz. short crust pastry
  (Recipe 252)
jam
1 egg white

3 oz. desiccated coconut
2 oz. sugar
few drops water

Line patty tins with the very thin pastry and little jam. Whisk up egg white, add coconut and sugar and just enough water to give soft consistency. Put into patty cases and bake for 15 minutes in centre of hot oven (425-450°F.—Gas Mark 6-7), then lower heat for a further 5 minutes.

## 279 Apple strudel

*For paste:*
8 oz. plain flour
pinch salt
2 tablespoons olive oil
1 egg yolk
5 tablespoons tepid water

*For filling:*
1½ oz. fresh white breadcrumbs
1 oz. butter
1 lb. cooking apples,
   weight when peeled,
   finely chopped

1 oz. castor sugar
½ teaspoon mixed spice
¼ teaspoon powdered
   cinnamon
2 oz. sultanas
finely grated zest ½ lemon
1 egg white
1 oz. hazelnuts (chopped)

Sieve the flour and salt into a warm mixing bowl. Add the olive oil, egg yolk and water. Mix and knead to a smooth dough. Wrap tightly in foil and allow it to rest for 30 minutes.

*For filling*
Fry the breadcrumbs in ½ oz. of the butter and mix with the remaining ingredients, except butter.
Roll the paste thinly on to a clean, floured teacloth. Stretch the paste by pulling it gently, until it is paper thin. Melt the remaining ½ oz. of butter and brush it over the surface of the paste. Scatter the filling over the top, to within one inch of the edges. Roll Swiss roll fashion. Press the ends together and slide the strudel onto a greased and floured baking sheet. Bake in a moderate oven 375°F.—Gas Mark 4) for 40-45 minutes. Serve hot or cold, dredged with icing sugar.
*(Illustrated in colour plate 11.)*

## 280 Welsh cheese cakes

4 oz. short crust pastry
   (Recipe 252)
raspberry jam
2 oz. butter
2 oz. sugar

1 egg
2 oz. flour
grated rind ½ lemon
pinch baking powder
little castor sugar

Line some patty tins with short crust pastry, then put a little raspberry jam into the bottom of each. Beat the butter and sugar together, then beat in the egg. Add the flour, lemon rind and lastly the baking powder. Put 1 teaspoon of this mixture over the jam in each patty tin and bake at once in a moderately hot oven (400°F.—Gas Mark 5) until nicely browned. Cool on a wire tray and before serving sprinkle with castor sugar.

## 281 Meringue cream slices

6 oz. short crust pastry
   (Recipe 252)

*Filling*
2 oz. plain flour
2 oz. sugar
2 egg yolks
½ pint milk
finely grated rind 1 orange

*Meringue*
2 egg whites
4 oz. castor sugar
few sultanas *or* raisins

Roll out pastry on to lightly floured board to rectangle approximately 8 × 10 inches. Place on a baking sheet.
Place flour and sugar in a basin. Stir in the egg yolks and blend with a little cold milk. Bring remainder of the milk to the boil and pour over the blended ingredients. Return to the pan and cook over a very low heat, whisking all the time until thick and the flour cooked. Stir in the grated orange rind. Leave to cool. When cold spread the filling down the centre of the pastry and fold the sides towards the middle, about 1½ inches on each side. Bake near the top of a hot oven (450°F.—Gas Mark 7) for 20-25 minutes.
Whisk the egg whites until stiff, add half the castor sugar and whisk again until stiff. Fold in the remaining sugar and pile roughly over the filling taking the meringue out to the edges. Decorate with lines of sultanas or raisins. Place in middle of a cool oven (300°F.—Gas Mark 2) for 10-15 minutes until lightly browned. Cut in slices. These slices are best served freshly made and just cold.

*Meringue cream slices*

## 282  Date fingers

8 oz. short crust pastry
  (Recipe 252)

| Filling | To decorate |
|---|---|
| 6 oz. dates | egg white *or* water |
| 1 oz. walnuts, chopped | castor sugar |
| juice ½ lemon | |

Make the pastry and roll out into a strip 10 × 6 inches. Cut
this into two lengthways.
Prepare the filling by chopping the dates finely and mixing
these with the chopped walnuts and enough lemon juice to
make soft paste. Spread this over one of the strips of pastry.
Place the other pastry strip on top and press down lightly.
Trim the edges, brush the top with egg white and sprinkle with
castor sugar. Cut the strip into 8 fingers and bake in centre of
hot oven (450°F.—Gas Mark 7) for approximately 20-25
minutes. Cool on a wire tray.

*Date fingers*

## 283  Coconut fingers

| | |
|---|---|
| 4 oz. short crust pastry | 3 oz. castor sugar |
|   (Recipe 252) | few drops water |
| jam | about 2 oz. plain *or* |
| 1 egg white |   milk chocolate |
| 4 oz. desiccated coconut | |

Roll out the pastry thinly to form a neat oblong shape. Put this on to the back
of a baking tin and spread thinly with jam. Whip egg white lightly, stir in the
coconut, sugar and just enough water to make soft consistency. Spread over
the pastry and bake for about 25 minutes in centre of moderately hot oven
(400°F.—Gas Mark 5), making sure the bottom of the pastry is crisp. Mark into
fingers and cool on a wire tray. When quite cold melt the chocolate in a basin
over hot water and spread a narrow strip of chocolate down the centre of each
finger.

## 284  Yorkshire curd cakes

| | |
|---|---|
| curds from 1 pint sour milk* | pinch salt |
| 1-2 oz. butter *or* margarine | 2 oz. dried fruit |
| 2 oz. sugar | 6 oz. flaky pastry (Recipe 257) |
| 1 large *or* 2 small eggs | little grated nutmeg |

*\* To speed souring of milk, warm milk to blood heat and stir in
1 teaspoon rennet*

To obtain the curds pour the sour milk into a muslin bag and allow to drip for
several hours. Cream the margarine and sugar together, add the curds, then the
well beaten eggs, the salt and dried fruit. Line rather deep patty tins or a deep
pie plate with the pastry and pour in the filling. Sprinkle on top with grated
nutmeg and put into centre of a hot oven (450°F.—Gas Mark 4) and bake for
15 minutes, after which time lower the heat to 400°F.—Gas Mark 4 for a further
10-15 minutes.

## 285  Banana chocolate flan

| | |
|---|---|
| ½ oz. cornflour | 1 9-inch baked pastry case |
| 5 oz. sugar | ¼ oz. gelatine |
| ½ pint milk | 1 tablespoon hot water |
| 3 eggs | |
| ½ teaspoon vanilla essence | *To decorate* |
| 4 oz. chocolate | grated chocolate |
| 2 bananas | banana |

Mix cornflour and 3 oz. sugar together. Add hot milk slowly to beaten egg
yolks, pour on to cornflour mixture. Cook very slowly over low heat until
custard thickens and coats back of spoon. Remove from heat and add vanilla
essence. To half this custard add chocolate and stir until melted. Arrange
sliced banana in bottom of pastry case and pour in chocolate custard. Chill.
To other half of custard add gelatine dissolved in hot water. Chill until slightly
thick. Beat egg whites until frothy, add rest of sugar and beat well together, then
fold into custard mixture. Pour over chocolate layer and leave until set. Decorate
with grated chocolate and banana slices.

*(Illustrated in colour plate 12.)*

## 286 *French apple flan*

6 large cooking apples
¼ pint water
4 oz. sugar
2 tablespoons butter

6 oz. short crust *or* fleur pastry
(Recipes 252, 260)
4 small cooking apples
apricot jam to glaze

Pare, core and quarter 6 cooking apples and put in saucepan with water, half the sugar and butter. Cover tightly and cook apples over moderate heat until tender. Press apples through a fine sieve, or purée them in an electric blender and let purée cool. Line a buttered flan ring with pastry and half fill with apple purée. Then peel, core and finely slice small cooking apples and arrange slices over apple purée in a spiral, starting at centre and working out, slices overlapping. Sprinkle fruit with rest of sugar and bake flan in moderately hot to hot oven (400-425°F. —Gas Mark 5-6) for 25-30 minutes, or until apples are tender and crust is golden. Glaze hot flan with apricot jam melted and thinned to spreading consistency with a little hot water. Top with thick cream if liked.

(*Also illustrated in colour on the jacket.*)

*French apple flan*

## 287 *Chocolate gâteau*

3 oz. unsweetened or plain
chocolate
8 *level* tablespoons clear
honey
6 oz. plain flour
1 level teaspoon bicarbonate
of soda
¾ teaspoon salt
4 oz. butter
3 oz. castor sugar
1 teaspoon vanilla essence
2 eggs

scant ¼ pint water

*For icing :*
6 oz. unsweetened or plain
chocolate
4 level tablespoons clear honey
8 oz. icing sugar
2 tablespoons warm water

*To decorate*
2 oz. walnut halves
angelica

Melt chocolate and honey in a basin over pan of hot water. Beat well. Cool. Sieve flour, bicarbonate of soda and salt three times. Cream butter and sugar until soft and light. Beat in chocolate mixture, then essence and eggs one at a time. Stir in flour, a little at a time, alternately with water. Beat well. Pour into two greased and bottom-lined 8-inch sandwich tins. Bake in centre of very moderate to moderate oven (350-375°F.—Gas Mark 4) for 45-50 minutes. To make icing, melt chocolate and honey in basin over hot water. Cool. Beat in half the sugar, stir in water and remaining sugar and beat well. Sandwich cakes with icing. Coat top and sides with remaining icing and rough up. Decorate with nuts and angelica.

(*Illustrated in colour plate 13.*)

## 288 *Cream cheese and apple flan*

3 dessert apples
8 oz. cream cheese
about 2 oz. castor sugar
1 short crust *or* fleur pastry
flan case (Recipes 252, 260)
redcurrant glaze
(Recipe 289)

angelica stalks

*Syrup*
4 oz. sugar
juice ½ lemon
½ pint water

Halve, core and peel the apples. Poach in boiling syrup made by boiling together sugar, lemon juice and water, until just tender. Drain well. Cream the cheese and sugar together, sweetening to taste. Spread evenly on the bottom of the flan case. Arrange the halved apples on top (cut side downwards). Coat carefully with the redcurrant glaze and decorate with angelica stalks. Serve cold.

## 289 *Redcurrant glaze*

4 dessertspoons redcurrant
jelly

1 dessertspoon water
2 dessertspoons lemon juice

Put jelly, water and lemon juice into a small thick saucepan and stir over gentle heat till dissolved. Boil briskly until slightly tacky, but do not overboil or the glaze will be of toffee consistency. Spoon the glaze very carefully over the fruit.

# SMALL CAKES

In this chapter you will find recipes for small cakes and biscuit-type cakes. The ordinary small cake will not keep well, so should be made in sufficiently limited quantities to be eaten while fresh. The biscuit-type of cake tends to keep better, but should be stored well away from ordinary cakes.

For children's parties you will find very tiny cakes are extremely popular and you can obtain patty tins that produce really midget cakes.

## 290 *Coconut castles*

4 oz. margarine
4 oz. castor sugar
1½ oz. desiccated coconut
2 eggs
5 oz. flour (with plain flour use 1¼ level teaspoons baking powder)
2 tablespoons milk

*To decorate*
raspberry jam
desiccated coconut

Cream margarine and sugar together until light and fluffy, then work in coconut. Add lightly whisked egg in tablespoons, beating in well after each addition. Fold in sieved flour, with baking powder, if used, and lastly mix in milk. Well grease 16 dariole tins and two-thirds fill with mixture. Place tins on a baking sheet and bake above centre of a moderately hot oven (400°F.—Gas Mark 5) for 15-20 minutes. Turn out on to a wire tray to cool. When cold, dip tops in warmed jam and then in coconut.

*Coconut castles*

## 291 *Madeleines*

4 oz. flour
4 eggs
4 oz. castor sugar
4 oz. butter *or* margarine
few drops vanilla essence

melted and sieved apricot jam
desiccated coconut
halved glacé cherries
angelica leaves

Sieve flour. Whisk together eggs and sugar over hot water until mixture is thick, pale in colour and will hold its own weight. Very lightly, and with a metal spoon, fold in flour and then melted butter or margarine and vanilla essence. Three-quarters fill 16-18 well-greased dariole moulds with mixture, and bake near top of a moderately hot oven (400°F.—Gas Mark 5) for 10-15 minutes. Turn out on to a wire tray to cool. When cold brush each madeleine with melted apricot jam and roll in desiccated coconut. Decorate top of each with ½ glacé cherry and angelica leaves.

## 292 *Chocolate madeleines*

2 oz. margarine
2 oz. castor sugar
1 egg
2½ oz. flour (with plain flour use ¾ level teaspoon baking powder)

2 teaspoons cocoa powder
sieved jam
desiccated coconut
glacé cherries
angelica

Cream fat and sugar until light and fluffy. Beat in lightly whisked egg. Fold in sieved flour, baking powder, if used, and cocoa adding a little warm water to form a soft dropping consistency. Half fill greased dariole moulds. Bake for 15 minutes just above centre of moderately hot oven (400°F.—Gas Mark 5). Cool on a wire tray. When cool, spread top and sides with a thin coating of sieved jam. Roll in coconut and top with glacé cherries and angelica.

To roll in coconut either insert skewer in cake and roll carefully or turn in coconut with two spoons.

## 293 *Orange madeleines*

3 oz. margarine
3 oz. castor sugar
2 teaspoons finely grated orange rind
1 egg
4 oz. flour (with plain flour use 1 teaspoon baking powder)

2 tablespoons orange juice
orange marmalade
desiccated coconut
12 crystallised orange slices (optional)

Cream margarine, sugar and orange rind together until soft and light. Add beaten egg and then stir in flour with baking powder, if used, and orange juice. Half fill well greased and floured dariole moulds and bake for about 10 minutes in a hot oven (450°F.—Gas Mark 7). Turn out and coat with warm marmalade, sieved if liked. Roll in coconut and top with butterfly of orange slice—made by cutting slice in half.

## 294 Ginger cakes

4 oz. self-raising flour
1½ level teaspoons baking
  powder *or* 4 oz. plain flour
  2½ level teaspoons baking
  powder
1 level teaspoon ground
  ginger
4 oz. castor sugar

3 oz. cooking fat *or* butter
2 eggs
2 oz. crystallised ginger,
  chopped
1 dessertspoon water
little glacé icing (Recipe 371)
small slices crystallised ginger

Sieve flour, baking powder, ground ginger and sugar into a
bowl. Add cooking fat, eggs, crystallised ginger and water, and
mixing all ingredients beat for 1 minute. Place one rounded
dessertspoon of the mixture in bun tins, brushed with melted
cooking fat. Bake near the top of a moderately hot oven (400°F.
—Gas Mark 5) for 20-25 minutes. When cold, ice with a little
white glacé icing and top with a slice of crystallised ginger.

*Ginger cakes*

## 295 Rich queen cakes

4 oz. margarine *or* butter
4 oz. castor sugar
½ teaspoon vanilla essence
2 eggs

4 oz. flour (with plain flour
  use 1 level teaspoon baking
  powder)
2 oz. sultanas, cut in half
1 tablespoon hot water

Cream together the margarine and sugar until light and fluffy,
and add the vanilla essence. Beat in the eggs one at a time. Fold
in the sieved flour, with baking powder, if used, and then the
sultanas and hot water. Two-thirds fill greased bun tins or
paper cases with the mixture and bake near top of a moderately
hot oven (400°F.—Gas Mark 5) for 15 minutes. Turn out and
cool on a cake rack. Ice, if liked, with plain glacé icing (Recipe
371).

*Rich queen cakes*

## 296 Fruity queen cakes

Use above recipe but add 1 oz. sultanas, 1 oz. glacé cherries, 1 oz. currants and
½ oz. chopped candied peel.

## 297 Economical queen cakes

Use above recipe but reduce the margarine or butter and sugar to 2 oz. each.
Bake near top of a hot oven (425-450°F.—Gas Mark 6-7).

## 298 Almond cakes

Ingredients as either Rich or Economical queen cakes (Recipes 295, 297) but
omit the sultanas and add 2 oz. chopped blanched almonds and a few drops
almond essence. Cover with few chopped almonds before baking.

## 299 Cherry cakes

Ingredients as either Rich or Economical queen cakes (Recipes 295, 297) but
omit the sultanas and add 2-3 oz. quartered glacé cherries. These should be
lightly floured before adding to the mixture.

## 300 Chocolate queen cakes

Ingredients as either Rich or Economical queen cakes (Recipes 295, 297) but omit ½ oz. flour and use ½ oz. cocoa powder instead. Sieve this with the flour. When cold ice the tops with butter icing (Recipe 388) and decorate with a walnut half.

*Chocolate queen cakes*

## 301 Coffee queen cakes

Ingredients as either Rich or Economical Queen cakes (Recipes 295, 297) but blend with very strong coffee instead of hot water. Cover with coffee glacé icing (Recipe 373) when cold.

## 302 Lemon or orange queen cakes

Ingredients as either Rich or Economical Queen cakes (Recipes 295, 297) but add finely grated rind of 1 lemon or 1 or 2 oranges and 1 tablespoon lemon juice or orange juice instead of water. Cover with lemon or orange glacé icing (Recipe 374) when cold.

## 303 Gingerbread squares

Make a rich gingerbread (Recipe 29). When cold, cut into squares and top with fresh whipped cream or frosting to which thick apple purée can be added.
*(Illustrated in colour plate 14.)*

## 304 Meringue baskets

Make up the meringue as Pavlova cake (Recipe 137). Place an oiled piece of greaseproof paper on a baking sheet. Put meringue mixture in a large piping bag with an open star nozzle. Pipe round base, pipe around edge to build a basket of meringue. Bake as Pavlova cake. Serve filled with fruit of choice.
*(Illustrated in colour plate 15.)*

## 305 Coffee butterfly cakes

| | |
|---|---|
| 4 oz. margarine | *Filling* |
| 4 oz. self-raising flour with 1 level teaspoon baking powder (with plain flour use 2 teaspoons baking powder) | 2 oz. margarine |
| | 1 oz. castor sugar |
| | 1 heaped teaspoon instant coffee powder |
| 4 oz. castor sugar | 1 dessertspoon warm water |
| 2 eggs | 1 dessertspoon milk |

Place all the cake ingredients in a mixing bowl. Quickly mix together, then beat thoroughly with a wooden spoon (pressing the margarine to the sides of the basin, if refrigerated). Place the mixture in 18 small bun tins, greased with margarine. Bake near top of a moderately hot oven (400°F.—Gas Mark 5) for 15-20 minutes. Cool on a cake rack.
Place the margarine, sugar, instant coffee powder and water in a small bowl. Whisk for 1-2 minutes, then add the milk, a little at a time, and whisk again.
Cut off tops of the buns (approximately 1½ inches wide), then cut tops in half. Place ½ teaspoon cream on each bun, and put the halves into the cream at an angle to form wings. Sieve icing sugar lightly on top. Pipe rosettes of remaining coffee filling down centre.

*Coffee butterfly cakes*

## 306 Coffee kisses

| | |
|---|---|
| 4 oz. margarine | use ½ teaspoon baking |
| 3 oz. sugar | powder) |
| 1 egg yolk | 2 teaspoons coffee essence |
| 8 oz. flour (with plain flour | coffee butter icing (Recipe |
| | 389) |

Cream margarine and sugar. Add egg yolk, flour with baking powder, if used, and coffee essence (adding little warm water if necessary but mixture *must* be dry).
Put into tiny heaps on greased baking tin and bake in moderately hot oven (425°F.—Gas Mark 5-6) for 10 minutes. When cakes are cold, sandwich together with coffee butter icing.

## 307 Chocolate kisses

As above, but use 1 tablespoon cocoa powder blended with little warm water instead of coffee essence.

## 308 Coconut kisses

| | |
|---|---|
| 3 oz. margarine *or* margarine | little milk |
| and cooking fat | jam |
| 2 oz. sugar | desiccated *or* fresh grated |
| 4 oz. flour (with plain flour | coconut |
| use 1 level teaspoon baking | |
| powder) | |

Cream the margarine and sugar, add the flour and just enough milk to make the dough firm enough to handle. If plain flour is used, the baking powder and flour should be sieved together. Take small pieces of the dough and roll into tiny balls about as big as hazel nuts. Put on to an ungreased baking tin and bake for 10 minutes in the centre of moderate oven (375°F.—Gas Mark 4). Cool on tin. When quite cold sandwich two of the balls together with jam; then cover all the outside with jam and roll in the coconut.

## 309 Walnut kisses

As above, but substitute finely chopped walnuts for the coconut.

## 310 Jam buns

| | |
|---|---|
| 4-5 oz. margarine *or* cooking | 4-5 oz. sugar |
| fat | 1 large *or* 2 small eggs |
| 8 oz. flour (with plain flour | milk to mix |
| use 2 level teaspoons baking | jam |
| powder) | |

Rub the margarine or fat into the flour, sieved with baking powder, if used. Add sugar, the egg or eggs and enough milk to make a sticky consistency. Put into small heaps on a greased baking tin, make a small 'hole' in the centre of each cake with the handle of a teaspoon and put a little jam in each 'hole'. Pull the edges of the mixture over the jam a little to prevent it boiling out during cooking. Bake for about 10 minutes near the top of a hot oven (450°F.—Gas Mark 7).
**Variations**
Put a little lemon curd in centre instead of jam and a small amount of grated lemon rind with the flour.
Put a small amount of marzipan (Recipe 385) in centre of each cake.
Flavour the cakes with a little lemon or orange rind and when cold cover with lemon or orange glacé icing (Recipes 374, 375).

## 311 Atholl cakes

| | |
|---|---|
| 3 oz. margarine *or* butter | 1 oz. rice flour* |
| 3 oz. sugar | 1 teaspoon baking powder |
| grated rind 1 lemon | little lemon juice |
| 1 egg | 1 tablespoon candied lemon |
| 3 oz. cornflour* | peel |

*\* Alternatively, use 4 oz. cornflour and omit rice flour*

Cream the margarine or butter, sugar and lemon rind together. Beat well until the mixture is very soft and light. Beat the egg into the margarine mixture gradually. Sieve all the dry ingredients together and gradually stir this into the margarine and egg mixture. Add enough lemon juice to make a mixture that just drops from the spoon, then stir in the candied peel. Put either into well greased and floured patty tins or paper cases, standing on flat baking sheet. Bake for about 10 minutes near the top of a hot oven (450°F.—Gas Mark 7).

## 312 Chocolate honey buns

| | |
|---|---|
| 4 oz. flour (with plain flour | 4 oz. honey* |
| use 1 teaspoon baking | 2 eggs |
| powder) | 2 oz. plain chocolate, |
| 4 oz. butter *or* margarine | chopped into small pieces |

*\* Either use spoon measure (4 tablespoons equal 4 oz. honey) dip spoon in boiling water, then spoon out honey—or flour scale pan and honey will run out after weighing quite easily.*

Sieve flour with baking powder, if used. Cream butter or margarine till soft, mix in honey and cream again. Add eggs, one at a time, beating thoroughly after each addition, and stir in chocolate. Lightly fold in flour with a metal spoon and transfer mixture into 14 well greased bun tins or paper cases. Bake towards top of a moderately hot oven (400°F.—Gas Mark 5) for 10-15 minutes. Cool on a wire tray.

*Chocolate honey buns*

### 313 One-stage cup cakes

4 oz. self-raising flour
½ level teaspoon baking
 powder
4 oz. luxury margarine
2 eggs
grated rind 1 orange *or* lemon
orange icing (Recipe 371)

*Decoration*
mimosa balls
chocolate buttons
angelica leaves
halved glacé cherries

Sieve the flour and baking powder then put all the ingredients in a mixing bowl and beat with a wooden spoon until well mixed. Place heaped teaspoons of the mixture in paper cases and bake just above the centre of a moderately hot oven (400°F. —Gas Mark 5) for 15-20 minutes. Allow to cool. Make the icing and place on top of the cakes; smooth with a palette knife. Decorate with mimosa balls etc. as shown in the photograph.

*One-stage cup cakes*

### 314 Chocolate squares

6 oz. margarine
6 oz. castor sugar
3 eggs
5 oz. flour (with plain flour
 use 1¼ level teaspoons
 baking powder)
1 oz. cocoa *or* chocolate
 powder
2 tablespoons water

*Chocolate icing*
1 tablespoon milk
1 rounded teaspoon cocoa *or*
 chocolate powder
4 oz. margarine
8 oz. icing sugar, sieved three
 times

Cream the margarine and sugar together until light and fluffy. Add the lightly whisked egg in tablespoonfuls, beating in thoroughly. Sieve the flour, baking powder, if used, and cocoa together and fold into the mixture. Stir in the water. Put into a lightly greased and floured cake tin 7 × 9 × 2½ inches deep. Bake just above centre of a moderate oven (375°F.—Gas Mark 4) for 30-40 minutes. Combine milk and cocoa, heat until dissolved and leave to cool. Cream margarine and sugar until light and fluffy, then gradually beat in cooled chocolate mixture. Spread over the surface of the cake when cold. Decorate with fork marks and cut into squares.

*Chocolate squares*

### 315 Lemon whispers

3 oz. margarine *or* butter
3 oz. sugar
1 egg
2 oz. flour (with plain flour
 use 2 level teaspoons baking
 powder)

2 oz. cornflour
1 teaspoon grated lemon rind
1 oz. chopped candied peel
1 dessertspoon lemon juice
very little milk
icing sugar

Cream margarine or butter and sugar until light and fluffy. Beat the egg well and add gradually to the margarine mixture. Sieve together flour, cornflour and baking powder, if used, and add gradually to the margarine mixture, taking care not to overbeat the cake. Add the lemon rind, candied peel, lemon juice and just enough milk to make a creamy consistency. Grease patty tins well and half fill with mixture. Bake for 10 minutes near the top of a hot oven (450°F.—Gas Mark 6-7). Turn out of the tins while still hot but handle carefully for the cakes are very delicate. When cold shake over dry icing sugar. These are very light— hence the name 'whispers'.

### 316 Lemon cakes

4 oz. butter *or* margarine
4 oz. castor sugar
grated rind 2 lemons
2 eggs
6 oz. flour (with plain flour
 use 1 level teaspoon baking
 powder)
2 oz. crystallised lemon peel

*To decorate*
little lemon glacé icing
 (Recipe 374)
glacé cherries

Cream butter, sugar and lemon rind together until light and fluffy, whisk eggs and beat in a little at a time. Sieve flour and baking powder, if used, and fold into creamed mixture with finely chopped crystallised peel. Half fill small paper cases with cake mixture and bake near top of a hot oven (425°F.—Gas Mark 6) for 15 minutes. When cakes are cold ice the top and decorate with half a glacé cherry.

## 317 Lemon star buns

2 oz. margarine
2 oz. castor sugar
grated rind ½ lemon
2 small eggs
3 oz. flour (with plain flour
   use ¾ level teaspoon
   baking powder)
juice ½ lemon

**To decorate**
icing sugar
silver balls

Cream the margarine and sugar together until light and fluffy, then work in grated lemon rind. Add the lightly whisked eggs in tablespoons, beating thoroughly. Fold in the sieved flour and baking powder, if used, and lastly add the lemon juice. Place 2 teaspoonfuls of the mixture in each of 18 paper cases. Bake near top of a moderately hot oven (400°F.—Gas Mark 5) for 10-15 minutes. Cut a star-shaped stencil the size of the top of the buns. Place stencil on top of the buns and dredge with the icing sugar. Place a silver ball in the centre of each.

*Lemon star buns*

## 318 Orange and lemon drops

4 oz. self-raising flour
1½ level teaspoons baking
   powder
4 oz. castor sugar
3 oz. cooking fat
2 eggs

grated rind 1 orange *or* lemon
1 dessertspoon orange *or*
   lemon juice
little lemon *or* orange glacé
   icing (Recipes 374, 375)
orange *or* lemon slices

Sieve flour, baking powder and sugar into a bowl. Add cooking fat, eggs, orange or lemon rind and orange or lemon juice and mixing all ingredients beat for 1 minute. Place 1 rounded dessertspoon of the mixture in bun tins brushed with melted cooking fat. Bake in a moderately hot oven (400°F.—Gas Mark 5, near the top of the oven) for 15-20 minutes.
When cold, ice with a little orange or lemon glacé icing and top with a section of crystallised orange or lemon.

*Orange and lemon drops*

## 319 Spiced ring doughnuts (*No yeast*)

12 oz. plain flour
2 level teaspoons cream of
   tartar
1 level teaspoon bicarbonate
   of soda
½ level teaspoon cinnamon
½ level teaspoon mixed spice

4 oz. margarine *or* butter
3 oz. castor sugar
1 egg
6 tablespoons milk
cooking fat for frying (enough
   to make 3-inch depth in pan)

Sieve together the flour, cream of tartar, bicarbonate of soda, cinnamon and spice. Rub in the margarine till the mixture resembles fine breadcrumbs, then mix in the sugar. Add the beaten egg and milk to make a soft but not sticky dough. Turn out on to a lightly floured board, knead quickly and roll out to about ¾ inch in thickness. Cut into 2-inch rounds and with a smaller cutter remove the centre from each. Fry the rings, a few at a time, in deep fat (360°F. or until a day-old cube of bread turns golden in 1 minute) for 2-3 minutes, till golden brown. Drain on crumpled kitchen paper. Roll in castor sugar. Sieve with hot chocolate or coffee.

*Spiced ring doughnuts*

### 320 Walnut griddle cakes

4 oz. plain flour
pinch salt
3 level teaspoons baking powder
2 oz. finest semolina
1 tablespoon castor sugar
2 eggs
¼ pint milk
1 tablespoon melted butter *or* margarine
2 oz. walnuts, chopped
butter and maple syrup

Sift flour, salt, baking powder and semolina into a bowl. Add sugar. Make a well in the centre of the mixture and add the eggs and milk. Beat thoroughly to form a thick, creamy batter. Stir in melted fat and chopped nuts. Drop spoonfuls on to a well greased, heated griddle, thick frying pan or hot plate of an electric cooker. Cook till brown on both sides, turning two or three times. Pile in a folded napkin to keep warm. Serve with butter and maple syrup.

*Adding the milk to the eggs and sieved ingredients.*

*Cooking the mixture on the hot plate.*

*Cooked and ready to serve with butter and maple syrup.*

### 321 Doughnuts (1) (No yeast)

8 oz. self-raising flour (with plain flour use 2 teaspoons baking powder)
1 egg
pinch salt
¼ pint milk
fat for frying
sugar

Beat flour, baking powder, if used, egg, salt and milk together and drop spoonfuls into hot fat. Fry until brown. If you wish to cut 'dunky' shapes you will get a better texture by rubbing 1 oz. margarine into the mixture and using slightly less milk so that you can roll out the dough. Drain and roll in castor sugar.

### 322 Welsh cakes

2 oz. margarine *or* butter
4 oz. flour (with plain flour use 1 teaspoon baking powder)
2 oz. sugar
2 oz. currants
little egg *or* milk to bind

Rub the margarine into the flour with baking powder, if used, add sugar, fruit and bind with egg or milk. Roll out to ¼ inch thick and cut into shapes. Heat solid grill, solid hotplate or griddle gently, grease and cook cakes for about 4 minutes, then turn and cook for a further 4 minutes. Turn heat off or very low and give a few more minutes cooking to make sure the cakes are cooked in the middle. To test if griddle is right heat before cooking, shake on a little flour: it should turn golden in 1 minute.

### 323 Hula hoops

8 oz. self-raising flour
1 level teaspoon baking powder
½ level teaspoon salt
1 level teaspoon mixed spice
2 oz. castor sugar
1 oz. cooking fat
4 oz. sultanas
6 tablespoons milk
cooking fat for frying
½ level teaspoon cinnamon
1 oz. castor sugar

Sieve the flour, baking powder, salt, mixed spice and sugar into a basin. Rub in the cooking fat. Add the sultanas and milk and mix into fairly soft dough. Roll out ¼ inch thick on a lightly floured board. Cut into rounds with a 3-inch plain cutter and remove the centre from each with a 2-inch cutter. Fry a few at a time, in a pan of deep fat, which has been heated to 360°F. (or until a cube of day-old bread turns golden brown in 1 minute). Cook until golden brown, approximately 2-3 minutes. Drain on crumpled kitchen paper and toss in cinnamon and sugar.

### 324 Gingerbread men

8 oz. flour (with plain flour use 1 level teaspoon baking powder*)
1 teaspoon ground ginger
3 oz. margarine
2 oz. sugar
1 level tablespoon golden syrup
milk to mix
few currants
few cherries
small quantity glacé icing (Recipe 371)

* *Plain flour is better in this recipe*

If you haven't a cutter in the shape of a 'man' make the shape in firm cardboard, and cut around this.
Sieve together flour baking powder, if used, and ginger, rub margarine into flour etc., then add sugar, golden syrup and work very firmly with a wooden spoon. Gradually add just enough milk to make a VERY FIRM rolling consistency. Roll out and cut into shapes. Transfer to greased baking tins, then put currants etc. in place of 'eyes'. Bake near top of a hot oven (425-450°F.—Gas Mark 6-7) for approximately 10 minutes. When cold decorate with little glacé icing (Recipe 371).

### 325 Chocolate butterflies

3 oz. self-raising flour
pinch salt
1½ level tablespoons cocoa powder
2 oz. cooking fat
2 oz. castor sugar
1 egg
3 dessertspoons milk

*Coffee icing*
1 oz. cooking fat
3 oz. icing sugar, sieved
1-2 teaspoons milk
1-2 teaspoons coffee essence

Sieve the flour, salt and cocoa together. Cream the fat and sugar together until light and fluffy, then beat in the egg thoroughly. Fold in the flour mixture lightly and mix with the milk to a dropping consistency. Half fill greased tins and bake near the top of a moderately hot oven (400°F.—Gas Mark 5) for 15-20 minutes. Cream together the cooking fat and half the icing sugar. Beat in the milk and coffee essence. Beat in the rest of the sugar and continue beating well until the icing is the consistency of whipped cream.
When cold cut a round out of the centre of each cake and cut round in half to resemble wings. Pipe a rosette of coffee icing in the middle of each cake and replace the 'wings' in the centre. Dredge with icing sugar.

## 326 Mariettas

4 oz. butter *or* margarine
4 oz. castor sugar
finely grated rind 1 orange
2 dashes Angostura aromatic
  bitters
2 eggs
6 oz. flour (with plain flour
  use 1½ level teaspoons
  baking powder)
1 tablespoon milk

*Fondant almond paste*
8 oz. icing sugar, sieved
4 oz. ground almonds
½ teaspoon Angostura
  aromatic bitters
beaten egg

*Chocolate cream*
4 oz. icing sugar, sieved
1 tablespoon cocoa powder
4 oz. butter *or* margarine

Cream the butter or margarine, sugar, orange rind and Angostura until light and fluffy. Gradually beat in the eggs and stir in the sifted flour with baking powder, if used, and milk. Bake in small, greased rounded patty tins in a moderately hot oven (375°F.—Gas Mark 5) for 10-15 minutes. Cool. Brush the flat sides of cakes with a little jam. Make the fondant paste by mixing the ingredients together. Take out enough to form tiny stalk shapes. Use the rest to make thin rounds. Press over the jam. Make the chocolate butter cream by beating the icing sugar, butter and cocoa well. Spread over the marzipan, mark with a fork and put stalks in position.

*Chocolate butterflies*

*Mariettas*

## 327 Mocha fancies

4 oz. cooking fat
4 oz. castor sugar
2 eggs
1 dessertspoon milk
4 oz. self-raising flour and 1
  teaspoon baking powder
  (replace 1 heaped dessertspoon flour by 1 heaped
  dessertspoon cocoa powder)

*Coffee icing*
3 oz. cooking fat
8 oz. icing sugar, sieved
2-3 dessertspoons milk
coffee essence
*To decorate*
crushed cornflakes
glacé cherries
chocolate drops
walnut halves

Beat all ingredients for about 1 minute (beating will NOT harm the cake) and when well mixed, place in a 7-inch square sandwich tin. Smooth top. Bake in middle of a moderate oven (375°F.—Gas Mark 4) for 30-35 minutes.
Cream together fat and half icing sugar. Beat in milk and coffee essence to taste. Beat in rest of sugar until light and fluffy. Cut half cake into rounds, using a 1½-inch plain cutter. Cover sides with a little icing and roll in crushed cornflakes; ice tops and place half a cherry in centre. Cut remaining half of cake into narrow strips. Ice tops, mark with a fork and cut into triangles or fingers. Decorate with chocolate drops or walnut halves.

## 328 Walnut diamonds

4 oz. margarine
4 oz. castor sugar
2 eggs
finely grated rind 1 orange
4 oz. flour (with plain flour
  use 1 level teaspoon baking
  powder)
2 oz. walnuts, chopped

*To decorate*
orange marshmallow frosting
  (Recipe 329)
walnut halves

Cream together margarine and sugar until light and fluffy. Add the eggs, one at a time, beating thoroughly after each addition. Stir in orange rind then lightly fold in the sieved flour with baking powder, if used, and walnuts with a metal spoon. Transfer mixture to a Swiss roll tin, 11 × 7 inches, well greased, and lined with greaseproof paper coming 1 inch above the top of the tin. Bake on second shelf from the top of a moderate oven (375°F.—Gas Mark 4) for 20 minutes. Cool on a wire tray. Spread top of cake with orange marshmallow frosting then cut into diamond shapes. Decorate each with half a walnut.

*Walnut diamonds*

## 329 Orange marshmallow frosting

1 egg white

3 tablespoons orange marmalade, heated, strained and re-heated

Whisk the egg white until stiff and peaky, then pour in the hot marmalade. Re-whisk until frosting is cool and stiff enough for spreading.

## 330 Iced fingers

6 oz. margarine
6 oz. castor sugar
3 eggs

6 oz. flour (with plain flour use 1½ level teaspoons baking powder)
8 oz. glacé icing (Recipe 371)
glacé cherries

Cream margarine and sugar together until light and fluffy. Add lightly whisked eggs in tablespoons, beating in thoroughly. Fold in sieved flour with baking powder, if used, and put mixture into a lightly greased and floured cake tin 7 × 9 × 2½ inches deep. Bake just above centre of a moderate oven (375°F. Gas Mark 4) for 30-40 minutes. When cool, cover top with glacé icing and leave to set. Trim edges of cake and cut into 18 fingers and place halved glacé cherry on each.

*Iced fingers*

## 331 Jellied slices

1 oblong sponge (use Recipe 237 for Battenburg cake)
little jam
1 pint jelly

few blanched almonds
mock cream (Recipe 416) or whipped cream

When the sponge is quite cold spread with jam on the top. Make the jelly, let it get quite cold and half set. Spread over the top of the cake, flattening it with a knife dipped in hot water. Let the jelly set completely, and cut into fingers with a sharp knife. Decorate with blanched almonds and piped roses of cream.

## 332 Apricot crispies

8 oz. short crust pastry (Recipe 252)
2 egg whites
4 oz. castor sugar

1 teaspoon grated lemon rind
2 oz. ready-cooked oat cereal
apricot jam

Roll out the pastry to an oblong shape about 10 × 8 inches, and place on a baking sheet. Prick well all over, and bake for 10-15 minutes just above centre in a moderately hot oven (400°F.— Gas Mark 5) until a light golden brown. Meanwhile, whisk up the egg whites until stiff, fold in the sugar, grated rind and oat cereal. Remove the pastry from the oven, and reduce the temperature to moderate (375°F.—Gas Mark 4). Spread the pastry with apricot jam, and pile the cereal mixture on top, spreading it out to the edges. Bake for a further 20-25 minutes at the lower temperature. Allow the crispies to cool for 5 minutes, and cut into slices while slightly warm.

*Apricot crispies*

## 333 Coconut squares

4 oz. margarine
4 oz. castor sugar
2 eggs
4 oz. flour (with plain flour use 1 level teaspoon baking powder)

*To coat*
3 dessertspoons lemon juice
½ tin sweetened condensed milk } mixed together
desiccated coconut

Cream margarine with sugar until light and fluffy. Add slightly whisked eggs in tablespoonfuls, beating well before adding more egg. Fold in sieved flour with baking powder, if used, mix thoroughly and turn into a greased and lined 6 × 8 inches shallow cake tin. Bake in centre of a moderate oven (375°F.— Gas Mark 4) for approximately 40-45 minutes. When cool cut into 2 halves and sandwich together with some of the lemon juice mixture. Cut into even-sized squares and brush all over with the remaining lemon juice mixture. Toss in desiccated coconut.

*Coconut squares*

14 Gingerbread squares

15. Meringue baskets

## 334 Chocolate rose cakes

3 eggs
3 oz. castor sugar
vanilla essence
½ oz. cocoa powder
2½ oz. flour (with plain flour
   use ½ teaspoon baking
   powder)
½ oz. margarine *or* butter,
   melted

*Decoration*
butter icing (Recipe 387)
chocolate vermicelli
4 oz. marzipan (Recipe 385)
cochineal
silver balls

Whisk the eggs and sugar until thick, light and fluffy. Add the vanilla essence. Very carefully fold in the sieved cocoa and flour with baking powder, if used. Add the melted margarine. Pour into a greased and lined Swiss roll tin. Bake in moderate oven (375°F.—Gas Mark 4) for about 15 minutes. Cool on a wire tray.

Cut into rounds using a 2-inch plain cutter. Using butter icing sandwich these together. Spread butter icing around the edges of each small cake and dip in chocolate vermicelli. Colour the marzipan pink with a little cochineal. Roll out thinly and cut into small rounds. Shape these to form petals. Pipe the top of the cakes with stars of butter cream or icing. Arrange the petals and silver balls to complete the decoration.

*Chocolate rose cakes*

## 335 Japonnaise cakes

small amount almond paste
   (Recipe 385)
green and red colouring
flour
4 egg whites
8 oz. castor sugar

8 oz. ground almonds *or* 6 oz.
   ground almonds and 2 oz.
   ground rice
almond essence
coffee butter icing (Recipe
   389)

Colour marzipan or almond paste with red or green colouring. Grease 2 baking tins and lightly sprinkle with flour. Whisk whites with half sugar until stiff and dry, fold in rest of sugar, almonds and ground rice, if used, add a few drops of essence. Spread mixture over tins evenly about ½ inch thick. Bake in a moderately slow oven (325°F.—Gas Mark 2) until almost set. Mark with a 1½-inch cutter into rounds. Return to oven and bake until golden and crisp. Cool rounds on a wire tray. Crush trimmings with a rolling pin and sieve. Put a large blob of coffee butter icing in centre of half biscuits. Place other rounds on top and press together. Any cream that comes out can be spread round sides and top, adding extra if necessary. Roll covered biscuits in crumbs. Decorate by piping with butter icing and topping with small diamonds, hearts, clubs, etc. of marzipan.

## 336 Macaroon biscuits

to each egg white* allow
   few drops almond essence
   2½-3 oz. castor sugar
   2½ oz. ground almonds

rice paper
glacé cherries *or* whole
   almonds

*\* One egg white will make about 6 small biscuits*

Whisk the egg white lightly. Add the almond essence, then sugar and ground almonds. If the egg white is exceptionally large then work in more ground almonds. Roll the mixture into rounds, and put, well spaced out, on rice paper. Put a cherry or almond on top of each biscuit. Bake for approximately 20-25 minutes in the centre of a moderate oven (375°F.—Gas Mark 4). When nearly cold, remove from the tin and tear or cut round the rice paper.

## 337 Chocolate macaroons

To each egg white allow 1 oz. ground almonds, 1 oz. grated chocolate or chocolate powder, and ½ oz. ground rice. Use same amount of sugar. Bake as above.

## 338 Coconut macaroons

Use 1½ oz. ground almonds and 1 oz. desiccated coconut to each egg white, together with 2½ oz. sugar. Proceed as above.

## 339 Cornflake macaroons

Use 1½ oz. ground almonds and 1 oz. crushed cornflakes, to each egg white, together with 2½ oz. sugar. Proceed as above.

## 340 Vienna finger macaroons

Recipe as for Macaroons, but work in enough ground almonds to allow you to roll out mixture. Cut into fingers and put on rice paper. Bake as above. When cold, cover with almond water icing (Recipe 379) and chopped nuts.

## 341 Coffee macaroons

To each egg white allow 1 teaspoon instant coffee, 2½ oz. sugar and 2½ oz. ground almonds. Bake as above.

### 342 *Rolled oat macaroons*

3 oz. margarine
2 oz. sugar
1 tablespoon golden syrup
4 oz. flour (with plain flour
use ½ teaspoon baking
powder)

4 oz. rolled oats
1 teaspoon almond essence
milk to mix

Cream margarine, sugar and syrup. Add all other ingredients. Knead well, then stir in just enough milk to make a mixture that just binds together. Roll into small balls and put on greased baking tin. Leave room for them to spread out. Bake for 20 minutes in centre of moderate oven (375°F.—Gas Mark 4). Cool on tin.

### 343 *Economical almond macaroons*

1 oz. margarine
½ teaspoon almond *or* ratafia
essence
1 dessertspoon semolina
2 oz. fine *or* medium oatmeal

2 oz. sugar
1 dessertspoon nuts, finely
chopped (optional)
1 egg yolk

Melt the margarine then mix with all other ingredients, binding with the egg yolk. The mixture should be only just soft enough to bind together. Put spoonfuls on a well greased baking tin, allow plenty of space between the biscuits as they spread out during cooking. Bake for 10 minutes in the centre of a moderate oven (375°F.—Gas Mark 4). Do not attempt to move these biscuits until they are absolutely cold as they crumble easily when warm, although they are very firm and crisp when cold. They are a good substitute for ground almond macaroons.

### 344 *Coconut cookies*

1 oz. rolled oats
2 oz. margarine *or* butter
2 oz. flour (with plain flour
use ½ level teaspoon
baking powder)
1 oz. castor sugar

1 oz. desiccated coconut
1 tablespoon golden syrup

*To decorate*
glacé cherries

Put all the ingredients into one bowl and knead thoroughly until it binds together in one ball. Break off pieces the size of a walnut, roll into balls and place on greased baking trays, allowing room to spread. Put a small piece of glacé cherry on top of each biscuit. Bake just above the centre of a very moderate oven (350°F.—Gas Mark 3) for 15-20 minutes. Allow to cool a short time before removing from baking trays. If wished the balls could be rolled in either coconut or more rolled oats before baking.

### 345 *Almond shorties*

12 oz. plain flour
4 oz. ground rice *or* fine
semolina
pinch salt
6 oz. cooking fat

4 oz. castor sugar
1 egg
few drops almond essence
1½ oz. split almonds

Sieve the flour, ground rice and salt into a bowl. Rub in the fat and stir in the sugar. Add the egg and a few drops of almond essence and mix to a dough. Roll into balls about 1½-inches in diameter. Place on a baking sheet brushed with melted cooking fat and dredged with flour, and flatten them slightly. Press a half almond on each biscuit, sprinkle with a little sugar. Bake in the middle of a moderate oven (350°F.—Gas Mark 4) for 25-30 minutes. Cool on a cake rack.

*Almond shorties*

### 346 *Oriental fingers*

4 oz. margarine
8 oz. flour, preferably plain
3 oz. sugar
milk to mix
2 oz. glacé cherries, quartered

2 oz. nuts, chopped
2 oz. dates, chopped
2 oz. sultanas
icing sugar

Rub 3 oz. of the margarine into the flour. Add 2 oz. sugar and enough milk to make a firm dough. Roll out half the dough into a neat oblong about ¼-inch thick and put on an ungreased baking tin. Put remainder of the margarine and sugar into a saucepan; heat until margarine has melted, then stir in the cherries, nuts, dates and sultanas. Mix well, then spread over the dough. Roll out the rest of the dough and cover the filling. Put into the middle of a moderate oven (375°F.—Gas Mark 4) for 25-30 minutes. Mark into fingers while still hot but leave on tin to cool. When quite cold put on to wire rack and dust with icing sugar.

### 347 *Jam whirls*

2 oz. cooking fat
3 oz. castor sugar
1 egg

5 oz. flour
pinch salt
raspberry jam

Cream cooking fat and sugar together until light and fluffy. Add the egg and beat in thoroughly. Fold in the sieved flour and salt and mix well. Put the mixture into a piping bag with a star tube. Form rounds on the greased baking sheet with a hollow in the centre of each round. Place half a teaspoon jam in the centre of each. Bake near the top of a moderately hot oven (400°F.—Gas Mark 5) for 15-20 minutes. Cool on a cake rack.

## 348 Shortbread flapjacks

**Shortbread**
2 oz. butter
1 oz. sugar
4 oz. plain flour
very little milk

**Topping**
1½ oz. cooking fat
1 tablespoon golden syrup
2 oz. cornflakes
1 oz. sugar
2 oz. rolled oats

Cream together the butter and sugar, work in the flour, kneading the mixture well, then add a few drops of milk. Roll out to about ¼-inch thick and make an oblong shape; place on to an ungreased baking tin.
Melt the cooking fat and syrup in a pan, stir in the cornflakes, sugar and rolled oats. Mix well, put on top of the shortbread mixture and, since the cornflake mixture is very crumbly, press this down firmly with damp hands. Bake in the centre of a moderate oven (375°F.—Gas Mark 4) for 25 minutes. Mark into fingers while the biscuit is still hot, but leave on the tin until quite cold.

## 349 Lemon almond shortcakes

3 oz. margarine
3 oz. soft brown sugar
grated rind 1 lemon

1 egg yolk
4 oz. plain flour
blanched almonds

Cream the margarine and sugar together until light and fluffy. Add the lemon rind; beat the egg yolk into the mixture. Mix in the flour. Press into greased 7-inch sandwich tin and place on whole blanched almonds. Bake in a very moderate oven (350°F.—Gas Mark 3) for 30-40 minutes. Mark into eight, cool slightly and turn out of the tin on to a wire tray.

## 350 Strawberry buttons

1 egg
3 oz. cooking fat
8 oz. plain flour
2½ oz. sugar

grated rind 1 lemon
1 tablespoon milk
little desiccated coconut
strawberry jam

Separate yolk from white of egg. Rub fat into sieved flour, stir in sugar and lemon rind and bind with egg yolk and milk. Roll into tiny balls. Dip each ball into egg white and roll in coconut. Place, not too closely together, on a greased and floured baking sheet. Make a dent in each ball with fingertip. Bake near top of moderately hot oven (400°F.—Gas Mark 5) for 15-20 minutes. While still hot, place a little strawberry jam in each dent. Cool on cake rack.

*Strawberry buttons*

## 351 Melting moments

3 oz. margarine *or* butter
3-4 oz. icing sugar
1 oz. flour

3 oz. cornflour
few drops milk
butter icing (Recipe 387)

Cream together margarine and sugar. Sieve flour and cornflour together. Work into the margarine mixture, then add a few drops of milk to make mixture that you can pipe. Put into forcing bag and use a large piping rose. Pipe into neat shapes on greased baking tray. Bake for 15 minutes in the centre of a moderate oven (375°F.—Gas Mark 4). Cool on tin. Sandwich two together with butter icing.
For Finger Melting Moments coat the ends with melted chocolate *before* sandwiching together.

## 352 Chocolate melting moments

Use 1 oz. cocoa powder instead of 1 oz. flour.

## 353 Almond melting moments

Use Recipe 351, adding few drops almond essence instead of milk. Sandwich together with either almond flavoured butter icing (Recipe 387) or rather soft marzipan (Recipe 385).

## 354 Ace biscuits

3 oz. flour
1 oz. cornflour
½ teaspoon baking powder
pinch salt
2 oz. margarine
2 oz. sugar
1 level tablespoon cocoa
  powder

1 teaspoon coffee essence
about 1 tablespoon milk

*To decorate*
water icing (Recipe 371)
chocolate butter icing
  (Recipe 388)

Sieve flour, cornflour, baking powder and salt into a bowl. Rub in the margarine. Mix in the sugar and cocoa. Add the coffee essence and milk to form a stiff dough. Knead lightly and roll out on a floured board. Cut into heart, diamond and other card shapes and place on a greased baking tray. Bake in a moderate oven (375°F.—Gas Mark 4) for 10-15 minutes. Ice and decorate when cold. Use various coloured water icings and pipe with chocolate butter icing.

## 355 Ginger cherry shortbreads

3 oz. margarine *or* butter
2 oz. castor sugar
4 oz. flour (with plain flour use 1 level teaspoon baking powder)
1 oz. crystallised ginger, finely chopped

1 oz. glacé cherries, chopped

*To decorate*
icing sugar *or* glacé icing (Recipe 371)
glacé cherries

Cream margarine and sugar well, work in flour with baking powder, if used, ginger and cherries. Form into small balls and put on to baking tins, allowing plenty of room to spread. Bake for about 15 minutes in centre of moderate oven (375°F.—Gas Mark 4). Cool on tin. Dust with icing sugar or decorate with a ring of icing and half a glacé cherry.

## 356 Pineapple cherry shortbreads

Recipe as above, but use 1-2 oz. finely chopped crystallised pineapple instead or crystallised ginger. Cover with glacé icing (Recipe 371) and pieces of crystallised pineapple.

## 357 Ginger shortbread

3 oz. butter *or* margarine
2 oz. sugar
3 oz. flour
1 oz. cornflour

1 teaspoon ground ginger
1 oz. crystallised ginger, chopped

Cream margarine and half sugar, work in the flour and other ingredients and lastly the rest of the sugar. Form into a round and put on to an ungreased baking tin. Make the biscuit about ⅓ inch thick. Cook for about 45 minutes in a very moderate oven (300-350°F.—Gas Mark 2-3) until quite firm. Cool on tin.

## 358 Caramel nut fingers

3 oz. cooking fat *or* butter
3 oz. castor sugar
2 eggs
4 oz. self-raising flour
pinch of salt

1 tablespoon milk
coffee icing (Recipe 359)
chopped almonds
caramel (Recipe 360)

Cream fat and sugar until soft and fluffy. Beat in eggs one at a time. Fold in sieved flour and salt lightly, add milk. Bake in an oblong tin 8 × 11 inches brushed with melted fat, in middle of a moderate oven (375°F.—Gas Mark 4) for 25-30 minutes. When cold cut into fingers 1 × 2 inches. Coat sides with coffee icing and press on finely chopped grilled almonds. Spoon a little caramel down centre of each.

## 359 Coffee icing

3 oz. cooking fat
6 oz. icing sugar, sieved

1 tablespoon milk
1 dessertspoon coffee essence

Cream together cooking fat and icing sugar. Add milk and essence. Beat until consistency of whipped cream.

## 360 Caramel

2 rounded tablespoons sugar

1 tablespoon water

Melt sugar in water in a saucepan, and stir until dissolved, then boil without stirring; gradually allow to become golden colour. Use at once.

## 361 Pantomime biscuits

8 oz. plain flour
pinch salt
5 oz. margarine
1½ oz. castor sugar
1 tablespoon water

*Fudge icing*
3 oz. margarine
4½ dessertspoons water
12 oz. icing sugar, sieved
few drops vanilla *or* orange flavouring

various vegetable colourings
1 rounded teaspoon cocoa powder, sieved

*Decorations*
angelica strips
red and green silver-type balls
strips and triangles of black and orange liquorice allsorts
chocolate-coloured sweets

Sieve together the flour and salt, add the margarine and rub in. Stir in sugar, mix with water to a firm dough. Form into a ball, and roll out thinly on a floured board. Using a cutter as for gingerbread men (Recipe 324) and a cat-shaped biscuit cutter to represent Dick Whittington and his cat, cut out 6 of each shape. Place on a baking sheet. Bake for 25-30 minutes in centre of a very moderate oven (350°F.—Gas Mark 3). Leave to cool.
Place the margarine and water in a saucepan, and stir over a moderate heat until the margarine is melted and the water boiling. Remove and stir in icing sugar; beat well. Beat in the flavouring. Remove about 3 tablesppons of the icing and place in a bowl for decorating. Divide the remaining icing and colour it. Ice the biscuits and leave to set. Trim off surplus icing from the sides. Divide the remaining 3 tablespoons of icing into two; beat the sieved cocoa into one portion, leave the other plain.
Pipe the chocolate and plain icing on the biscuits. Decorate as liked with angelica strips etc.

## 362 Viennese tarts or Swiss tarts

4 oz. margarine *or* butter
1½ oz. icing sugar, sieved
2 oz. flour

2 oz. cornflour
glacé icing (Recipe 371) *or* jam

Cream together margarine and icing sugar. Work in flour and cornflour, then pipe into small paper cases. Bake for about 45 minutes in centre of very moderate oven (350°F.—Gas Mark 3) until pale brown. Fill centres with glacé icing or jam. Dust with sieved icing sugar.

## 363 Honey crisps

4 oz. margarine
2 oz. sugar
2 tablespoons honey

3 oz. flour
3 oz. fine *or* medium oatmeal

Cream together margarine, sugar and honey. Work in flour and oatmeal. If needed, add a little more honey to bind. Roll into balls and flatten slightly. Put on a well greased baking tray, allowing room to spread. Bake for 15 minutes in centre of a moderate oven (375°F.—Gas Mark 4). Cool on tin.

## 364 Syrup crisps

As above, but use syrup instead of honey.

## 365 Brandy snaps

2 oz. flour
2 oz. margarine *or* butter *or* cooking fat
2 oz. sugar

2 level tablespoons golden syrup
½ level teaspoon ground ginger

Take 1 teaspoon of flour away, so scales no longer give quite 2 oz. Put margarine, sugar and golden syrup into a saucepan. Mix flour and ginger together. Allow margarine to melt slowly, then take pan off heat and stir in flour. Grease 2 or 3 baking tins very well indeed—do not flour. Put teaspoons of mixture on the trays, allowing about 3 inches all round, since they spread out a great deal. As rolling takes several minutes put one tray into the oven to begin with, setting it at a very moderate heat (325-350°F.—Gas Mark 3). The biscuits take 8-12 minutes to cook, but you can look into the oven after 5 and again a little later. They are ready to remove from the oven when uniformly golden brown. Put a second tin into the oven after about 5 minutes, then the third tin after about 10 minutes. Keep trays as near middle of oven as possible. When first tray comes out of oven do not touch the biscuits for about 2 minutes, since they are very soft. Test after 2 minutes to see if you can slip a palette knife under them; if so they are ready to roll. Grease the handle of a wooden spoon, lift biscuit from tray, then press round spoon. Hold in position a few seconds to give biscuit a chance to set. Slip out handle of spoon and put biscuit on a wire sieve. Do the same with the next biscuit. Try and work quickly with each tray, as you will find when biscuits start to harden they cannot be removed from tin. If this does happen to the last one or two, just put baking tin back into oven for a minute and start testing again when you bring it out. Store *away from all* other biscuits, cakes, etc. in airtight jar or tin.

If wished biscuits can be filled with whipped cream just before serving.

## 366 Lemon and honey snaps

2 oz. margarine *or* butter
2 oz. sugar
2 oz. honey

scant 2 oz. flour
finely grated rind 1 lemon

Method of mixing and baking as brandy snaps (Recipe 365), substituting honey for golden syrup, and lemon rind for ginger.

## 367 Parisienne biscuits

2 oz. butter *or* margarine
2 oz. sugar
2 oz. golden syrup

2 oz. plain *or* self-raising flour
1 oz. chopped candied peel

Put butter, sugar and golden syrup into a saucepan, and heat until butter has melted. Remove from heat and stir in flour. Put small spoonfuls on well greased baking tins, allowing space to spread out. Bake for 5-7 minutes just above centre of moderate oven (375°F.—Gas Mark 4), then remove from oven. Sprinkle peel on top of biscuits, then return to oven for a further 5-7 minutes, until golden brown. Allow to cool for approximately 1 minute, then insert palette knife under each biscuit. Complete cooling on a wire tray.

## 368 Florentines

4 oz. butter
4 oz. castor sugar
4 oz. blanched almonds, chopped
2 oz. chopped candied peel
1 oz. glacé cherries, chopped

1 oz. walnuts, chopped
1 oz. sultanas
1 egg
1 oz. flaked almonds
3-4 oz. plain chocolate couverture

Put butter and sugar into a saucepan and heat gently until melted. Stir in chopped almonds and other ingredients, except flaked almonds and chocolate. Add well beaten egg last. Put small teaspoons of mixture on well greased baking tins, allowing plenty of space for biscuits to spread out. Bake just above centre of a moderate oven (375°F.—Gas Mark 4) for approximately 20 minutes until crisp and golden brown. After biscuits have been in oven for about 5 minutes, remove trays from oven, and sprinkle flaked almonds over the top. If edges of biscuits seem to be spreading out very widely, draw them together with a palette knife, then return trays to oven. When cooked, allow biscuits to cool for a few minutes, then remove from baking trays. Heat chocolate in a basin over hot water until softened, then coat one side only, i.e. bottom surface, with chocolate.

## 369 Mock Florentines

ingredients as brandy snaps (Recipe 365)
1 oz. chopped candied peel

1 oz. glacé cherries, chopped
3 oz. almonds, chopped
3-4 oz. chocolate

Prepare mixture as in brandy snaps, but stir in peel, chopped cherries and almonds. Cook as brandy snaps, but do not roll. Coat as described in Recipe 368.

# ICING

You will find the basic icings in this chapter and also some lesser known recipes. In addition, many of the decorated cakes have special icing recipes given with them, so that in time you will build up a very big selection of ideas for decorating and filling your cakes.

## 370 Secrets of successful icing

To ice cakes successfully is largely a matter of practice—no one can expect to 'do the job' perfectly at the beginning but there are hints which will assist.

**1** Remember glacé or water icing is not a piping icing, except for writing names or feathering (Recipe 381). Use a royal or butter icing (Recipes 382, 387).

**2** Be sure when piping that the icing is the right consistency—if so stiff you need to press very hard on the piping bag, syringe or cloth bag, it needs more moisture —but it should be stiff enough to hold a shape. Many more details on piping will be found in Recipe 384.

**3** To coat the top of a cake only with icing, tie a band of very stiff paper (several thicknesses of greaseproof paper can be used), foil or thin cardboard round the cake. Tie tightly or secure with pin. Pour the icing over the top and leave until quite firm. Untie or remove pin from paper, and remove carefully. You will then have a neat edge.

**4** Details for coating cakes with royal icing will be found under Recipe 383, but if using softer icing allow it to flow down the sides of the cake, spreading lightly with a palette knife.

**5** When the sides of a cake are coated with icing, then with chopped nuts, coconut or crisp meringue crumbs, put these on to a sheet of paper. Hold the cake rather like a hoop, and roll firmly over the nuts etc. so that they adhere to the sides. After coating the sides ice the top in the usual way.

**6** IF YOU DO NOT HAVE AN ICING TURNTABLE, stand cake on its board or plate on an upturned basin. This gives a better working height, and the basin can be turned round like a turntable.

## 371 Water icing or glacé icing

8 oz. icing sugar*          about 1½ dessertspoons warm water

\* To cover the top of a 6-inch sponge use 4 oz. icing sugar; for a 7-inch cake or sponge 6 oz. and for an 8-9 inch sponge 8 oz. If covering top and sides use at least double quantities.

If the icing sugar seems rather lumpy you can sieve it, but if you add the water and let it stand for some time, unless the lumps are very hard indeed, it will become smooth by itself. Add the water gradually.

## 372 Chocolate glacé icing

Add 1 good dessertspoon cocoa powder to the icing and then beat in a knob of melted butter about the size of an acorn.

## 373 Coffee glacé icing

Mix with strong coffee instead of water or with soluble coffee powder, blended with little warm water.

## 374 Lemon glacé icing

Mix with lemon juice instead of water.

## 375 Orange glacé icing

Mix with orange juice instead of water.

## 376 Vanilla glacé icing

Add a few drops of vanilla essence.

## 377 Mocha glacé icing

Add 1 good dessertspoon cocoa to the icing sugar, and use strong coffee instead of water. A small knob of butter, melted, can be added if wished.

## 378 Spiced glacé icing

Blend ½ teaspoon mixed spice, ½ teaspoon grated nutmeg and ½ teaspoon cinnamon with the icing sugar.

## 379 Almond glacé icing

Add a few drops of almond essence.

## 380 Using glacé or water icing

Glacé or water icing is a soft icing ideal for coating small cakes, sponges, etc. As stated in Recipe 370, it is not suitable for piping, except for writing, feathering, etc., for it does not hold the shape of stars, flowers or other designs. You will find that after a day or so glacé icing tends to crack, so for a cake that needs long keeping it is advisable to use royal icing. Various flavours are given above, but any flavouring essence and colouring can be added to glacé icing.

## 381 Feather icing

Sieve the icing sugar into a bowl. Add sufficient warm water to make a stiff glacé icing (see Recipe 371). Remove about 1 tablespoonful, and add to this enough sieved cocoa powder to give a dark chocolate colour. If necessary add a little more water to maintain the correct consistency. Put the chocolate icing into a paper piping bag and cut off the tip.

Spread about 1 teaspoonful of white icing on to a biscuit, and immediately pipe on to this straight lines of chocolate icing.
While still wet use a fine skewer or writing pipe to draw straight lines at right angles to the chocolate lines.
Repeat in the opposite direction to give a feathered effect.
**Note**
The decoration of each biscuit must be completed before starting on the next. This type of icing may also be used on top of sponges or cakes.

## 382 Royal icing

To give a somewhat softer icing omit a little egg white and use water instead or add 1 teaspoon glycerine to each 8 oz. icing sugar.
*For the top only of 7-inch cake—one layer and little piping:*
8 oz. icing sugar, sieved
1 egg white
1 dessertspoon lemon juice
*For the top and sides of 7-inch cake—one layer and piping:*
1¼ lb. icing sugar, sieved
2½ egg whites
1¼ tablespoons lemon juice
*For the top only of a 9-inch round or 8-inch square cake—one layer and piping:*
12 oz. icing sugar, sieved
1½ egg whites
1½ dessertspoons lemon juice
*For top and sides of 9-inch round or 8-inch square cake—one layer and piping:*
2 lb. icing sugar, sieved
4 egg whites
2 tablespoons lemon juice
*For top of 10-inch round or 9-inch square cake—one layer and piping:*
1 lb. icing sugar, sieved
2 egg whites
2 tablespoons lemon juice
*For top and sides of 10-inch round or 9-inch square cake—one layer and piping:*
2½ lb. icing sugar, sieved
5 egg whites
2½ tablespoons lemon juice
**Note**
You can economise on egg whites by using partly the whites and partly water, and as explained above this gives you a softer icing.
Whisk the egg whites lightly, stir in the icing sugar and lemon juice and *beat well* until very white and smooth.

## 383 How to coat a cake with marzipan and icing

1 Brush away loose crumbs from cake.
2 Spread the sides of the cake either with egg white or with sieved apricot jam.
3 Roll out marzipan on sugared board or table.
4 Measure circumference of the cake and depth.
5 Cut a strip exactly the length of the circumference, plus about ⅛ inch—but to be 1 inch deeper than the cake. Use approximately half, or just over half the total amount of marzipan. Cut a round of marzipan the size of the top of the cake.
6 Hold the cake on its side, then just as if you were rolling a hoop, roll along the strip of marzipan. If you do this firmly you will find the marzipan sticks to the cake. Make sure extra inch is at the top edge.
7 Turn cake on to the base again, seal the join firmly and press down the extra inch on top.
8 Brush top with egg white or jam, press round of marzipan into position.
9 Tidy sides by rolling jam jar, or rolling pin held upright, round sides of the cake. Roll top and give neat edge—this makes icing the cake much easier.
There are two schools of thought about putting icing straight on to the marzipan. If you are very experienced at icing cakes and you do not handle the marzipan too much the icing can be put on at once. This has the advantage of keeping the marzipan very moist. If, on the other hand, you over-handle the marzipan even a *little* too much, the oil will come through the icing and spoil the colour—that is why it is essential, if in doubt, to leave the cake with marzipan on for at least 48 hours before icing.
With a Christmas cake one good layer of icing and then the piping is enough, but for a very professionally piped cake, and certainly for a wedding cake that needs keeping for a very long time, use 2 layers of icing before putting on the piping.

*To put on the icing:*
1 Lift cake on to cake board—if possible stand cake on turntable or upturned basin.
2 Use most of the royal icing and put in one 'pile' on the top.
3 Spread icing away from the centre of the cake down the sides. Cover the whole of the cake before neatening icing. To spread icing easily use broad-bladed palette knife and dip in a jug of hot water. Shake knife reasonably dry but use while warm.
4 To neaten sides of cake hold blade of knife against icing and gently, but firmly, draw round sides of cake, removing any uneven surplus icing—this should be returned to basin. If your cake is on a turntable or upturned basin, you can then turn the cake round with your left hand while using the knife in your right hand.
5 To neaten top of cake—hold either an icing spatula or the edge of the palette knife across the top of the cake, holding one end in each hand, and draw slowly across the cake to neaten icing.
6 If piping, allow to harden—keep rest of icing in basin covered with damp cloth so that it is soft enough for piping.
*To give 'snow' effect on Christmas cake:*
Make sure you have a good layer of icing. When the cake is covered, and before the icing has time to harden, pick it up in peaks. Use either the handle of a teaspoon or the tip of a knife and sweep the icing up in points—don't expose any of the marzipan.

## 384 To pipe and decorate cakes

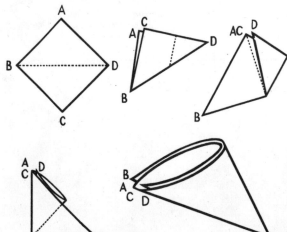

Use an icing pipe and syringe or pipe and paper bag. The best icings for piping are butter and royal. Make sure they are the right consistency—firm enough to stand up in peaks in the bowl but soft enough to handle. There are a very wide range of icing pipes available—those illustrated are a small proportion but you can see the various effects to be obtained. The numbers are those on the pipes, so you are sure of buying the right shape.
The secret of good piping is, of course, practice, also to have the right consistency of icing and to learn the correct pressure of the pipe, so that you get just the right amount of icing on to the cake.

**How to make an icing bag**
The bag is made from a square piece of white paper, which eventually is folded over 4 times to give a firm bag. Drop the icing pipe at the bottom of this, cut or tear away a small piece of the paper so that the icing comes through the pipe. Secure the top by either tucking it under or with a pin.

16 & 17.  Lemon fingers/Yeast tea ring

18. Brownies

19. Peanut crackers

20. Rich fruit bread

### 385 Almond paste or marzipan

*For* generous *layer on top of 7-inch cake:*
4 oz. ground almonds
2 oz. castor sugar
2 oz. icing sugar
few drops almond essence*
egg yolk to mix
*For top and sides of 7-inch cake (thin layer):*
8 oz. ground almonds
4 oz. castor sugar
4 oz. icing sugar
few drops almond essence*
2 egg yolks to mix
*For a generous layer on top of 9-inch round cake or 8-inch square cake:*
6 oz. ground almonds
3 oz. castor sugar
3 oz. icing sugar
few drops almond essence*
1½ egg yolks to mix
*For top and sides of 9-inch round cake or 8-inch square cake (thin layer):*
12 oz. ground almonds
6 oz. castor sugar
6 oz. icing sugar
few drops almond essence*
3 egg yolks to mix
*For top layer of 10-inch round cake or 9-inch square:*
6-8 oz. ground almonds
3-4 oz. castor sugar
3-4 oz. icing sugar
few drops almond essence*
1½-2 egg yolks to mix
*For top and sides of 10-inch round or 9-inch square (thin layer):*
12 oz.-1 lb. ground almonds
6-8 oz. castor sugar
6-8 oz. icing sugar
few drops almond essence*
3-4 egg yolks to mix
* *The amount of almond essence should, of course, be increased proportionately*

Mix all ingredients together, adding enough egg yolk to make a firm mixture. Knead thoroughly. Do not over-handle.

### 386 Cooked marzipan or almond paste

8 oz. granulated *or* loaf sugar
4 tablespoons water
pinch cream of tartar
6 oz. ground almonds

few drops almond essence
egg white
2 tablespoons icing sugar

Put the sugar and water in a strong saucepan, stir until the sugar dissolves, then add the cream of tartar. Boil steadily until the mixture reaches 240°F. or forms a soft ball when a little is dropped into cold water. Remove from the heat and beat for a minute or two until the mixture becomes cloudy. Add the ground almonds, almond essence and the lightly whisked egg white and stir over the heat for about 2 minutes. Turn out on to a board dusted with the icing sugar. When cool knead as uncooked marzipan, adding a little extra icing sugar if desired. This amount is sufficient for top and sides of a 7-inch cake.

### 387 Butter icing

2 oz. butter
3-4 oz. icing sugar, sieved

(to make a firmer icing use the larger quantity of sugar)
flavouring as individual recipe

Cream the butter until very soft and white—it is essential not to warm it. Work in the sugar and flavouring.

### 388 Chocolate butter icing

Add good dessertspoon chocolate powder or 1 oz. melted chocolate and few drops vanilla essence.

### 389 Coffee butter icing

Work in good dessertspoon coffee essence or 1 teaspoon soluble coffee powder dissolved in 2 teaspoons water. Do this gradually or mixture will curdle.

### 390 Lemon or orange butter icing

Add 2 teaspoons finely grated lemon rind or 3 teaspoons grated orange rind and gradually beat in 1 dessertspoon lemon or orange juice.

### 391 Honey butter icing

Follow the basic recipe for butter icing, adding a dessertspoon of honey to each 2 oz. of butter. Flavour as desired.
Honey butter icing is used in the honey sponge (Recipe 102)

**392** *Rum butter icing*

Add few drops rum essence or about dessertspoon rum.

**393** *Vanilla butter icing*

Add ½ teaspoon vanilla essence to icing.

**394** *Caramel icing*

3 oz. margarine         9 oz. icing sugar, sieved
about 4 tablespoons caramel
  (see note)

Beat the margarine. Add the caramel and sieved icing sugar alternately, beating the mixture to keep it smooth and fluffy.
**Note**
To make the caramel, put 8 oz. of granulated sugar and ¼ pint water into a small strong pan and stir over gentle heat until the sugar has dissolved. Bring to the boil, and boil to a rich golden brown. Add 4 tablespoons cold water and allow the caramel to cool. Use as required. Surplus caramel can be kept in a bottle for future use.

**395** *Melted chocolate icing*

Chocolate makes an excellent icing for cakes. If possible use the real chocolate couverture; otherwise use block plain or milk chocolate.
It is essential that this is melted over hot, but not boiling, water and is NOT allowed to become too hot, otherwise the shine and gloss will be lost. When the chocolate begins to melt beat hard with a spoon, and add a few drops melted butter or oil to make it easier to spread.

**396** *Frosting*

6 oz. loaf *or* granulated sugar    1 egg white
4 tablespoons water            pinch cream of tartar

This is the boiled type of icing that never becomes too hard. It is brittle and crisp on the outside, but far softer inside than a royal icing. It is not suitable for piping, but keeps very well on a cake.

Put the sugar and water into a saucepan and stir until the sugar has dissolved. Boil steadily, until mixture reaches soft ball stage, i.e. when a little is dropped into cold water it forms a soft, pliable ball (238°F.).
Beat until the syrup turns cloudy, then pour on to the *stiffly-beaten* egg white, adding the cream of tartar. Continue beating until the mixture thickens, then spread on cake. Pick up at intervals to form peaks on top of the cake.
(*Illustrated in colour plate 6 American Bride's Cake.*)

**397** *Almond frosting*

Add 1 teaspoon almond essence to the mixture.

**398** *Chocolate frosting*

Stir ½ oz. sieved cocoa powder into the icing when it reaches 238°F.

**399** *Coffee frosting*

Use 4 tablespoons strong coffee instead of water.

**400** *Pineapple frosting*

Use either 1 teaspoon pineapple essence in the icing or 4 tablespoons pineapple juice instead of water.

**401** *Orange frosting*

Use 4 tablespoons fresh orange juice instead of 4 tablespoons of water and add ½-1 teaspoon very finely grated orange rind.

**402** *Lemon frosting*

Use 2 tablespoons lemon juice and add enough water to give 4 tablespoons.
Also add ½ teaspoon very finely grated lemon rind if wished.

**403** *Coconut frosting*

Boil icing until it reaches 238°F., then add 3 oz. desiccated coconut or freshly shredded coconut, stir well then continue as before.
For the top only of a 7- or 8-inch cake use the above quantities. For top and sides of a 7- or 8-inch cake use double quantity.

**404** *Seven-minute frosting*

1 egg white               ¼ teaspoon cream of tartar
3 dessertspoons cold water  ½ teaspoon vanilla essence
7 oz. granulated sugar

Put all the ingredients except the vanilla into a double saucepan or a heat-proof basin that fits over a small saucepan. Whisk until well mixed. Place over rapidly boiling water. Beat and cook for 7 minutes until frosting stands up in peaks. Then add vanilla essence.

## 405 Jam or jelly frosting

1 egg white

2 tablespoons sieved jam or jelly

Whisk the egg white until very stiff, then gradually beat in the jam or jelly. If possible this should be melted; allow to cool but NOT become set, before being added.
This gives a soft, marshmallow type of frosting, which is excellent for sponge cakes, or cakes for children.
If the jam or jelly is not melted you get a slightly mottled effect, but this does not spoil the flavour of the frosting.

## 406 Butterscotch frosting

6 oz. brown sugar
4 tablespoons water

1 egg white
pinch cream of tartar

Put the sugar and water into a saucepan and stir until the sugar has dissolved. Boil steadily, until mixture reaches soft ball stage, i.e. when a little dropped into cold water forms a soft, pliable ball (238°F.). Beat until the syrup turns cloudy, then pour on to the stiffly beaten egg white, adding the cream of tartar. Continue beating until the mixture thickens, then spread on cake. Pick up at intervals to form peaks on top of cake if wished.

## 407 White fudge icing

8 oz. icing sugar
3 oz. cooking fat
3 tablespoons water

3 oz. granulated sugar
vanilla essence to flavour

Sieve the icing sugar into a bowl. Dissolve remaining ingredients gently over low heat. Bring to the boil and pour gradually over the icing sugar, stirring all the time. When cold, beat with a wooden spoon until light and fluffy. Use either as a filling or coating.

## 408 Chocolate fudge icing

Use ½ oz. cocoa powder and ½ oz. less icing sugar.

## 409 Coffee fudge icing

Use 3 tablespoons diluted coffee made from essence or powdered coffee instead of water.

## 410 Orange or lemon fudge icing

Use 3 tablespoons fruit juice instead of water and a little grated lemon or orange rind.

## 411 To decorate small cakes

These can be decorated in many ways, a simple coating of glacé icing being the easiest. When the icing is nearly set arrange attractive shapes of cherries, nuts or crystallised rose or violet petals on top. For very small cakes the best way to coat with the icing is to insert a fine fork or skewer in the base of each small cake and dip it into the rather soft icing.
A moist coating for small cakes is given by spreading with sieved apricot jam, then covering with butter or glacé icing.
Here are some ideas for decorating small cakes:
Orange glacé icing (Recipe 375) decorated with a line of melted chocolate and an orange jelly sweet.
Lemon glacé icing (Recipe 374) with a flower and leaf of crystallised lemon.
Coffee glacé icing (Recipe 373) with piping in melted chocolate and white glacé icing decorated with either a coffee bean or nut.
*Chocolate mice*
Cut pieces of sponge to resemble the shape of a mouse. Spread with a little sieved apricot jam, press almonds into position for ears. Pour over melted chocolate or chocolate glacé icing (Recipe 372). When set, decorate with tiny blobs of white glacé icing (Recipe 371).

## 412 Petits fours (1)

Use Genoese pastry (Recipe 86) or one of the sponge recipes in that section. Cut into long strips or tiny shapes and ice and decorate.

## 413 Petits fours (2)

1 oz. butter
1 oz. castor sugar
2 oz. flour (with plain flour use ½ teaspoon baking powder)

marzipan made with 4 oz. ground almonds etc. (Recipe 385)

This recipe gives a much more 'biscuity' type of petits fours.

Cream butter and sugar together, work in the sieved flour with baking powder, if used, then knead well. Add the marzipan and knead again. Colour if desired, then roll and cut into fancy shapes. Put on to lightly greased tin and bake for 15 minutes in the centre of a very moderate oven (350°F.—Gas Mark 3). Cool on tin then decorate as desired.

## 414 Confectioner's custard or vanilla cream (1)

1 level tablespoon cornflour
¼ pint milk
1-2 teaspoons sugar
vanilla essence

2 egg yolks
4 tablespoons thick whipped cream

Blend the cornflour with the milk. Put into saucepan with sugar and vanilla essence and gradually bring to the boil, stirring all the time. Cook until mixture is very thick. Take off the heat and cool slightly. Add the egg yolks and return to the heat for a few minutes, without allowing mixture to boil. When the mixture is a little cooler add the cream.

## 415 Vanilla cream (2)

2 egg yolks
2 tablespoons castor sugar
1 tablespoon cornflour

½ pint milk
1 vanilla pod

Whisk together the egg yolks, sugar and cornflour, then add a little warm milk. Boil remainder of milk with vanilla pod. Gradually add egg and sugar mixture to boiled milk and then return to heat, warming gradually till mixture cooks and thickens. This cream should be thick enough to spread over a cake.

## 416 Whipped cream and mock cream fillings

Both real cream and mock cream make an excellent filling and decoration for cakes.

REAL CREAM Take care not to over-whip this, as it will then separate and it is not possible to pipe it. Put the cream into a dry bowl and whip briskly until it starts to thicken, then whip very slowly until the mixture holds its shape. Add a little sugar to taste if desired.

CRÈME CHANTILLY Whipped cream, to which a little sugar and vanilla essence is added.

LIGHT WHIPPED CREAM To give a lighter and less rich cream, whip ¼ pint cream in one bowl and 1 or 2 egg whites in another. Fold the egg whites into the cream, add sugar and vanilla to taste.

MOCK CREAM WITH BUTTER Make the butter icing, Recipe 387, then very gradually beat in enough water or milk to give a very soft consistency.

MOCK CREAM WITH EVAPORATED MILK Boil the evaporated milk in the tin for 15 minutes, then open tin; do this carefully so the milk will not come out too quickly. Soften a level teaspoon powder gelatine in 1 tablespoon hot water, add to the very hot evaporated milk and stir until dissolved. Pour into a bowl and allow to become very cold, then whip until stiff. Add a little sugar and flavouring to taste.

## 417 Fondant icing

6 oz. loaf or granulated sugar
4 tablespoons water

pinch cream of tartar
1 dessertspoon warm water

This is a good filling or topping to a cake, but it tends to harden with keeping. It is a good substitute for marzipan under royal icing.

Put the sugar and 4 tablespoons water into a saucepan, stir until the sugar has dissolved, add the cream of tartar and boil until the mixture reaches 237-238°F., i.e. forms a soft ball when tested in cold water. Beat until the mixture starts to turn cloudy, add the warm water, then spread on the cake or through the centre. If desired to use instead of marzipan turn on to a sugared board, knead well, and roll out like marzipan.
This quantity gives a good layer on an 8-inch cake.

## 418 Fudge icing

8 oz. granulated sugar
3 tablespoons water
1 oz. butter
flavouring*
1 small can condensed milk

*flavourings:
½-1 teaspoon vanilla essence or
½ oz. cocoa powder or strong coffee instead of water

This is delicious, either as a filling or a topping.

Put the sugar and water into a saucepan with the butter, and stir over a gentle heat until the sugar has dissolved. Add the flavouring and condensed milk (use full cream milk if possible), and boil steadily, stirring from time to time, until the mixture reaches 237-238°F., i.e. forms a soft ball when tested in cold water. Beat until cloudy, then spread through the centre and on top of the cake.
This quantity is enough for a thin layer through centre and on top of a 7-inch cake.

**Note**
For a slightly softer icing beat in 1 tablespoon cream when the icing has reached correct temperature.

## 419 Toppings for cakes

1 oz. butter
2 oz. flour

1 oz. brown sugar
1 oz. nuts, chopped

In addition to the icings in this section and those given with individual cakes in this book, there are many other quick and easy ways of decorating the tops of cakes. For example:

**1** Spread with jam and chopped nuts.
**2** Spread with jam and coconut.
**3** Spread with sieved apricot jam and grated chocolate.
If you do not wish to ice a cake, but want an attractive decoration, try:
*Toasted marshmallow topping*
Put marshmallows on the cake, then put under a low grill for a minute until they commence to melt.
For fruit and plain cakes try a CRISP TOPPED mixture—this is put on the cake BEFORE baking.

Rub the butter into the flour, add the sugar and nuts. Press on top of the cake and bake in the usual way.
This can be varied by adding more sugar or spices to taste.

## 420 Chocolate piping icing

Make a glacé icing (Recipe 371). Set aside a tablespoon of this icing, add 1 teaspoon cocoa powder with a few drops of water to make a chocolate piping icing.
*Chocolate piping icing is illustrated in Walnut Cherry Gâteau, colour plate 3 made from the Honey Sponge recipe No. 102.*

## 421 Meringues

2 egg whites
2 oz. castor sugar AND

2 oz. icing sugar, sieved *or*
4 oz. castor sugar

Whisk egg whites until stiff, fold in the sugar gradually or beat in half the sugar and fold in the rest. Then pipe or pile small spoonfuls on to a well oiled or buttered tin or oiled or buttered paper on a baking tin. Bake for about 2-3 hours, depending on size, in a very low oven (225-250°F.—Gas Mark 0-½) until crisp, but still white. Lift from the tin with a warmed palette knife, cool, then store in airtight tins. Sandwich together with cream, ice cream or fruit and cream, or butter icing (Recipe 387). Do not put in cream until nearly time to serve.

*Whisking the egg whites until stiff.*

*Sandwiched together with cream and ready to serve.*

## 422 Chocolate meringues

3 level teaspoons cocoa powder
6 oz. sugar, icing and castor mixed

3 egg whites
whipped cream *or* flavoured butter icing (Recipe 387)

Mix cocoa with sugar, then proceed as for meringues (Recipe 421)

*Chocolate Meringues*

### 423 Mushrooms

ingredients as for meringues
(Recipe 421)

little chocolate powder
small quantity marzipan

Having made the meringues, pipe into tiny rounds on oiled paper and shake on a little chocolate powder. Bake as before. When set you will find the chocolate powder has melted slightly and formed a layer of icing. Make small stalks of marzipan and stick these on to the meringue tops.

### 424 Almond meringue fingers

3 egg whites
6 oz. sugar, icing and castor mixed

2 oz. almonds, chopped
whipped cream

Proceed as for meringues (Recipe 421), then pipe the mixture into equal shaped fingers. Dust with the chopped almonds and bake in the centre of a *very cool oven* (200-250°F.—Gas Mark 0-½), until quite firm. This should take about 1½ hours. When cold, sandwich together with the whipped cream.

### 425 Nut meringues

6 oz. sugar, icing and castor mixed
pinch salt

3 oz. nuts, chopped
3 egg whites

Sieve together the sugars and salt. Mix in the nuts. Beat the egg whites until stiff, fold in the sugar mixture. Proceed as in Recipe 421.

# BISCUITS

In this section you will find a selection of easy-to-make biscuits—sweet and savoury.

Biscuits are ideal to cook when you have a few spare minutes, because they store well for a considerable length of time without deteriorating in flavour.

You will find the essential points given below, but it is important to remember that most biscuit doughs are very short in texture; too much liquid should never be added.

### 426 Hints on biscuit making

1 Biscuits should not rise like cakes so unless the recipe says to the contrary it is better to use plain flour.
2 Do not be afraid of handling the dough; it can be kneaded well and rolled firmly. You will find it extremely helpful to do both. Keep your hands as warm as possible.
3 Avoid using too much liquid in biscuit recipes as this causes the mixture to spread badly and tends to make the biscuit soft instead of crisp right through to the middle.
4 Most biscuits should cool on the baking tins as this helps to crisp them. It saves baking twice, as used to be the rule for biscuit making.
5 If in doubt as to baking temperatures, use a moderate oven—the biscuit should be crisped right through, not just browned on the outside.
6 Use ungreased trays except where otherwise stated.

### 427 Shrewsbury biscuits
### Basic recipe

8 oz. plain flour
4 oz. margarine

4 oz. castor sugar
beaten egg to mix

Sieve the flour, then rub in the margarine till the mixture resembles fine breadcrumbs. Add the sugar, then mix to a very stiff dough with the beaten egg. Turn on to a lightly floured board, knead quickly to remove cracks and roll out thinly. Cut out into desired shapes, put on to greased baking sheets and bake towards the top of a moderate oven (375°F.—Gas Mark 4) for 12-15 minutes. Cool on baking tin.
**Variations**
In all cases blend in any additions before forming the mixture into a dough with the egg.

### 428 Cinnamon

Add 1 teaspoon cinnamon.

### 429 Lemon

Add finely grated rind ½ lemon.

### 430 Almond

Add 1 small teaspoon almond essence and 2 oz. ground almonds.

### 431 Fruit

Add 2 oz. currants or chopped glacé cherries or dates.

### 432 Coconut

Add 2 oz. desiccated coconut.

## 433 Spice

Add 1 teaspoon mixed spice.
The biscuits may be left plain, or:
**1** Brushed with beaten egg white and sprinkled with chopped nuts before baking.
**2** Sandwiched together with jam or cream when cool and, if liked, dusted with sieved icing sugar.
**3** The tops iced with glacé icing or butter cream (Recipes 371, 387) and decorated to taste with glacé cherries, angelica, whole nuts, silver balls, etc.

## 434 Shortbread
## Rich recipe

| | |
|---|---|
| 3 oz. butter | 1 oz. cornflour *or* rice flour |
| 1½-2 oz. sugar | castor sugar, to sprinkle |
| 3 oz. plain flour | |

Cream butter and half sugar, work in flour and the cornflour then the last of the sugar. Knead well, then press into a 7-inch fluted flan ring placed on a baking tray and prick with a fork; shape on the back of an ungreased tin, or into a floured shortbread mould. Bake for 30-40 minutes in a slow oven (300-325°F.—Gas Mark 2). Cool in the ring. Sprinkle with castor sugar.

*Shortbread*

## 435 Shortbread
## Economical recipe

| | |
|---|---|
| 2 oz. margarine | 4 oz. flour |
| 1 oz. sugar | |

Slightly melt the margarine, then work in other ingredients. Proceed as before, but bake for 25 minutes (350°F.—Gas Mark 3).

## 436 Orange and lemon crunchies

| | |
|---|---|
| 4 oz. margarine *or* butter | *Filling* |
| 2 oz. castor sugar | orange *or* lemon curd |
| 5 oz. plain flour | |

Place all the ingredients in a mixing bowl. Mix together quickly, then beat very thoroughly with a wooden spoon until the mixture is soft and creamy. Place in a Swiss roll tin. Spread evenly, and mark the top in lines with the back of a fork. Bake near the top of a moderate oven (375°F.—Gas Mark 4) for 20-25 minutes. Cut into fingers. Cool on a cake rack and sandwich in pairs with orange or lemon curd.

*Orange and lemon crunchies*

## 437 Shortbread crisps

Use the same recipe as for the rich shortbread (Recipe 434). Add a few drops of vanilla or almond essence. Roll the mixture into balls, and put on to ungreased baking trays, allowing room for them to spread during cooking. Decorate with a cherry or nut on top before cooking, and bake for approximately 14 minutes in the centre of a moderate oven (375°F.—Gas Mark 4). Cool on the tin.
If liked 1 oz. desiccated coconut can be substituted for 1 oz. flour.

## 438 Coconut shortbread

| | |
|---|---|
| 3 oz. margarine *or* butter | 2 dessertspoons ground rice |
| 1½-2 oz. granulated sugar | *or* fine semolina |
| 3 oz. plain flour | 2 oz. desiccated coconut |

Cream the margarine or butter and half the sugar. Work in the other ingredients. Put in the last of the sugar, knead thoroughly then press on to an ungreased baking sheet, forming a neat round. Prick and mark into sections. Bake in the centre of a very moderate oven (350°F.—Gas Mark 3) for approximately 45 minutes. Cool on the tin.

### 439 Savoury oatmeal biscuits

1 oz. margarine
4 oz. fine oatmeal
good pinch salt

water, milk or diluted
vegetable extract to mix

Rub the margarine into the oatmeal, add the salt and sufficient liquid to give a dry mixture. Roll out until wafer thin. Then cut into rounds and bake on a lightly greased tin for about 10 minutes in centre of a moderately hot oven (425°F.—Gas Mark 6).

### 440 Oatmeal biscuits (Semi-sweet)

4 oz. margarine
2 oz. sugar
4 oz. flour
good pinch salt

4 oz. fine oatmeal
milk to mix
2 oz. almonds, finely chopped

Cream margarine and sugar together. Sieve flour and salt into margarine together with oatmeal. Add enough milk to make a firm dough. Roll out fairly thinly and press into a greased 7-inch sandwich tin. Sprinkle with finely chopped almonds. Bake in the centre of a moderate oven (375°F.—Gas Mark 4) for 20-25 minutes. Cool in the tin; cut into portions.

Oatmeal biscuits

### 441 Cheese biscuits

4 oz. plain flour
seasoning
3 oz. margarine *or* butter

2-3 oz. cheese
egg yolk

Sieve flour and seasoning together. Rub in margarine, add finely grated cheese and bind with egg yolk. Roll out firmly, cut into desired shapes. Put on to lightly greased baking trays and bake for about 7-10 minutes near top of a hot oven (450°F.—Gas Mark 7). Cool on tray as they are very short and brittle.

### 442 Cream crackers

8 oz. flour
½ teaspoon salt

1-1½ oz. fat
water to mix

Sieve flour and salt together, rub in the fat, and mix to a very dry dough with the water. Roll out very thinly. Fold into three, roll again lightly, then cut into squares. Bake at the top of a very hot oven—(475°F.—Gas Mark 8) for approximately 7 minutes.

### 443 Cracknell biscuits

3 oz. butter
6 oz. plain flour
good pinch salt

2 oz. cornflour
milk and water to mix

Rub the butter into the flour, sieved with salt and cornflour, blend with the milk and water until a very *dry* dough—you need very little liquid and dough must be kneaded very well to bind the ingredients together. Cut into small rounds, press the centre down slightly with the back of a spoon and bake in the centre of a moderate oven (375°F.—Gas Mark 4) for about 12 minutes.

### 444 Digestive biscuits

1 tablespoon sugar
3 oz. cooking fat, margarine
  *or* butter
6 oz. plain flour, preferably
  wholemeal flour

2 oz. oatmeal
½ teaspoon salt
water to mix

Cream together the sugar and fat. Firmly knead this into the dry ingredients and mix with sufficient water to make a rolling consistency. Roll firmly until the mixture is about a good ¼ inch in thickness. Cut into rounds, prick and bake on a greased baking tin in the centre of a moderate oven (375°F.—Gas Mark 4) for 15 minutes.

### 445 Chocolate peppermint creams

5½ oz. plain flour
½ oz. cocoa powder
3 oz. butter *or* margarine
3 oz. castor sugar
few drops vanilla essence
beaten egg to mix

*Peppermint butter cream*
1½ oz. butter
3 oz. icing sugar, sieved
few drops peppermint essence

Sift flour and cocoa powder into a bowl and rub in fat until the mixture resembles fine breadcrumbs. Add sugar and mix to a stiff paste with vanilla essence and egg. Turn out on to a lightly floured board and roll out thinly. Cut into rounds with a 2½-inch plain cutter.
From half the rounds remove centres with a 1½-inch plain cutter. (These can be re-rolled to make more biscuits.) Transfer to greased baking trays and bake at 375°F.—Gas Mark 4 for 15 minutes. Cool. Cream the butter and icing sugar together until light and fluffy. Add few drops peppermint essence. Spread the rounds with peppermint butter cream and top with the rings.

## 446 Lemon fingers

**For pastry**
4 oz. plain flour
pinch salt
1 oz. lard
1 oz. margarine
½ oz. castor sugar
about ½ egg to bind

**For biscuit mixture**
4 oz. butter

1½ oz. castor sugar
about ½ egg
½ teaspoon vanilla essence
1 oz. ground almonds
4 oz. plain flour
¼ level teaspoon baking
   powder

**For decoration**
lemon curd

Sieve flour and salt. Rub in the fats, stir in sugar and mix to a firm dough with beaten egg. Roll out pastry thinly into a rectangle about 9 × 7 inches. Trim edges. Cut into 2 long strips about 3½ inches wide. Lift on to lightly greased baking sheet and prick well. Make up biscuit mixture. Cream butter and sugar. Beat in egg and vanilla essence. Work in the ground almonds. Sift in flour and baking powder and beat to a soft piping consistency. Put into piping bag with medium star tube and pipe a border down the long sides of each strip. Use remaining mixture to pipe a line down the centre of each strip. Bake above centre of a moderate oven (375°F.—Gas Mark 4) until firm. Leave on the baking sheet. Pipe lemon curd between the borders of biscuit mixture, using a paper piping bag with a ½-inch end snipped off. Mark into fingers while still warm, but do not cut through until almost cold. Cut straight across or slantwise. *(Illustrated in colour plate 16.)*

## 447 Hungarian biscuits

2 oz. margarine, butter *or*
   cooking fat
2 oz. castor sugar
few drops almond *or*
   ratafia essence

2 oz. flour (with plain flour
   use ½ level teaspoon baking
   powder)
2 oz. ground almonds
few blanched almonds

Cream margarine, sugar and essence. Work in flour and ground almonds. Knead well and add no extra liquid. Roll out thinly, cut into fingers or rounds, put on to lightly greased tin. Press halved almond on each and bake for 8–10 minutes in centre of moderate oven (375°F.—Gas Mark 4). Allow to cool on the tin.

## 448 Marshmallow spring hats

ingredients as for shortbread
   (Recipes 434, 435)

**Decoration**
marshmallows

glacé icing (Recipe 371)
crystallised violets
angelica
glacé cherries

Roll out the shortbread mixture and cut into rounds about ¼ inch thick. Bake in the centre of a moderate oven (375°F.—Gas Mark 4) for 15 minutes. Cool on tin. Put a marshmallow in the centre of each biscuit, and coat with a thin layer of icing. Arrange tiny pieces of cherry, etc. to look like the decorations on a hat.

## 449 Tutti frutti rounds

Ingredients as for shortbread
   (Recipes 434, 435)

**To decorate**
little jam *or* honey

dates, chopped
walnuts, chopped
glacé cherries, halved
small quantity glacé icing
   (Recipe 371)

Roll out the shortbread mixture and cut into rounds about ¼ inch thick. Bake in the centre of a moderate oven (375°F.—Gas Mark 4) for 15 minutes. Cool on tin. Sandwich together with jam or honey. Mix together the dates, walnuts and cherries. Spread the sandwiched biscuits with a little jam or honey, then add a teaspoon of the date mixture. Coat with a thin layer of glacé icing.

## 450 Mont Blanc shortbreads

ingredients as for shortbread
   (Recipes 434, 435)

*\* Obtainable from good grocers*

**To decorate**
tube of chestnut purée\* or
   chestnut butter icing
whipped cream
grated chocolate

Roll out the shortbread mixture to ¼ inch thick. Cut into 2½-inch rounds, and bake in the centre of a moderate oven (375°F.—Gas Mark 4) for approximately 15 minutes. Cool on tin. Put the chestnut purée or butter icing into an icing bag with a plain nozzle, and pipe round the edge of the biscuits to give a nest shape. Fill the centre with whipped cream and grated chocolate. *Do this only a short time before serving* otherwise the biscuits become too soft. To make chestnut butter icing add little sieved chestnuts to butter icing (Recipe 387).

## 451 Almond fingers

ingredients as for shortbread
   (Recipes 434, 435)

**To decorate**
blanched almonds
glacé icing (Recipe 371)

Shred the almonds and brown slightly under the grill or in the oven. Roll out the shortbread mixture to ¼ inch thick. Cut into fingers and bake in the centre of a moderate oven (375°F.—Gas Mark 4) for approximately 15 minutes. Cool on tin. When cold cover with the icing and the almonds.

## 452 Vanilla biscuits

4 oz. margarine
4 oz. castor sugar
1 egg yolk
1 tablespoon milk
few drops vanilla essence

6 oz. plain flour (with self-
   raising flour omit baking
   powder but plain flour is
   better in this recipe)
1 teaspoon baking powder
2 oz. fine semolina
pinch salt
2 tablespoons cornflour

Cream margarine. Add sugar and beat together until soft and light. Whisk egg yolk with milk and vanilla, add to creamed fat and sugar, mixing until blended. Sift remaining ingredients and work into mixture, which will be a soft one. If liked, pipe through biscuit machine to make small shapes, or chill and roll out on floured board and cut into shapes.
Bake in the centre of a moderate oven (375°F.—Gas Mark 4) for approximately 5 minutes and allow to cool on the baking tray.
*(Illustrated in colour on the jacket.)*

## 453 Sugary finish

Brush with white of egg and sprinkle with castor sugar before baking.

## 454 Sandwiches

Sandwich two biscuits together with melted chocolate, butter cream, icing or jam.

## 455 Cockle shells

Make marbles of paste and space apart on a greased baking tin. Press flatter with a fork. When baked, sandwich together with lemon butter cream or icing, or melted chocolate, etc. and dust with icing sugar.
(*Illustrated in colour on the jacket.*)

## 456 Jam sandwich

Press some of the mixture through the ribbed nozzle of biscuit maker. When baked, sandwich together with jam.
(*Illustrated in colour on the jacket.*)

## 457 Nut fingers

Pipe some of the mixture through a broader nozzle to 3-inch lengths. When cooked, sandwich together with melted chocolate or jam. Dip each end in melted chocolate and then into chopped nuts.
**Note**
To vary the basic mixture include 2-3 oz. finely chopped nuts and substitute a few drops almond essence for vanilla. If liked add 1 teaspoon cocoa powder or currants or chopped peel.
(*Illustrated in colour on the jacket.*)

## 458 Overnight nut cookies

8 oz. plain flour
2 oz. fine semolina
6 oz. butter *or* margarine
5 oz. castor sugar
1 egg yolk mixed with
   2 dessertspoons cold water
1 egg white
2½-3 oz. walnuts

Sift flour and semolina into a bowl. Rub in fat till mixture resembles fine breadcrumbs, add sugar then mix to a stiff paste with the egg yolk and water. Draw together lightly with the finger tips, turn out on to a floured board and divide in half. Shape each piece into a smooth roll, wrap in greaseproof paper and chill till firm—about 2-3 hours, or overnight, or even for a day or two. Unwrap, then cut rolls into very thin slices. Transfer cookies to greased baking trays, brush with lightly beaten egg white, and top each with a small piece of shelled walnut. Bake in centre of a moderately hot oven (400°F.—Gas Mark 5) for 8-10 minutes or till golden. Cool. Store in an airtight tin.

*Forming the mixture into a stiff paste with egg yolk and water.*

*Shaping the mixture into 2 rolls.*

*Cutting the chilled rolls into thin slices.*

*The cookies baked and ready to serve.*

## 459 Flapjacks (1)

6 oz. butter *or* margarine
6 oz. Demerara sugar

8 oz. quick cooking rolled oats
pinch salt

Melt the fat in a saucepan over a very gentle heat. Mix in the sugar, oats and salt. Stir well and turn the mixture into a well greased Swiss roll tin and press lightly together. Smooth the surface with a knife and bake for approximately 30-35 minutes in the centre of a moderate oven (375°F.—Gas Mark 4). When cooked golden brown leave to stand in the tin a few minutes, then cut across into 16 squares or fingers. Leave in the tin until quite cold before removing.
**Note**
For a slightly stickier flapjack use 3 oz. Demerara sugar and 3 tablespoons golden syrup instead of all sugar.

## 460 Spiced walnut flapjack

As above, but add 2 oz. chopped walnuts and 1 teaspoon mixed spice to ingredients.

## 461 Chocolate flapjacks

As above, but use only 6 oz. quick cooking rolled oats and 2 oz. cocoa powder. Bake as before. When cold these biscuits can be covered on top with melted chocolate.

## 462 Flapjacks (2)

3 oz. cooking fat
2 oz. soft brown sugar

1 heaped tablespoon golden syrup
6 oz. rolled oats

Heat the fat, sugar and syrup in a small saucepan over a low heat, until the sugar dissolves. Cool. Place the rolled oats in a basin. Stir in the cooled fat and sugar mixture and mix well. Spread in a shallow 8-inch square tin, brushed with heated fat. Bake near the top of a very moderate oven (350°F.—Gas Mark 3) for 30-35 minutes. Leave to cool a little, then cut into finger-size pieces and leave to finish cooling on a cake rack.

## 463 Ginger nuts (1)

4 oz. syrup
4 oz. castor sugar
3 oz. cooking fat
8 oz. self-raising flour
½ level teaspoon bicarbonate of soda

2 rounded teaspoons ground ginger
1 level teaspoon mixed spice
1 egg
1-2 oz. almonds, halved

Place syrup, sugar and fat in a saucepan and heat gently until sugar dissolves. Leave to cool. Sieve flour, bicarbonate, ginger and mixed spice into a basin. Then add egg and cooled syrup and fat mixture. Mix well together, then form into walnut-sized balls, rolling between the fingers. Place well apart on a baking sheet, brushed with melted cooking fat. Place a sliced almond on each. Bake near the top of a very moderate oven (350°F.—Gas Mark 3) for 20-30 minutes. Remove and cool on a cake rack. When cold, store in an airtight tin.

## 464 Ginger nuts (2)

4 oz. plain flour
1 oz. sugar
1 level teaspoon bicarbonate of soda
1 level teaspoon each mixed spice, cinnamon, ground ginger

2 oz. fat—margarine, cooking fat, dripping *or* peanut butter can be used
2 level tablespoons golden syrup

Mix all the dry ingredients together. Melt the fat and syrup and pour on to the flour mixture. Roll into balls about the size of a walnut, and put on to a well greased baking tin, allowing room between the balls, for as they cook they will spread out. Put the tin on the second shelf from the top of the oven and bake for 5 minutes at 450°F.—Gas Mark 7. At the end of this time, transfer the tin to the middle of the oven, and lower heat to Gas Mark 4, or if using an electric oven, switch OFF. Cook for a further 10 minutes in the middle. Cool on the tin.

## 465 Chocolate nut biscuits

Ingredients as above, but use 3 level teaspoons cocoa powder instead of spices.

## 466 Lemon cinnamon biscuits

2 oz. cooking fat *or* lard
2 oz. sugar
1 level tablespoon golden syrup
6 oz. plain flour

½ teaspoon powdered cinnamon
1 dessertspoon finely grated lemon rind
1 dessertspoon lemon juice

Cream the lard, sugar and golden syrup together. Add all the other ingredients. Mix thoroughly, first with a spoon, then with your fingers. Knead the dough thoroughly. If necessary add a few drops of water to make into a firm ball—you will probably find that no extra liquid is necessary. Roll out until very thin. Cut into rounds or fancy shapes and put on to a well greased baking tin. Bake in the centre of a very moderate oven (350°F.—Gas Mark 3) for 10 minutes.

## 467 Danish brune kager (brown biscuits)

4 oz. black treacle *or* golden syrup
2 oz. brown sugar
1 oz. cooking fat
1 level teaspoon ground cloves
1 level teaspoon cinnamon
½ level teaspoon ground ginger

grated rind ½ orange
¼ level teaspoon bicarbonate of soda
6 oz. plain flour

*Topping*
almonds, chopped
candied peel, chopped

Place the treacle, sugar, cooking fat, cloves, cinnamon, ginger and orange rind in a saucepan and allow to dissolve over a low heat. When only warm stir in the bicarbonate of soda. Sieve the flour into a bowl and pour in the melted ingredients. Form into a dough and roll out thinly on a floured board to a square. Cut into finger-shaped pieces approximately 3½ × 1¼ inches and place on a baking sheet brushed with melted cooking fat. Brush over with a little milk or water and decorate with chopped almonds and chopped peel. Bake near the top of moderately hot oven (375°F.—Gas Mark 5) for 8-10 minutes. Remove and cool on a cake rack.

*Danish brune ager (brown biscuits)*

## 468 Brownies

6 oz. butter *or* margarine
2 oz. cocoa
6 oz. castor sugar
2 eggs
2 oz. plain flour

2 oz. walnuts chopped

*To decorate*
castor sugar
walnuts

Melt 2 oz. butter and add the cocoa. Mix well and set this aside. Cream remaining 4 oz. butter and sugar, gradually beat in the eggs. Beat well and add the flour, walnuts and cocoa mixture. Put into greased and floured 7-inch square tin and bake in the centre of the oven (375°F.—Gas Mark 4) for about 45 minutes. Leave to cool in the tin. When cold, turn out and cut into small squares. Sprinkle with castor sugar, top each square with a walnut. (*Illustrated in colour plate 18.*)

## 469 Maple walnut biscuits

2 oz. walnuts
4 oz. margarine
3 oz. sugar*

2 level teaspoons maple syrup*
7 oz. plain flour
1 teaspoon instant coffee

* *If maple syrup is unobtainable in your shops use golden syrup and brown sugar*

Chop or mince the walnuts, cream margarine, sugar and syrup, work in the flour, coffee and walnuts, and knead together very well. If too dry add 2 or 3 drops of milk, but this should not be necessary. Roll out very thinly—this must be done firmly so that the biscuits do not break. Cut into rounds with a fluted cutter. Put on to lightly greased and floured baking trays and bake for 10 minutes in the centre of a moderate oven (375°F.—Gas Mark 4). Cool on the tray. Store in an airtight tin and serve dusted with icing sugar, or sandwich two biscuits together with coffee butter icing (Recipe 389). Cover the top with a thin layer of coffee butter icing and decorate with chopped walnuts.

## 470 Coffee walnut biscuits

Ingredients as above but *omit* maple syrup and use 6 oz. flour only. If necessary add little milk or egg to bind. Before baking brush with a little milk and sprinkle with chopped walnuts.

*Coffee walnut biscuits*

## 471 Peanut crackers

2 oz. butter
1½ oz. soft brown sugar
2 oz. granulated sugar
½ egg

few drops vanilla essence
5 rounded dessertspoons crunchy peanut butter
4 oz. plain flour

Cream butter and sugars. Beat in the egg and vanilla essence, then work in the peanut butter. Sift in the flour and mix to a smooth dough. Roll into small balls and place on greased baking sheets, well apart. Press out with the prongs of a fork. Bake above centre of moderate to a moderately hot oven (375-400°F.—Gas Mark 5-6) until firm (about 15 minutes). Cool on a rack. (*Illustrated in colour plate 19.*)

# BREAD

There is a returning interest in home-baked bread, and it surprises many people, when using yeast for the first time, to find that it is not difficult and that the results are very rewarding.

Yeast, unlike baking powder, is a living organism. It can be killed by too much heat, so follow the directions for 'proving' carefully. Fresh yeast is a pale putty colour, crumbles easily and smells fresh: stale yeast is dry in texture and smells unpleasant.

## 472 Terms used in yeast cooking

Cooking with yeast is very well worth doing, for it provides a more interesting variety of cakes, buns, bread, etc., at very economical prices. Do not be frightened by the terms used in yeast cookery—they are quite simple.

If a recipe states *let the sponge break through* it simply means that having creamed the yeast and sugar and added liquid and a sprinkling of flour, you put the mixture in a warm place until its surface is covered with small bubbles.

In most recipes using yeast mention is made of allowing the dough to *prove*. This means allowing it to rise, and this is done by putting the dough in a warm place—NOT TOO HOT—until it has increased its bulk to twice the original size. Never allow it to become more than twice the original size, or the dough will be 'over-proved' and its taste and texture spoiled.

To *knock back* the dough means that when it has *proved* it is then kneaded gently but firmly until it remains its original size.

*KNEADING* is a process that must be done efficiently if good-textured bread and buns are to result. Use the heel of the hand—the part of the palm near the wrist—and pull the dough gently and firmly.

*Success in yeast cooking*

This depends on correct handling of the dough—see explanations of terms used given above.

Have all ingredients, utensils, etc., at a comfortable temperature, just warm —NOT TOO HOT and not very COLD.

Bake at the right temperatures. Most yeast cooking needs a hot oven at the beginning, to kill the yeast directly the food is put into the oven.

Handle the dough firmly, but not too roughly.

The fact that in some recipes the quantity of water is given rather approximately is not a fault, for flours vary considerably in the amount of liquid they absorb. An ideal bread dough is easy to handle, yet not too stiff. You can always tell when it is sufficiently handled by testing with a firm pressure of your finger—if the mark comes out the bread is kneaded enough.

## 473 Bread

3 lb. plain or bread flour
3-7 teaspoons salt*
1 oz. yeast†

1-2 level teaspoons sugar (use 2 teaspoons only with fruit bread)
at least 1¼ pints tepid water

* For amounts of salt see Recipe 478
† For bread with dried yeast, see Recipe 478

Sieve flour and salt into a warm basin, then put in warm place. Cream yeast and sugar in another basin, add part of liquid. Put this into a well made in centre of flour, giving a light dusting of flour over top. Cover with a clean cloth and leave in a warm place for a good 15 minutes, until top is covered with bubbles. Add rest of liquid—you may need a little more to give a soft dough. Knead well until dough is smooth and leaves bowl clean. Put to rise in a warm place for about 1½ hours, then knead again. Form into loaves and put into warm and lightly greased bread tins, half filling them. To give very crisp crust, brush with melted margarine or use milk or egg and water. Prove for a final time, about 20 minutes. Bake in centre of a hot oven (425-450°F.—Gas Mark 6-7) for the first ten minutes. Reduce heat to moderate (375°F.—Gas Mark 4) for a further 30-45 minutes, depending on size of loaves. To test, knock on bottom of loaves: they should sound hollow. Cool away from draught.

**Note**

An ounce of lard or margarine rubbed into flour helps to keep bread moist.

## 474 Brown bread

1½ lb. plain *or* bread flour
1½ lb. wholemeal flour
3-7 level teaspoons salt*

1 level teaspoon sugar
1 oz. yeast†
at least 1½ pints tepid water

* For amounts of salt see Recipe 478
† For bread with dried yeast see Recipe 478

Method as Recipe 473 but a lighter and better result is obtained with brown bread if the dough is slightly slacker (i.e. more moist).

## 475 *Wholemeal bread*

3 lb. wholemeal flour
3-7 teaspoons salt*
1 teaspoon sugar

1 oz. yeast†
2-2½ pints tepid water

*\* For amounts of salt see Recipe 478*
*† For bread with dried yeast see Recipe 478*

Method as for bread, Recipe 473, until the liquid is added, then add enough water to give a very soft dough that is much too slack to knead. Beat well with a wooden spoon. Allow to prove in a warm place for approximately 1½ hours, then beat again and put into warmed bread tins, half filling these. Prove for the final time, about 20 minutes, then bake as Recipe 474.

The additional water in this recipe gives a more moist and light wholemeal bread.

*Brown bread*

*Wholemeal bread*

## 476 *Shaping bread*

After you have experimented with ordinary tin loaves, i.e. baking in loaf tins, you will be anxious to make more ambitious shapes.

**Bloomer loaf**
Form the dough into a rather 'fat' roll. Flatten the top slightly, then mark on top with a sharp knife before final proving. Bake on flat baking tins.

**Cottage loaf**
Form the dough into two rounds—one considerably smaller than the other. Press the small round on top of the larger and make a deep thumb mark in the middle of the top round. Bake on flat baking tins.

**French stick**
Form the dough into long 'stick' shape. Score on top with sharp knife before proving. Bake on flat baking tins.

**Coburg**
Form dough into large rounds. Mark with wide cross on top before proving. Bake on flat baking tins.

**French or Vienna loaf**
Form into a rather shorter and thicker 'stick' than the French stick.

**Farmhouse or Danish loaf**
If using the basic bread dough, mix with rather more milk than water. This can be baked in a loaf tin, but fill the loaf tin slightly fuller than usual, so you get the typical rounded edges. Score well on top before final proving. Brush with a little milk and sprinkle top with light dusting of flour before baking.

## 477 *Malt yeast bread*

good ½ oz. yeast
3 teaspoons sugar
about ½ pint tepid milk
  and water

2 tablespoons malt
1½ lb. plain *or* bread flour
1 teaspoon salt
3-5 oz. dried fruit (optional)

Cream the yeast and 1 teaspoon sugar in a warm basin, add half the tepid liquid, the malt and a good sprinkling of flour. Leave in a warm place for 20-25 minutes until the top is covered with bubbles. Sieve the flour and salt together, add rest of the sugar and the dried fruit. Stir in the yeast mixture and enough liquid to give a soft pliable dough. Knead well, then continue as Recipe 473, allowing mixture to prove first in the bowl, then in the tin or tins. Bake one large loaf for approximately 55 minutes or two smaller loaves for approximately 35-40 minutes. Allow 10 minutes in a very hot oven (450-475°F.—Gas Mark 7-8), then lower the heat to moderate (375°F.—Gas Mark 4). Bake the loaves in the centre of the oven.

## 478 *Bread with dried yeast*

With dried yeast, mix with the sugar and a little tepid liquid. Allow to stand in warm place until soft—approximately 20 minutes, then cream. Continue after this as for fresh yeast. Makes of dried yeast vary, so follow instructions for each particular make—generally speaking 1 oz. fresh yeast is equivalent to 1 level tablespoon dried yeast.

The amount of salt varies according to individual tastes—for the first time use smaller quantity of salt.

## 479 Plain rolls

Use Recipes 473, 474, 475, depending on whether white, brown or wholemeal rolls are desired. Allow to prove as in Recipe 473, when instead of putting dough into bread tins form into some of the shapes illustrated. Put on warmed greased baking tins, allowing room for rolls to rise and spread out slightly. Allow to prove for 10-15 minutes in a warm place, then bake for a good 10 minutes near top of a hot to very hot oven (450-475°F.—Gas Mark 7-8).

To give a *shiny top* to the rolls, brush with beaten egg mixed with water or milk before baking.

To give a *soft outside* to the rolls, make the dough rather soft, and brush with milk after they have been cooking for about 8 minutes.

To give a '*floury*' coating to the rolls, toss very gently in sieved flour before putting on to the trays.

For *milk rolls*, mix the dough with all milk—this will slow up proving slightly, and you need to be rather generous in weighing out the yeast.

## 480 Mixed fancy rolls

½ oz. fresh yeast*

1 teaspoon sugar

about ½ pint warm milk

1 lb. plain flour

1 level teaspoon salt

2 oz. butter *or* margarine

1 egg, beaten

* *See directions for using dried yeast Recipe 478*

Cream yeast with sugar, add little warm milk and sprinkling of flour. Stand in warm place until mixture bubbles. Put flour and salt into bowl then rub in butter or margarine. Make a well in centre of mixture and pour in yeast mixture, egg and sufficient milk to make an elastic dough. Knead thoroughly by hand, cover bowl, then leave to rise in a warm place until dough has doubled in bulk. Turn on to a lightly floured board, knead lightly and divide into 14 pieces. Shape into plaits, round rolls, miniature cottage loaves and crescents and place on greased baking trays. Cover with greased polythene and leave to rise in a warm place for a further 15 minutes. Brush with beaten egg and bake just above centre of a hot to very hot oven (450-475°F.—Gas Mark 7-8) for approximately 15 minutes.

## 481 Coffee-time rolls (no yeast)

1 lb. self-raising flour

¼ level teaspoon salt

4 oz. margarine

2 oz. castor sugar

2 eggs

⅓ pint milk

1 rounded teaspoon cinnamon

1 rounded tablespoon granulated sugar

Sieve flour and salt into a bowl. Add margarine and rub in until mixture resembles fine breadcrumbs. Add castor sugar and mix well. Whisk eggs and milk together. Add beaten eggs and milk (keeping back 1 tablespoon for glazing) and mix lightly. Turn out on to a lightly-floured board, roll to ⅓ inch thickness. Cut into rounds with a 3-inch cutter, moisten tops and fold over. Place on a baking sheet brushed with margarine. Brush tops with egg and milk kept for glaze. Bake on second shelf from top in a hot oven (450°F.—Gas Mark 7) for 15-20 minutes. Remove. Brush again with glaze and sprinkle with cinnamon and sugar. Return to oven for 1 minute. Serve either hot or cold.

*Coffee-time rolls*

## 482 Currant loaf

4 oz. margarine

2 lb. flour

pinch salt

5 oz. currants

5 oz. sultanas

3 oz. chopped candied peel

3 oz. sugar

generous 1 oz. yeast

2 eggs

¾ pint warm milk

Rub fat into flour and salt, add fruit and all but a teaspoon of the sugar. Cream yeast with a teaspoon sugar until liquid, and add to beaten eggs and warm milk. Sprinkle lightly with flour. Put in warm place for approximately 20 minutes, then add to the rest of ingredients, mixing to a dough. Turn out on to a floured board and knead. Put to prove until twice its size (this takes approximately 1½-2 hours). Knead well again, then put into two warmed greased loaf tins and allow to prove again. Bake in centre of a hot oven (450°F.—Gas Mark 7) for 15 minutes. Reduce heat to moderate and bake for further 40 minutes.

## 483 Rich fruit bread

4 oz. lard

2 lb. plain flour

pinch salt

5 oz. sultanas

3 oz. chopped candied peel

5 oz. currants

3 oz. sugar

generous 1 oz. yeast

2 eggs

¾ pint warm milk *or* milk and water

Rub lard into flour and salt, add fruit and all but 1 teaspoon of the sugar. Mix yeast with a teaspoon of sugar until liquid, and add to beaten eggs and warm milk. Set aside for a little while then add to the rest of the ingredients, mixing to a dough. Turn out on to a floured board and knead. Put to prove until twice its size. Put in two 2-lb. bread tins and allow to prove for approximately 20 minutes. Bake in centre of hot oven (450°F.—Gas Mark 7) reducing the heat after the first 10 minutes to moderately hot (400°F.—Gas Mark 5) for approximately 40-50 minutes. Brush with glaze made of 2 tablespoons sugar and 2 tablespoons water on removing from oven.

*(Illustrated in colour plate 20.)*

## 484 Wiener striezel (Viennese fruit bread)

½ oz. yeast
1½ oz. sugar
4 tablespoons lukewarm milk
10 oz. plain flour
2 eggs

1½ oz. cooking fat
1½ oz. sultanas
grated rind ½ lemon
½ oz. almonds, finely chopped

Cream the yeast and sugar together, and mix in the warm milk. Sieve the flour into a warm bowl, then pour in the yeast mixture, mixing with a wooden spoon, lastly adding the beaten eggs and cooking fat. Leave covered with a damp cloth in a warm place to rise until double in bulk (about 1 hour). Knead well on a floured board and add the sultanas and lemon peel. Divide the dough in half. Roll out one portion to an oval about 8 inches long and 4 inches across the widest point. Roll out the second portion and cut into three lengths and form into a plait. Place down the centre of the flat dough, securing the ends well. Place on a baking sheet brushed with melted cooking fat. Brush with egg or milk and sprinkle with the chopped almonds. Leave in a warm place to prove for 15 minutes. Bake in the middle of a moderately hot oven (400°F.—Gas Mark 5) for 20-25 minutes. Allow to cool a little on the baking sheet, then finish cooling on a cake rack.

*Wiener striezel (Vienneze fruit bread)*

## 485 Bara brith (Speckled bread or fruit loaf)

1 oz. barm *or* yeast
8 oz. brown sugar
1¼-1½ pints warm milk*
3 lb. flour
½ teaspoon salt

4 oz. lard *or* butter
1 lb. currants
8 oz. stoned raisins
4 oz. chopped candied peel
3 eggs

* *Depending on strength of flour*

Cream yeast with teaspoon sugar and sprinkling flour and milk, or make a light soft dough with half the flour, salt, all the yeast and milk. Cover and set to rise in a warm place for 45 minutes. Then melt fat and when slightly cooled, pour into the dough, add the rest of flour, sugar, fruit and beaten eggs and mix thoroughly with the hands or a wooden spoon. Cover and allow to rise in a warm place until the size is doubled, about 1-1½ hours. Fill large greased bread tins three quarters full, put them to stand in a warm place for 20 minutes. Bake in centre of a hot oven (425-450°F.—Gas Mark 6-7) for 30 minutes, then decrease the heat to very moderate and bake slowly for 1½-2 hours more. This should not be eaten fresh, and will keep 2 or 3 weeks.

## 486 Orange bread

½ oz. yeast
1 level teaspoon sugar
2 tablespoons tepid water
2 oz. lard
1 teaspoon salt
1 heaped tablespoon golden syrup

1 oz. brown sugar
3 oz. quick cooking rolled oats
1 orange
6 tablespoons boiling water
cold water
8 oz. plain flour
crystallised orange slices

Cream yeast and sugar, bind with tepid water in bowl. Set in warm place until bubbly. Combine lard, salt, syrup, brown sugar, oats and grated orange rind in a large bowl. Add the boiling water and the orange juice—made up to ¼ pint with cold water. Add yeast mixture and blend. Add flour gradually and mix to a soft dough. Knead dough on floured board until smooth. Place in greased bowl and brush with melted fat. Cover and let rise in warm place until double its bulk—about 1 hour. Shape dough into a loaf. Place in a greased loaf tin 8½ × 4½ × 2½ inches. Let rise until double in bulk. Sprinkle on few oats and bake in a hot oven (425-450°F.—Gas Mark 7) for 15 minutes, reduce temperature to moderate (375°F.—Gas Mark 4) and bake 30 minutes longer or until cooked. Remove from tin and cool; decorate with orange slices.

## 487 Easter plait

1 oz. yeast
3 oz. sugar
about ¼ pint milk *or* milk and water
12 oz. plain flour

2 oz. butter *or* margarine
2 egg yolks
good pinch salt
4 oz. chopped candied peel
few finely chopped almonds

Cream the yeast with 1 teaspoon sugar, add the *tepid* milk and water, and a sprinkling of flour. Leave in a warm place to rise for about 20 minutes until the surface is covered with little bubbles. Meanwhile, cream the butter and the rest of the sugar, add the egg yolks. Work in the flour, sieved with the pinch of salt, and the yeast liquid. It should be a soft yet pliable mixture. Lastly add the peel. Knead lightly but firmly with your hands until a smooth dough. Return to the bowl, cover with a cloth and leave in a warm place for about 1 hour until nearly double its original size. Knead again and form 3 long equal-sized strips. Plait these *loosely*—this is important to allow the dough to rise. Lift on to a warm and greased baking tray, cover with the chopped almonds. Allow to prove for approximately 20 minutes, then bake for approximately 30 minutes in the centre of the oven. Use a hot oven (450°F.—Gas Mark 7) for the first 20 minutes, then lower the heat slightly for the final 10 minutes. If you wish to decorate with a coloured egg, then mark a deep 'depression' with your finger just before baking the loaf.

21. Battenburg and hot cross buns

22. Wiltshire lardy cake

23. Mocha shell cake

24. Hazelnut and chocolate gâteau

## 488 Easter round

Ingredients as for the Easter plait (Recipe 487) but instead of almonds use coloured sugar strands (obtainable in tubes) and a small quantity of marzipan (Recipe 385).

Make the dough as before but when ready to prove for the final time use two-thirds of this and press into a greased round cake tin. Roll out the rest of the dough, make into thin strips. Form the marzipan into 4 or 5 Easter egg shapes —arrange on top of the dough, then cover these with crossing strips of dough. Brush the top lavishly with sugar strands and bake as before.

## 489 Cherry bread

plain yeast dough
  (Recipe 548)
3-4 oz. glacé cherries

few very finely chopped nuts
little milk *or* egg white

Prepare the yeast dough, adding chopped glacé cherries, but save about 8 or 9 whole large cherries and the nuts for decoration. Form the dough into a long rather flat loaf shape, score the top with a knife, and brush with a little milk or egg white. Press the finely chopped nuts against the sides and the whole cherries in the centre. Prove for about 20 minutes then bake for approximately 35 minutes in the centre of a hot oven (450°F.—Gas Mark 7) for the first 15 minutes then lower the heat to moderate for the rest of the time.

## 490 Scotch butteries

1 oz. yeast
1 level tablespoon castor sugar
6 tablespoons tepid water
1 lb. flour

6 oz. lard
6 oz. butter *or* margarine
1 level teaspoon salt

Cream the yeast with teaspoon of sugar, add the tepid water and a sprinkling of flour. Put on one side and allow to rise. Meanwhile rub 2 oz. lard, 2 oz. butter into flour, mixed with salt and rest of sugar, blend with the yeast liquid and roll out to a neat oblong. Mix the remainder of lard and butter together. Put half of this on to the dough in small pieces exactly as if making flaky pastry. Fold, turn and roll out again, doing exactly the same thing with the rest of the lard and butter. Re-roll into a neat square and then make your butteries. Allow the individual shapes to prove and then bake in a hot oven for approximately 15 minutes (425°F.—Gas Mark 6-7).

**Note**

Although recipe states 6 tablespoons tepid water, use only 4 to begin with and add a little more, *if needed*, when you mix into the flour.

## 491 Harlequin loaf

plain yeast dough
  (Recipe 548)
2 oz. butter
2 oz. sugar
about 2 oz. glacé cherries,
  chopped
2 oz. chopped candied peel

*To decorate*
small quantity glacé icing
  (Recipe 371)
about 1 oz. glacé cherries,
  and 1 oz. chopped candied
  peel *or* crystallised fruits

Make the plain yeast dough, allow to prove then roll out into an oblong shape. Brush with half the butter and half the sugar and half the cherries and peel. Fold like flaky pastry and roll out once again and repeat the process using the rest of the butter, sugar and fruit and peel. Fold once again and form into a neat oblong shape. Lift on to a warmed and greased baking tin, and allow to prove for approximately 20 minutes. Bake for approximately 30 minutes—for the first 15 minutes in a hot oven (450°F.—Gas Mark 7), then lower the heat for the rest of the time. Make up the glacé icing, coat the loaf while still warm and put the cherries and peel on top.

## 492 Herb bread
### (delicious with savouries)

good pinch oregano *or*
  marjoram
2 teaspoons chopped parsley
½ teaspoon chopped sage
½ teaspoon chopped thyme

pinch garlic salt
plain yeast dough (Recipe 548),
  but use only 1 teaspoon
  sugar

Work all the flavourings into the dough. Allow to prove, then knead well and put into a warmed, greased and floured loaf tin. Brush the top with egg or milk, and allow to prove in a warm place for about 20 minutes.

Bake for approximately 30 minutes in the centre of the oven—allow a hot oven (450°F.—Gas Mark 7) for the first 20 minutes, then if the loaf is browning too much, lower the heat for a further 10-15 minutes. To test if this loaf is cooked remove it from the tin and tap the base; it should sound hollow. If in doubt return it to the oven for a little longer.

## 493 Apricot bread

4 oz. dried apricots (weight
  after cooking) *or* canned
  fruit
3 tablespoons apricot syrup
¾ oz. yeast
1 tablespoon sugar

12 tablespoons tepid milk
  and water
1 lb. plain flour
good pinch salt
1 oz. butter

**Note**

To give 4 oz. cooked dried apricots only about 1½ oz. need be soaked and cooked until just tender. *DO NOT OVERCOOK.* If using canned apricots choose very firm ones, or you can use raw apricots and little extra sugar and water to take place of syrup.

Cream yeast with 1 teaspoon sugar, add the apricot syrup, some of the tepid milk and a sprinkling of flour. Allow to stand in a warm place until the mixture bubbles; this will take approximately 20 minutes. Chop the apricots. Sieve flour and salt together, add rest of sugar and rub in butter. Stir in the chopped fruit, the yeast liquid and the rest of the tepid milk, adding this gradually. The mixture must not be too soft; it must be firm enough to handle. Knead well and put into warmed greased loaf tin, allowing the mixture to come halfway up the tin. Bake in the centre of a really hot oven (450°F.—Gas Mark 7) for 15 minutes, then lower the heat to moderate (375°F.—Gas Mark 4) for a further 20 minutes.

**Variations**

2-3 oz. sultanas can be added to the apricots. Chopped walnuts or hazelnuts can be added. Peaches or figs can be used instead of apricots.

## 494 *Apple sauce and fruit loaves*

1½ lb. plain flour
1 teaspoon salt
1 oz. butter
6 oz. raisins
½ oz. yeast

1 teaspoon castor sugar
½ pint warmed milk
¼ pint thick sweetened apple
    sauce

Sieve the flour and salt together into a large bowl. Rub in butter, add washed raisins, make a well in the centre. Cream the yeast in a smaller bowl with sugar, add warmed milk and pour into centre of flour mixture. Stir in apple sauce. slowly beat into flour until a soft dough is formed. Cover with a damp cloth, prove until dough has doubled its size (about 1 hour). Knead well on floured board and divide into 2 greased and floured 1½-2 lb. loaf tins. Cover again with a damp cloth and allow to rise until dough has again doubled its size (about ¾ hour). Bake in the centre of a hot oven (450°F.—Gas Mark 7) until golden brown.

## 495 *Iced fruit loaves*

8-10 oz. icing sugar
little water *or* lemon juice
sliced dessert apple

walnuts
angelica

Blend icing sugar with water or lemon juice to give soft mixture. Pour over top of loaves when cold. Decorate with sliced apple—dipped in lemon juice to keep white, or walnuts and angelica leaves.

## 496 *Speedy celery bread*

1 egg
½ pint water
1 packet celery soup
1 lb. self-raising flour

1 level teaspoon salt
3 oz. butter *or* margarine
little milk

Mix egg and water together. Blend in the dry soup mix and allow to stand for 10 minutes. Sieve flour and salt and rub in butter or margarine. Pour in the soup mixture and work ingredients together. Knead into a round. Lift on to a greased baking sheet, flatten slightly and brush with milk. Mark off into eight sections and bake in a moderately hot oven (400°F.—Gas Mark 5) for 35-40 minutes. Serve freshly baked with cheese or salad.

## 497 *Soda bread without yeast*

about 1 oz. margarine
8 oz. plain flour
pinch salt
1 level teaspoon bicarbonate
    of soda

1 level teaspoon cream of
    tartar
¼ pint milk

Rub the margarine into the flour; this is not essential, but helps to keep the bread moist. Add the salt, dissolve the bicarbonate of soda and cream of tartar in the milk, add to the flour. Knead lightly and form into a round loaf. Brush with a little milk and bake on a flat tin in the centre of very hot oven (475°F.—Gas Mark 8) for 15 minutes. After this time, lower the gas to moderately hot (Gas Mark 5) or re-set electric cooker to 400°F. for another 10-15 minutes.

## 498 *Farmhouse loaf cake*

5 oz. margarine
5 oz. castor sugar
2 eggs
6 oz. flour (with plain flour
    use ½ level teaspoon baking
    powder)

2 oz. glacé cherries
3 oz. ground almonds
3 large chocolate flake bars

Cream the margarine and sugar together until soft and fluffy. Beat in the lightly whipped eggs. Fold in the sieved flour with baking powder, if used. Add the glacé cherries, ground almonds and crumbled flake bars. Put into a greased loaf tin approximately 8½ × 4½ inches. Bake in centre of moderate oven (375°F.—Gas Mark 4) for about 20 minutes and then reduce to very moderate (350°F.—Gas Mark 3) and continue cooking until firm. Cool on a wire tray, sprinkle with castor sugar.

## 499 *Holiday banana tea bread*

7 oz. flour (with plain flour
    use 2 level teaspoons
    baking powder)
½ level teaspoon salt
2½ oz. butter, margarine *or*
    lard
5 oz. sugar
2 eggs
1 oz. walnuts

2 oz. finely cut candied
    pineapple
2 oz. finely cut candied
    cherries
2 oz. thinly sliced citron peel
2 oz. finely cut candied
    orange peel
2 oz. raisins
2-3 ripe bananas, mashed

Sift together flour and salt. Beat fat until creamy in mixing bowl. Add sugar gradually to fat and continue beating until light and fluffy. Add eggs and beat well. Mix in nuts, pineapple, cherries, citron, orange peel and raisins; add flour mixture alternately with bananas, a small amount at a time, mixing after each addition only enough to moisten dry ingredients. Turn into a well greased loaf tin (8½ × 4½ inches) and bake in a very moderate oven (350°F.—Gas Mark 3) about 1 hour 10 minutes or until bread is firm to touch.

*Holiday banana tea bread*

## 500 *Malt fruit loaf*

2 tablespoons malt
2 tablespoons golden syrup
5 tablespoons milk
8 oz. flour (with plain flour
   use 2 teaspoons baking
   powder)

pinch salt
4 oz. dried fruit
1 egg
1 level teaspoon bicarbonate
   soda
1 tablespoon water

Melt the malt and syrup with the milk in a saucepan. Sieve the flour with baking powder, if used, and pinch of salt and add the dried fruit and egg. Pour in the melted ingredients and mix very thoroughly. Line a loaf shaped tin with greased paper. Mix the bicarbonate of soda with a tablespoon water and add it to the malt mixture. Beat well and pour immediately into the lined tin. Bake in centre of a moderate oven (375°F.—Gas Mark 4) for about 1 hour.

## 501 *Banana bread without yeast*

8 oz. flour (with plain flour
   use 3 level teaspoons
   baking powder)
pinch salt
2 oz. margarine *or*
   vegetable cooking fat

2 oz. sugar
grated rind 1 lemon
1 egg
2-3 bananas, mashed
milk

Sieve the dry ingredients. Rub in the margarine or cooking fat, then add the sugar, lemon rind, egg and mashed banana pulp. Mix thoroughly. If necessary add enough milk to give sticky consistency. Put into greased and floured loaf tin and bake for approximately 45 minutes in centre of moderate oven (375°F. —Gas Mark 4) until golden brown and firm. Just before serving, decorate the top with slices of banana.
(*Illustrated in colour on jacket.*)

## 502 *Orange banana bread*

Use ingredients as above, but instead of lemon rind add the grated rind of 2 oranges, and mix with a little orange juice instead of milk.

## 503 *Banana tea bread*

Ingredients as above, but add 2 oz. finely chopped walnuts and 1 oz. crystallised lemon peel, cut very finely.

*Banana tea bread*

## 504 *Malt walnut bread without yeast*

12 tablespoons milk
1 oz. margarine
2 tablespoons malt extract
8 oz. flour (with plain flour
   use 2 level teaspoons
   baking powder)

½ teaspoon bicarbonate
   of soda
1½ level tablespoons sugar
4 oz. walnuts, chopped

Warm the milk, margarine and malt together. Sieve dry ingredients, then beat in the milk mixture. Add the sugar and nuts and stir well. Pour into well greased and floured loaf tin and bake for approximately 30-35 minutes in the centre of a moderately hot oven (400°F.—Gas Mark 5).

## 505 *Date and walnut bread without yeast*

8 oz. flour (with plain flour
   use 2 teaspoons baking
   powder)
1 level teaspoon bicarbonate
   of soda
2 oz. sugar

1 oz. margarine
12 oz. dates, chopped
¼ pint water
1 egg
4 oz. walnuts, chopped

Sieve all dry ingredients. Put the sugar, margarine and dates into a basin. Boil the water and pour over these. Leave and allow to cool. Stir in flour, egg and nuts. Put into 8-inch greased cake tin or small loaf tin and bake approximately 50 minutes in centre of moderate oven (375°F.—Gas Mark 4).

## 506 *Raisin bread*

As above, but add 8 oz. chopped raisins instead of dates.

# SCONES

Home-made scones are quickly prepared, in fact in most cases the more quickly you make them the better they will be.
Do not worry about the dough being rather soft—it gives a better result.

## 507 *Secrets of successful scones*

Scones are very easy to make, and quite delicious when good.
Remember:
**1** Scones are meant to be eaten fresh; if you have some left over they should either be split and toasted the next day or just before serving brushed with a little milk and warmed in a hot oven.
**2** A good scone dough should not be too stiff; it should leave one's fingers slightly 'sticky' when mixing, and be quite soft to handle.
**3** Do not roll scones too much. Roll quickly then cut into required shapes.
**4** Bake as soon as possible after preparing.
**5** Use a really hot oven and bake near the top of the oven, unless recipe states to the contrary.

## 508 *Plain scones*

8 oz. flour*                    1 oz. sugar
good pinch salt               milk to mix†
1-2 oz. margarine

*\* With plain flour use either 4 level teaspoons baking powder or 1 level teaspoon cream of tartar and ½ teaspoon bicarbonate of soda. With self-raising flour use half these quantities.*
*† If using sour milk, which is excellent for mixing scones, then you can omit the cream of tartar—or if using baking powder use half quantity only.*

Sieve together flour, salt, bicarbonate of soda and cream of tartar. Rub in the margarine, add the sugar. Mix to a *soft* rolling consistency with the milk. Roll out and cut into required shapes. Put on to an ungreased tin baking sheet and bake near the top of a very hot oven (475°F.—Gas Mark 8) for approximately 10 minutes. To test if cooked press firmly at the sides. Scones are cooked when they feel firm to the touch.

## 509 *Brown scones*

Use above recipe, but use 4 oz. wholemeal flour, and 4 oz. white flour.

## 510 *Fruit scones*

Use above recipe, but add 2-4 oz. chopped dried fruit, sultanas, raisins, currants, dates, glacé cherries, or a mixture.

## 511 *Almond scones*

As above, but add 1 extra oz. sugar and 2-3 oz. blanched chopped almonds. Stir a few drops almond essence into milk for mixing. Sprinkle chopped almonds on top before baking.

## 512 *Marmalade scones*

As above, but substitute 2 tablespoons marmalade for the sugar.

## 513 *Rich egg scones*

As above, but use butter and mix with 2 eggs and milk instead of all milk.

## 514 *Treacle scones*

As above, but add 2 tablespoons black treacle and use less milk in mixing. The sugar can be omitted if liked.

## 515 *Orange scones*

As above, but add the finely grated rind of 2 oranges. Mix with the juice of 2 oranges, then add milk as required. 1-2 oz. crystallised orange rind can also be included if liked.

## 516 *Walnut scones*

As above, but add 2 oz. chopped walnuts. Mix as before, cut into rounds and decorate with a walnut half before baking. A few finely chopped dates can be added if desired.

*Walnut scones*

## 517 Rich cheese scones

8 oz. flour (with plain flour add 3 level teaspoons baking powder)

¼ teaspoon salt

2 oz. butter

4 oz. cheese, grated

milk to mix

Sift together the flour, baking powder, if used, and salt. Rub in the butter and add the grated cheese. Gradually stir in enough milk to give a soft dough. Turn out on to floured board, knead lightly, then roll out to about ¾ inch thick. Cut into rounds, put on to baking tin and brush with beaten egg or milk for a glaze. Bake near the top of a hot oven (450°F.—Gas Mark 7) for 7-10 minutes.

## 518 Economical cheese scones

As above, but use only 1 oz. butter and 2 oz. grated cheese. Season very well, and bake in a very hot oven (475°F.—Gas Mark 8).

## 519 Rich scones

8 oz. self-raising flour*

½ level teaspoon baking powder

good pinch salt

2 oz. butter *or* margarine

1 oz. castor sugar

1 egg

scant ¼ pint milk

*\* With plain flour use 3 level teaspoons baking powder*

Sift flour, baking powder and salt. Rub in fat. Add sugar. Mix to a soft dough with beaten egg and milk. Turn on to lightly floured board and knead quickly. Roll to ½-¾ inch thickness. Cut with knife or floured cutter. Place on hot baking tray and brush with milk. Bake in very hot oven (450-475°F.—Gas Mark 7-8) for 12-15 minutes.

## 520 Cottage cheese scones

As above, but omit the sugar, reduce butter to 1 oz. and add 4 oz. sieved cottage cheese and a dusting of nutmeg.

Mix with sour milk or cream, using 8 oz. plain flour and sifting it with 1 level teaspoon bicarbonate of soda and 1 level teaspoon cream of tartar and good pinch salt.

Delicious served with cottage cheese and strawberries.

*Cottage cheese scones*

## 521 Honey scones

As above, but omit sugar and add 2 tablespoons honey to the egg, with grated orange rind. Brush while hot with butter and sprinkle with sugar and cinnamon.

## 522 Luxury fruit scones

As above, but add 3 oz. mixed dried fruit, 1 oz. chopped nuts, and 1 oz. chopped glacé cherries.

## 523 Orange nut scones

As above, but add grated rind and juice of 1 orange, and 2 tablespoons marmalade instead of sugar and less milk. Sprinkle chopped nuts on top.

## 524 Rich spiced scones

As above, but sieve ½ teaspoon mixed spice, ½ teaspoon grated nutmeg, and ¼ teaspoon cinnamon with the flour. Add dried fruit if wished.

## 525 Swedish scone ring

4 oz. butter *or* margarine

8 oz. flour (with plain flour use 3 level teaspoons baking powder)

2 oz. fine semolina

pinch salt

2 oz. castor sugar

1 egg and milk to mix

*Filling*

3 oz. mixed fruit

3 oz. dates, chopped

3 tablespoons marmalade

*Topping*

glacé icing (Recipe 371)

chopped nuts

Rub margarine into flour to resemble fine breadcrumbs. Add semolina, salt and sugar. Add beaten egg and milk and mix to a soft but not sticky dough. Roll to a rectangle. Cover with fruit and dates bound together with the marmalade. Roll up lengthwise, shape into a ring and place on greased oven tray with small mould in the centre so the mixture keeps its shape. Snip halfway through with scissors from outer edge, about every inch, and glaze with a little milk. Bake towards top of moderately hot oven (400°F.—Gas Mark 5) for about 30 minutes. Cool. Run little glacé icing over top and sprinkle with chopped nuts.

*Swedish scone ring*

## 526 *Butterscotch scones*

*Topping*
1 oz. melted butter *or*
  margarine
1 oz. brown sugar

12 oz. self-raising flour
pinch salt
2 oz. butter *or* margarine
1½ tablespoons castor sugar

1 finely grated rind orange
1 egg
about 6 tablespoons water or
  milk

*Filling*
2 rounded tablespoons orange
  marmalade
2 oz. currants

**To prepare the topping**
Grease an 8-inch square cake tin and pour in melted fat. Sprinkle base with brown sugar.
Sift flour and salt into a basin. Rub in fat till mixture resembles fine breadcrumbs, add sugar and grated rind then mix to a soft, but not sticky, dough with egg and milk. Turn out on to a floured board, knead quickly and roll into an oblong approximately 12 × 9 inches. Spread with marmalade to within 1 inch of edges and sprinkle with currants. Moisten edges with water then roll up like a Swiss roll, starting from one of the longer sides. Cut into twelve 1 inch thick slices and arrange in prepared tin, leaving a little room between each for spreading. Bake in the centre of a very hot oven (450–475°F.—Gas Mark 7-8) for about 15 minutes. Turn out on to a wire tray and break apart when cool.

*Butterscotch scones*

## 527 *Cherry scone ring*

12 oz. flour (with plain flour
  use 3 level teaspoons
  baking powder)
pinch salt

2 oz. butter *or* margarine
1 tablespoon sugar
3 oz. glacé cherries, chopped
milk to mix

Sieve dry ingredients, rub in butter, add sugar and cherries and mix with milk to a soft rolling consistency. Either cut into rounds and pack these into an 8-inch cake tin, which can be lightly greased, or roll out the dough, form into a well shaped round, mark into sections with a knife, but do not cut right through. Bake on a flat tin in this case. Bake for approximately 15-20 minutes near the top of a hot oven (450°F.—Gas Mark 7).
**Note**
Any of the scone recipes can be baked in a round, rather than cutting into individual shapes.

## 528 *Syrup scone ring*

As above, but omit the cherries and use 2 tablespoons golden syrup. The sugar can also be left out if wished; you will need less milk for mixing.

## 529 *Potato scones*

8 oz. freshly boiled mashed
  potatoes
4 oz. flour*
salt

2 oz. melted butter *or*
  margarine
1 egg

*\* With plain flour use 2 level teaspoons baking powder; with self-raising flour use 1 level teaspoon baking powder*

Mash or sieve the potatoes while they are still hot, add them to the flour, baking powder and salt, also the melted butter. Mix well, add enough of the beaten egg to make a stiff mixture. Roll this out to about ¾ inch thickness, cut into rounds or triangles, put on baking sheet or greased dish and bake near top of a hot oven (450°F.—Gas Mark 7) until they are golden brown, approximately 10-12 minutes. Serve hot, split, with plenty of butter.
For the potato apple cake see Recipe 59.

## 530 *Sweet potato scones*

As above, but add 2 oz. sugar and 2 oz. sultanas.

## 531 *Oatmeal scones*

1 oz. margarine
2 oz. fine oatmeal
2 oz. medium oatmeal

pinch salt
1 good teaspoon sugar
milk to mix

Rub the margarine into the fine oatmeal, add other ingredients, then work in sufficient milk to give a soft rolling consistency. Roll to ½-inch thick, cut into shapes and bake on a lightly greased tin for 10 minutes, near the top of a hot oven (450-475°F.—Gas Mark 7-8). More sugar can be added if wished—or omit sugar and add 1 oz. of finely grated cheese and plenty of seasoning.

## 532 *Oatmeal and potato scones*

As above, but replace the fine oatmeal with 2 oz. mashed potato.

## 533 *Hot apple muffins*

1 cooking apple
8 oz. flour (with plain flour
  use 2 rounded teaspoons
  baking powder)

pinch salt
2 oz. cooking fat *or* butter
2 oz. sugar
2 tablespoons water

Peel, core and chop the apple finely. Sieve the flour, salt and baking powder, if used, into a mixing bowl. Rub in the cooking fat until the mixture resembles fine breadcrumbs. Add the sugar and chopped apple and mix to a soft dough with water. Roll out to ½ inch thickness and cut with a 2-inch cutter. Place the muffins on a baking sheet lightly greased with cooking fat. Bake in a moderate oven (375°F.—Gas Mark 4) near the top for 25-30 minutes. Split while hot and spread with margarine or butter.

## 534 Drop scones or Scotch pancakes (1)

| | |
|---|---|
| 8 oz. plain flour | pinch salt |
| 1 level teaspoon bicarbonate of soda | 2 oz. castor sugar |
| 2 level teaspoons cream of tartar | 1 oz. cooking fat |
| | 1 egg |
| | 12 tablespoons milk |

Sieve together all the dry ingredients into a basin. Add sugar. Rub in the cooking fat until the mixture resembles fine breadcrumbs. Beat in the egg and two-thirds of the milk and stir until the mixture is smooth. Stir in the remaining milk to make a batter the consistency of thick cream. Lightly brush a hot girdle or electric hot plate with melted cooking fat and drop the batter on in dessert-spoonfuls, well apart. Cook over a gentle heat and when the bubbles rise to the surfaces of the scones turn over with a palette knife and cook the other sides. When the second sides are golden brown and the edges are dry, the scones are cooked. Cool in a folded tea towel on a cake rack.

*Hot apple muffins*

*Drop scones or scotch pancakes*

## 535 Drop scones or Scotch pancakes (2)

| | |
|---|---|
| 4 oz. flour (with plain flour use either 2 teaspoons baking powder or ½ small teaspoon bicarbonate of soda and 1 small teaspoon cream of tartar) | pinch salt |
| | 1 oz. sugar |
| | 1 egg |
| | ¼ pint milk |
| | 1 oz. melted margarine (optional) |

Sieve together dry ingredients. Beat in first egg, then milk. Lastly, stir in melted margarine. This is not essential but it does help to keep the scones moist. Grease and warm the girdle, electric hot-plate or frying pan. It is best to use the bottom of the frying pan—the part that usually goes over the heat. To test if correct heat, drop a teaspoon of the mixture on this and if it goes golden brown within 1 minute the plate is ready. Drop spoonfuls of the batter on to the plate. Cook for about 2 minutes, then turn and cook for a further 2 minutes. To test whether cooked press firmly with the back of a knife, and if no batter comes from the sides and the scones feel firm, cool on a wire sieve.

## 536 Quick to make drop scones or Scotch pancakes

A packet of scone mix gives drop scones very quickly. Use either half the contents of the packet with 1 egg and approximately 7 tablespoons milk, or 2 eggs and just over ¼ pint milk. Blend to a smooth batter and cook as the preceding recipe.

## 537 Tangy surprise muffins

| | |
|---|---|
| 2 oz. Cheddar cheese | ½ level teaspoon dry mustard |
| 2 oz. seedless raisins | pinch pepper |
| 8 oz. flour (with plain flour use 2 level teaspoons baking powder) | 4 oz. margarine |
| | 1 egg |
| ½ level teaspoon salt | ¼ pint milk *plus* 1 tablespoon milk |

Grate cheese and chop raisins. Sift flour, baking powder, if used, salt, mustard and pepper into a basin. Rub in margarine till mixture resembles fine breadcrumbs. Stir in cheese and raisins. Mix to a fairly soft dough with egg and milk, beating with a wooden spoon. Put mixture in 18 well greased bun tins. Bake near top of a moderately hot oven (425°F.—Gas Mark 6) for 20 minutes. Split open while still warm. Spread with margarine and serve immediately.

*Tangy surprise muffins*

## 538 Apple girdle scones

| | |
|---|---|
| 4 oz. flour (with plain flour use 1 level teaspoon baking powder) | 1 oz. sugar |
| | 1 small cooking apple, peeled and grated |
| 2 oz. margarine | little milk to mix |

Sieve flour and baking powder, if used, together, rub in margarine, add sugar and apple. Mix thoroughly together, then if necessary add few drops milk to make soft rolling consistency. Roll to about ½ inch thick, cut into shapes. Heat and lightly grease solid hot plate, griddle, or bottom of frying pan. Put on the cakes and cook slowly for about 10 minutes, turning as necessary. Spread with butter, dust with sugar and serve hot.

## 539 Fruit girdle scones

| | |
|---|---|
| 8 oz. flour (with plain flour use 3 level teaspoons baking powder) | 1-2 oz. butter, cooking fat *or* lard |
| pinch salt | 3-4 oz. dried fruit |
| 1 oz. sugar | milk to mix |

Sieve dry ingredients together, rub in butter or lard, add other ingredients. Mix to a soft rolling consistency with the milk, and roll out to about ½ inch thick (do not make any thicker than this). Grease the top of the girdle or solid hot plate lightly or if using a frying pan grease this. With a very heavy frying pan it is possible to cook the scones on the upturned base, rather than inside the pan and this gives slower, and rather better cooking. Test to see if the right heat is obtained by shaking on a little flour, and this should turn golden brown within 1 minute. Cook the scones steadily for approximately 10 minutes, turning them as they brown on to the second side.

**Note**

Most of the scones in this section are suitable for cooking by this method, rather than baking in the oven. Take care they are not too thick, otherwise they will brown too much on the outside, and be uncooked in the centre, and do not try to cook them too rapidly.

## 540 Teatime rusks

| | |
|---|---|
| 4 oz. flour (with plain flour use 1 teaspoon baking powder) | 1 oz. margarine |
| | 1 dessertspoon sugar |
| good pinch salt | milk to mix |

Sieve the dry ingredients together. Rub in margarine. Add sugar and just enough liquid to make a firm dough. Roll out and cut into rounds about ⅓ inch thick. Put on to ungreased baking sheet and bake for a good 5 minutes in a hot oven (450°F.—Gas Mark 7). Remove the trays from the oven and split the rusks through the centre. Put on to the trays, cut side down. You will, of course, need more baking trays since you now have twice the original number of rounds. Bake for a further 10 minutes in a moderate oven (375°F.—Gas Mark 4). Cool on rack and put into a tin the moment they are quite cold.

## 541 Yeast rusks

| | |
|---|---|
| ½ oz. yeast | 8 oz. flour |
| 1 teaspoon sugar | good pinch salt |
| ¼ pint tepid water | 1 egg |

Cream yeast and sugar. Add liquid and sprinkle top with little flour. Leave in warm place for about 15 minutes until surface is covered with little bubbles. Sieve flour and salt, add yeast liquid and egg. Knead well and leave to rise in warm place until double original bulk. Knead again and roll out until very thin. Cut into rounds and put on greased baking tray. Prove for 5 minutes, then bake for about 30 minutes in very moderate oven (300-350°F.—Gas Mark 2-3) until crisp and golden brown.

## 542 Crumpets

| | |
|---|---|
| 4 oz. plain flour | 1 egg |
| pinch salt | scant ¼ oz. yeast |
| ½ oz. margarine *or* butter | 1 teaspoon sugar |
| about 10 tablespoons milk | |

Sieve flour and salt into warm basin. Melt the butter, add the warm milk, then pour on to egg. Cream yeast and sugar, add the tepid milk mixture, with a sprinkling of flour. Allow to prove for about 15 minutes, until surface is covered with little bubbles. Stir into the flour mixture and beat thoroughly. The mixture should be fairly soft. Cover the bowl and put to rise for about 45 minutes, until just about twice the original size. Grease a hot girdle and drop spoonfuls on this. Cook until pale brown, then turn and cook until pale brown on other side.

## 543 Croissants

| | |
|---|---|
| 8 oz. plain flour | ¼ pint tepid milk |
| pinch salt | 4 oz. butter |
| good ½ oz. yeast | little egg for brushing |
| 1 teaspoon sugar | |

Sieve flour and salt. Cream yeast and sugar, add the tepid milk and strain on to the flour. Mix together well, then prove for an hour. Have a warm, but not too hot place for this. Turn on to floured board, knead lightly then roll out to oblong shape. Put 1-1½ oz. butter on to the dough in small pieces as though making flaky pastry. Fold, turn and roll out again. Repeat twice, using the rest of the butter. Roll out, cut into triangles and twist, then form into a horse-shoe shape and put on to warmed lightly greased baking trays. Brush with beaten egg and prove in warm place for 15 minutes. Bake 12-15 minutes in a hot oven (450°F.—Gas Mark 7).

## 544 Brioche

| | |
|---|---|
| ½ oz. yeast | 12 oz. plain flour |
| 1 oz. sugar | pinch salt |
| generous 4 tablespoons tepid milk | 5 oz. margarine |
| | 2 eggs |

Cream the yeast with teaspoon sugar. Add the tepid milk and enough flour to make thick batter. Put into a warm place for 15 minutes. Sieve flour and salt into warm bowl. Rub in margarine, add the rest of the sugar. Work in yeast mixture and lastly beaten eggs. Put this dough to prove for 2 hours. Knead lightly until smooth. Put the brioches into greased and floured fluted tins—then prove for 10-15 minutes. Bake in a hot oven (450°F.—Gas Mark 7) for about 12 minutes.

## 545 Flaky brioche (1)

**Quick recipe:** Mix together 8 oz. plain bread dough (Recipe 473) and 8 oz. puff pastry dough (Recipe 262) by laying one on top of the other. Roll and fold about 3 times (the puff pastry having already been folded). Form into desired shapes. Prove for 15 minutes, then bake for 12-15 minutes in hot oven (450°F.—Gas Mark 7).

## 546 Flaky brioche (2)

| | |
|---|---|
| 8 oz. flour | 1 teaspoon sugar |
| pinch salt | ¼ pint tepid milk |
| generous ½ oz. yeast | 3 oz. butter *or* margarine |

Sieve flour and salt. Cream yeast and sugar, then add the tepid milk and strain into flour. Mix together, then prove for an hour. Turn on to floured board, knead lightly then roll out to oblong. Put on 1 oz. margarine or butter in small pieces, exactly as though making flaky pastry. Fold, turn and roll out again. Repeat twice again using the rest of the margarine. Roll out and then make desired shapes. Prove on warmed greased baking tray for 15 minutes, then brush lightly with beaten egg or milk and bake for 12-15 minutes in hot oven (450°F.—Gas Mark 7).

# YEAST BUNS AND YEAST CAKES

If you have tried yeast for bread making you will be anxious to make your own yeast buns and cakes. Most of the recipes using yeast are extremely economical and, like bread making, *NOT* difficult.

## 547 *Successful buns and cakes with yeast*

The same methods of mixing, proving etc. as described in Recipes 472, 473 and onwards in the bread section are used for buns and yeast cakes. It is important to remember:

1 In most cases a richer dough is used for buns, and certainly for cakes, and it will take longer to prove and to bake the mixture.

2 The proportion of yeast used in these recipes seems much higher than the amount used in bread making—this is essential to give a good result.

3 To give good buns make the mixture fairly soft, otherwise they tend to dry rather quickly after being cooked.

4 Rich yeast cakes keep well if stored in airtight tins, but they are not considered a long keeping type of cake, as is a Dundee, for example.

## 548 *Basic or plain yeast mixture*

½ oz. yeast
1-2 oz. sugar
about 12 tablespoons tepid water, milk and water, *or* milk

12 oz. plain flour
good pinch salt
1 oz. margarine *or* fat

Cream the yeast with a teaspoon of the sugar. Add the tepid liquid and a sprinkling of flour. Put into a warm place until the sponge breaks through. Meanwhile, sieve the flour and salt into a warm bowl, rub in the margarine and add the sugar. When ready work in the yeast liquid and knead thoroughly. Put into a warm place for approximately 1 hour to prove, that is until the dough just about doubles its original size. Knead again until smooth, then shape into desired shape or loaves. Cook as the recipe.

## 549 *Fruit buns*

½ oz. yeast
1-2 oz. sugar
about 12 tablespoons tepid water, milk and water, *or* milk
12 oz. plain flour
good pinch salt

1 oz. table margarine
2-4 oz. dried fruit
1-2 oz. chopped candied peel
1 oz. sugar for glaze
1 tablespoon water

Cream the yeast with a teaspoon of the sugar. Add the tepid liquid and a sprinkling of flour. Put into a warm place until the sponge breaks through. Meanwhile sieve the flour and salt into a warm bowl, rub in the margarine and add the sugar, fruit and peel. When ready work in the yeast liquid and knead thoroughly. Put into a warm place for approximately 1 hour to prove, that is, until the dough just about doubles its original size. Form into round buns, prove for 15 minutes on warm tray, and bake for 10 minutes near the top of a very hot oven (475°F.— Gas Mark 8). Mix the sugar with a tablespoon of water and the moment the buns come from the oven, brush with this to give an attractive glaze.

## 550 *Swiss buns*

10 oz. plain flour
pinch salt
1½ heaped teaspoons yeast
1 teaspoon sugar
1 oz. margarine
warm milk *or* water

*Icing*
6 oz. icing sugar, sieved
cochineal
1½ teaspoons cocoa powder, sieved
½ oz. butter

Sieve the flour and salt into a warmed mixing bowl. Cream the yeast and sugar together in a small basin. Rub the margarine into the flour, and add the creamed yeast. Pour in sufficient warm milk or water to form a soft dough. Beat with the hand until smooth. Stand in a warm place for about 1 hour to prove. Knead on a floured board and cut into 12-16 even-sized pieces. Knead each piece and roll into finger shapes. Place on a warm greased baking tray, far enough apart to allow for rising. Stand in a warm place to prove. When the buns are twice their original size, bake near top of a very hot oven (475°F.—Gas Mark 8) for about 10 minutes. Cool on a wire tray before icing.

**To decorate**

Using the sieved icing sugar and a little warm water, mix to a stiff glacé icing. Divide the mixture. Add a little cochineal to one half and to the other the sieved cocoa. Also beat into this the butter to keep the chocolate icing glossy. Holding each bun between the thumb and finger of the right hand dip the top into the icing. Remove any excess icing. Stand on a wire tray and allow to set.

## 551 *Assorted buns*

The picture on this page shows some of the favourite buns—Recipe 554 for Chelsea buns, 555 for Bath buns, 549 for fruit buns. Rich rolls and a plaited tea loaf are also shown. You can make this tea loaf with any of the recipes in the bread section—but those particularly suitable are Recipes 480, 481, 482, 483 and 484. Instead of forming the dough into small rolls or a loaf, form into thick strips. You will need 3 of these, plaited loosely—allowing room for the dough to rise. Lift on to a warmed greased tin and bake for 10 minutes in the centre of a hot oven (450°F.—Gas Mark 7), then reduce heat to moderate for approximately 20 minutes depending on the richness of the recipe chosen.

## To make assorted buns very quickly

**To make assorted buns very quickly**
Make up the basic yeast dough, Recipe 548. Allow to prove, then divide into 3 or 4 parts.
Form the first part into Swiss buns (Recipe 550).
Work fruit into the second part for fruit buns (Recipe 549).
Make the third into round balls and bake as Devonshire splits (Recipe 556).
Roll out the fourth part, add a little extra warmed butter or margarine, sugar, spice and fruit and roll up like Chelsea buns (Recipe 554).

*Assorted buns*

*Hot cross buns*

## 552 Hot cross buns

Ingredients as for fruit buns (Recipe 549) but add 4 oz. dried fruit, 2 oz. chopped candied peel, 1 teaspoon spice

The spice should be sieved with the flour. Proceed as for fruit buns, proving the buns for 15 minutes. The cross should be marked before the buns are proved. Do this with the back of a knife or by cutting very thin strips of pastry and arranging on the top. Bake for 10 minutes near the top of a very hot oven (475°F.—Gas Mark 8). If the buns are to be eaten straight away mix 1 oz. sugar and 1 tablespoon of water, and brush with this to give a glaze. If, as so often happens, the buns are to be warmed again on Good Friday, make up the glaze and brush after they are re-heated.

*(Also illustrated in colour plate 21.)*

## 553 Hot cross bun variations

*Alternatives:*
a little dried fruit and spice;

marzipan (Recipe 385) and chopped candied peel;
marzipan (Recipe 385) and coloured sugar strands.

For the dough use the same recipe as for the Easter plait (Recipe 487) but omit the chopped candied peel.

Make the dough, allow to prove in one large amount then divide into three. Into one part work a little mixed spice and dried fruit, roll into rounds, put on to warmed baking tins, which should be lightly greased, and mark the cross with a knife. Prove for 15 minutes then bake for approximately 12 minutes in a hot oven (450°F.—Gas Mark 7). For the second amount of dough just work in a little candied peel. Form into rounds and make the cross of marzipan. Prove and bake as before. If you do not wish the marzipan to become too hard, this cross can be added when the buns are cooked.
For the third amount of dough, roll into rounds, put a piece of marzipan on top, make a cross with thin strips of dough. Scatter with the sugar strands and prove and bake as before.

## 554 Chelsea buns

½ oz. yeast
4 oz. sugar
¼ pint tepid milk *or* milk and water
12 oz. plain flour
4 oz. margarine
pinch salt

1 egg (this can be omitted and a little more milk used)
3-5 oz. mixed fruit
1 oz. chopped candied peel
1 oz. sugar for glaze
1 tablespoon water

Cream yeast with a teaspoon of sugar. Add tepid milk and a sprinkling of flour. Leave in a warm place for about 20 minutes. Rub 2 oz. margarine into flour, adding salt, 1 oz. sugar and egg. Work in yeast liquid, knead lightly, then prove for about 1 hour or until just about twice original bulk. Knead dough again and roll out to an oblong shape. Spread with warmed margarine, then sprinkle over sugar, fruit and peel. Roll firmly like a Swiss roll, then cut into 12 equal shapes. Put on to greased and warmed baking trays. Prove for 15 minutes, then bake near top of a hot oven (450°F.—Gas Mark 7), for nearly 15 minutes. Either dust buns with very fine castor sugar or glaze them immediately they come from the oven. To make glaze mix 1 oz. sugar with 1 tablespoon water.

## 555 Bath buns

| | |
|---|---|
| ½ oz. yeast* | 4 oz. mixed dried fruit |
| 2 oz. sugar | 2 oz. chopped candied peel |
| about ¼ pint tepid milk | good pinch salt |
| 12 oz. plain flour | 2 whole eggs *or* 3 egg yolks |
| 4 oz. margarine | 4 lumps sugar |

*\* See remarks on dried yeast in Recipe 478*

Cream the yeast with a teaspoon of sugar. Add just under the ¼ pint tepid milk and a sprinkling of flour. Put into a warm place for about 20 minutes for the sponge to break through. Meanwhile rub the margarine into the flour, adding sugar, fruit, peel and salt. Work in the yeast liquid and the beaten eggs. The mixture should be just firm enough to handle, and definitely softer than most buns, bread or rolls. It may be necessary to add a little more warm milk. Allow to prove for 1 hour, then knead again and form into 12 round shapes. Put on to warmed, greased baking trays, allowing room to spread. Break the lumps of sugar with a rolling pin and sprinkle on top of the buns. Prove for 15 minutes in a warm place, then bake for 15 minutes near the top of a hot oven (450°F.— Gas Mark 7).

## 556 Devonshire splits

| | |
|---|---|
| ingredients as for plain yeast dough (Recipe 548) | whipped cream |
| jam | icing sugar |

Make the plain yeast dough, and allow to prove. Knead it well and cut into about 12 equal-sized pieces. Form into neat rounds and put on to warm, greased baking trays. Prove for 15 minutes in a warm place then bake for 10 minutes near the top of a very hot oven (475°F.—Gas Mark 8). When cold split through the centre, fill with jam and cream, and dust with sieved icing sugar.

## 557 Danish pastry

| | |
|---|---|
| ¾ oz. yeast | ½ level teaspoon salt |
| 1½ oz. castor sugar | ¼ pint lukewarm milk |
| 9 oz. plain flour | 4 oz. margarine |

Cream the yeast to a liquid with 1 teaspoon of the sugar. Sieve together the flour and salt, add remaining sugar and warm slightly. Make a well in the centre. Pour in the liquid yeast and sufficient milk to make a soft but not sticky paste. Beat thoroughly by hand, then knead till smooth. Turn out on to a floured board, roll into an oblong ½ inch in thickness and cover all over with the margarine, divided into pieces the size of small walnuts. Fold in three and seal the edges as for flaky pastry. Give the pastry a quarter turn to the left. Repeat the rolling, folding and turning twice more so that the margarine is well blended into the pastry. If the pastry is sticky and too elastic to roll, rest 15-20 minutes between each turn. Wrap in waxed or greaseproof paper and leave in a cool place for at least 1 hour.

The pastry can be formed into various bun shapes with fillings such as lemon curd, slightly sweetened cream cheese, or almond paste. For example, roll out the pastry to ¼ inch in thickness and, for crescents, cut into triangles, put a spoonful of almond paste in the centre of each, moisten the uncovered surface and roll up to form a crescent shape. For turnovers, cut pastry into squares, put 1 teaspoon of cream cheese in the centre, moisten edges and fold over to form triangles. For Danish pinwheels, roll pastry into a strip, brush with melted syrup or jam, sprinkle liberally with currants (cleaned and dried) and 1 small teaspoon cinnamon, roll up like a Swiss roll and cut in ½ inch thick slices.

Put the buns on to greased baking trays and leave in a warm place to rise for about 20-30 minutes. Bake in a hot oven (425-450°F.—Gas Mark 6-7) for 15-20 minutes. Leave to cool on a wire rack, then coat the buns, if liked, with thin water icing (Recipe 371) and sprinkle with chopped nuts.

## 558 Doughnuts

| | |
|---|---|
| scant ½ oz. yeast | 1 oz. margarine, melted |
| 1 oz. sugar | fat for frying |
| about ¼ pint tepid milk | |
| 8 oz. plain flour | *To fill and coat* |
| pinch salt | little jam |
| 1 egg | 2 oz. castor sugar for rolling |

Cream the yeast with a tablespoon of the sugar. Add the tepid milk and the rest of the ingredients, working in the melted margarine at the end. Allow the dough to prove for approximately 1 hour, until just twice its original bulk. Knead well, then divide into required number of pieces. Roll into neat rounds; make a hole in each round, put in a little jam, then re-roll so that the jam is completely covered; put on to warmed and greased trays to prove for a further 15 minutes. While proving, heat the pan of deep fat. Test this and it should be just sufficiently hot to turn a cube of bread pale brown within a minute. Lift about 3 or 4 doughnuts off the tray and drop into the hot fat. Turn the doughnuts in the hot fat with either a fish slice or two spoons so that they become golden brown all over. It is advisable to lower the heat the moment the doughnuts are dropped into the fat, otherwise they will become too brown on the outside before they are cooked through to the middle. Drain them a second on a fish slice, then coat with the sugar. Re-heat and fry a second batch.

*Doughnuts*

## 559 Spiced doughnuts

plain yeast mixture (Recipe 548)
1-2 teaspoons mixed spice
fat for frying

jam
castor sugar
cream

Sieve spice with the flour then continue as for plain yeast dough (Recipe 548). Allow dough to prove as described in Recipe 548, knead well and form into the various shapes for the doughnuts.

**Round doughnuts**

Form into balls—remembering they will double their size in cooking. Make a deep hole and put in jam, re-roll the balls to cover the jam.

**Crescents**

Form into half moon shapes—if wished these can be cut out rather thinly and two halves sandwiched together with jam.

**Ring doughnuts**

Roll out dough and cut into rings with pastry cutters.

Put the shapes on to a warmed baking tin to prove again for 15 minutes. Meanwhile heat the cooking fat in a saucepan. Lift the doughnuts carefully from the tin and lower into the frying basket. Make sure the fat is hot—but not too hot—it should turn a small cube of bread golden brown within 1 minute—no sooner. Put in the doughnuts and cook steadily for 5-10 minutes—the ring doughnuts cook more quickly. Lift out, drain for 1 minute on absorbent or kitchen paper, then roll in castor sugar. If putting whipped cream into the doughnuts wait until quite cold, then split and put in the cream.

## 560 Raisin fingers

plain yeast dough (Recipe 548)
1 oz. butter
1 oz. brown sugar
3 oz. raisins

2 oz. dates, chopped
1 oz. figs, chopped
1 oz. chopped nuts (optional)

Make and prove the dough, then roll out very thinly and cut into 5-inch squares. Cream the butter and sugar, add the other ingredients. Put a line of this filling into each square, and bring over the two opposite corners to cover most of it. Allow to prove on warmed greased baking tins for about 20 minutes, brush with a little milk then bake for about 12 minutes in a hot oven (450°F.—Gas Mark 7).

## 561 Lardy cake

basic yeast dough (Recipe 548)
4 oz. lard

2 oz. castor sugar
2 oz. currants
1 teaspoon mixed spice

Follow basic recipe and method to initial proving. After that, turn dough on to a floured board, knead lightly then roll into an oblong. Spread surface of the top two-thirds with half the lard (divided into small pieces) and half the sugar, currants and spice. Dredge with flour then fold the lower third of pastry over the centre third and bring the top third over. Seal edges with a rolling pin. Give the dough a quarter turn, then repeat the rolling and folding processes again, using up rest of lard, sugar, currants and spice. Give the dough a quarter turn, roll into an oblong, dredge surface lightly with flour and fold in three as before. Give the dough a quarter turn, then roll into a large oval of about ½ inch in thickness. Score the top in criss-cross pattern with a knife and transfer to a greased baking sheet. Cover with greased paper, polythene or a cloth and leave to rise in a warm place for 15 minutes. Brush with milk. Bake in the centre of a hot oven (425-450°F.—Gas Mark 6-7) for approximately 30 minutes. Serve hot with butter or cold as a cake.

## 562 Wiltshire lardy cake

ingredients as plain yeast dough (Recipe 548)
4 oz. lard

4 oz. sugar
4 oz. dried fruit
little spice

Make the dough as described in Recipe 548, allow to prove, then roll out to an oblong shape. If a little 'sticky' flour the board well. Divide the lard and sugar into two equal portions, cutting the lard into tiny pieces. Put half the lard and half the sugar and fruit, with a light dusting of spice, on the dough. Fold in the same way as for flaky pastry. Re-roll the dough, and do exactly the same thing with the rest of the lard, sugar, fruit and spice. Fold again and roll into a neat square or oblong shape, to fit into a 7- or 8-inch tin. If using a round tin then mould with the hands to required shape. Put the mixture into a warmed, greased and floured cake tin, making certain it comes no more than two-thirds of the way up the tin. Prove for 20 minutes in a warm place, then bake in the centre of a hot oven (425-450°F.—Gas Mark 6-7) for 15 minutes. Lower the heat to moderate (375°F.—Gas Mark 4) and cook for a further 20-25 minutes. Either dust the cake with castor sugar when cold or brush with glaze while still hot. To make glaze mix together 1 tablespoon sugar and 1 tablespoon hot water.

*(Illustrated in colour plate 22 .)*

## 563 Barm brack

½ oz. yeast *or* barm
1 teaspoon sugar
½ pint tepid milk
12 oz.-1 lb. margarine *or* butter
1¼ lb. plain flour

2-3 eggs
12 oz. currants *or* raisins
1½ oz. chopped candied peel
1 dessertspoon caraway seeds
grated rind 1 lemon

Cream yeast with 1 teaspoon sugar. Add tepid milk and leave for a short time in a warm place until the mixture starts to bubble. If using barm, then blend this with the lukewarm liquid. Melt the margarine or butter, but make sure this is not too hot. Add this to the yeast liquid—pour on to the flour, together with the well beaten eggs, the fruit etc. Put into a warm place to prove (rise), which will take just about 1½-2 hours. Knead very well, adding a little more flour if necessary. Put into a greased tin—allow to prove for a further 25-30 minutes, then bake in a moderate to moderately hot oven—(375-400°F.—Gas Mark 4-5) for 1¼-1½ hours, reducing the heat slightly if the cake is getting too brown.

## 564 Chelsea ring

Use same ingredients as for Chelsea buns and the same method of mixing as described in Recipe 554. Make the roll, cut into the pieces, and then pack these into a warmed greased 8-inch cake tin. They should be packed loosely enough for the dough to rise well. Prove and bake as Recipe 554, but it is advisable to bake just above the middle of the oven, and to allow 20-25 minutes total cooking time, since it is more difficult for the heat to penetrate through to the centre of the dough. Serve as a cake, rather than pulling the buns apart. The mixture can be dusted with castor or icing sugar before serving, or covered with a thin layer of lemon flavoured glacé icing (Recipe 374).

## 565 Yeast tea ring

½ oz. fresh yeast or 2 level teaspoons dried yeast
1 teaspoon sugar
about ¼ pint tepid milk
12 oz. plain flour
good pinch salt
2 oz. margarine or butter
2 oz. sugar
1 egg

*Filling*
2 large apples
1 oz. butter

2 oz. sugar
2 tablespoons water
4 oz. dried fruit
2 oz. chopped or ground almonds

*Icing*
glacé icing (Recipe 371)
few chopped nuts

Cream yeast with sugar, add tepid milk, little flour OR blend dried yeast with sugar, little liquid, stand until softened, cream, add rest of liquid. Put in warm place until covered with bubbles. Sieve flour with salt, rub in margarine, add sugar, then yeast liquid. Knead thoroughly, add egg and extra milk, if needed, to give soft dough. Knead thoroughly, cover with tea towel or polythene. Allow to 'prove'—rise until double original size. Knead again until smooth, roll out on a floured board to a neat oblong. Cover with cold filling, made by cooking sliced apples with butter, sugar, water, until soft, then adding fruit and almonds. Brush edges of dough with water, fold over to make a long strip, then form into a round. Seal firmly. Lift on to warmed greased tin, snip dough at intervals to show filling. Cover, allow to 'prove' until well risen, bake in centre of oven (400°F.—Gas Mark 5-6) until golden brown. Test by knocking base, tea ring should sound hollow. Then cover with icing and nuts.

*(Illustrated in colour plate 17)*

## 566 Gugelhupf

scant ¾ oz. yeast
2 oz. sugar
approx. 4 tablespoons tepid milk *or* milk and water
8 oz. plain flour
2 oz. butter
2 oz. blanched almonds, chopped
2 oz. raisins*

grated rind 1 orange and/or lemon
1 tablespoon lemon *or* orange juice
2 eggs

*To decorate*
icing sugar

* For a specially delicious flavour soak the raisins in a little rum

Cream the yeast with 1 teaspoon of the sugar, add the liquid and a sprinkling of flour. Allow to stand in a warm place for about 20 minutes. Meanwhile melt the butter and mix the flour with the rest of the ingredients. Add the yeast liquid to the flour mixture, and lastly the melted butter. The mixture should be a fairly soft consistency, but the amount of liquid flours absorb varies, so if too stiff work in a very little extra warm milk. Beat the dough very well with a wooden spoon, then put into a warmed, greased and floured fluted ring mould.* Allow to rise, prove for about 30 minutes, and bake for approximately 35-40 minutes in the centre of a hot oven (450°F.—Gas Mark 7) for the first 20 minutes, then lower the heat slightly for the rest of the time. Dust with icing sugar while warm.
* This type of mould is often called a Savarin tin or Angel cake tin; if you do not have one stand a small cake tin inside a large one.

## 567 Coffee nut ring

1 lb. plain flour
1 level teaspoon salt
1 level tablespoon instant coffee powder
1 oz. yeast
1 level teaspoon granulated sugar
scant ½ pint tepid milk
2 oz. butter
2 eggs

*Filling*
2 oz. butter
3 oz. castor sugar
1 teaspoon instant coffee powder
4 oz. walnuts, chopped

*Decoration*
glacé icing (Recipe 371)
walnut halves

Sieve the flour, salt and coffee powder together in a warmed basin. Cream the yeast with the granulated sugar and add half the tepid milk. Melt the butter and add the remainder of the milk. Beat the eggs and add to the melted butter together with the yeast mixture. Pour all into the flour. Beat well. Turn out on to a floured board and knead well until smooth and even in texture. Divide the mixture into two.
To make the filling, melt the butter and add the sugar, coffee powder and walnuts.
Roll half the dough into a 4-inch wide strip, then roll up like a Swiss roll. Place in the base of a deep ring tin. Spoon in the walnut filling and spread evenly over the dough. Shape the remaining dough into a roll and place over the nut filling. Leave in a warm place to rise to the top of the tin—cover with a sheet of polythene to keep moist. Bake in a moderately hot oven (400°F.—Gas Mark 5) for 10 minutes, then reduce heat to 350°F.—Gas Mark 3 and bake for a further 35-40 minutes. Turn out onto a rack and cool.
When cool decorate the top with glacé icing and walnut halves.

*Coffee nut ring*

# USING READY-PREPARED MIXES

**568** *Using ready-prepared mixes*

When using these ready-prepared mixes, remember that a great deal of time and testing has gone into the preparation not only of the mix itself, but the instructions for using it, and it is essential to follow these implicitly for the first time. After that you will be able to experiment, as with other recipes.

Leave all loaves about 15 minutes between shaping and baking.

---

**569** *Spiced fruit loaf*

5 tablespoons water
2 tablespoons mincemeat

scone mix
little milk

Add the water and mincemeat to the scone mix. Blend thoroughly, and put into a 1 lb. loaf tin. Smooth the top, and brush with a little milk. Bake for 40-45 minutes in the centre of a very moderate oven (350°F.—Gas Mark 3).

---

**570** *Curly cob*

2 oz. cheese, grated
seasoning
scone mix
6 tablespoons milk

little extra milk
extra grated cheese for
 topping

Add the grated cheese and a little seasoning to the scone mix, and bind with the milk. Knead the soft dough lightly, form into a long roll, then twist this into a pyramid shape. Place on a greased baking tin, brush with milk and sprinkle with cheese. Bake for 40-45 minutes in the centre of a very moderate oven (350°F.—Gas Mark 3).

---

**571** *Orange plait*

grated rind 1 orange
juice 1 orange
scone mix
about 5 tablespoons water
little milk

*To decorate*
glacé icing (Recipe 371)
chopped candied peel

Add orange rind and juice to the scone mix, and water to bind. Mix well, and divide into three long strips. Plait these and put on to lightly greased baking tin. Brush top with milk and bake for 25-30 minutes just above the centre of a moderately hot oven (400°F.—Gas Mark 5). When cold this can be covered with glacé icing (Recipe 371) and decorated with candied peel.

---

**572** *Cherry horseshoe*

2 oz. dried fruit
2 oz. glacé cherries
6 tablespoons milk
scone mix

*To decorate*
glacé icing (Recipe 371)
chopped cherries *or* sieved
 icing sugar *or* golden syrup
 and chopped nuts

Add fruit, cherries and milk to scone mix, form into roll about 12 inches long, and shape into a horseshoe. Lift on to a lightly greased baking tin, and bake for 25-30 minutes, just above centre of moderately hot oven (400°F.—Gas Mark 5). When cold this can be decorated with glacé icing (Recipe 371) and chopped cherries or with sieved icing sugar, or it can be covered with a little golden syrup and chopped nuts *before* baking.

---

**573** *Date loaf*

2 oz. dates, chopped
6 tablespoons milk

scone mix
little extra milk

Add the dates and milk to the scone mix. Shape into an oval and slash the top 3 or 4 times. Brush with milk.
Bake for 35-40 minutes in the centre of a very moderate oven (350°F.—Gas Mark 3).

---

**574** *Crescent*

6 tablespoons milk

scone mix

Add milk to scone mix, and roll out dough into a large triangle. Trim edges and roll from wide end to point of triangle. Place on lightly greased baking tin forming crescent. Brush with extra milk, baking in centre of very moderate oven (350°F.—Gas Mark 3) for 30-35 minutes.

---

**575** *Scone loaf*

6 tablespoons milk

scone mix

Add milk to scone mix, and knead lightly. Put into a 1 lb. loaf tin and smooth top. This can be brushed with milk or rubbed with a little melted margarine or butter to give a crisp top. Bake for 40-45 minutes in centre of very moderate oven (350°F.—Gas Mark 3).

---

**576** *Petal ring*

6 tablespoons milk
scone mix

glacé icing (Recipe 371)
glacé cherries

Add the milk to the scone mix and knead lightly. Divide the dough into 7 even-sized pieces. Place 6 of these on to a lightly greased baking tin, and put the seventh into the middle. Bake for 10-15 minutes near the top of a moderately hot oven (400°F.—Gas Mark 5). When cold decorate with the glacé icing (Recipe 371) and cherries.

---

**577** *Seed Loaf*

As above, but sprinkle the top with caraway or poppy seeds before baking.

## 578 Cottage loaf

6 tablespoons milk  
scone mix  
little extra milk

Add the milk to the scone mix, and knead lightly. Divide the dough into two portions—the first two-thirds and the second one-third. Shape into rounds, press the smaller on top of the larger, which should be moistened with milk. Brush the top with milk and bake for approximately 30-35 minutes on a flat baking tin in the centre of a very moderate oven (350°F.—Gas Mark 3).

## 579 Using ready-prepared cake mixes

The very excellent cake mixes available today enable you to prepare cakes even when you are in a hurry. It is important to follow the directions for them, and not vary quantities of liquid etc., at any rate for the first time. There are a variety of flavours today, so they need not become monotonous.

## 580 Cherry basket

1 packet Madeira cake mix  
1 egg  
5 tablespoons milk  
cherry jam  
little cream  
blanched almonds  
1 lb. ripe cherries  
long strip angelica

Make up Madeira cake mix, as instructions on packet, adding egg and milk. Bake in a well greased cake tin or straight-sided pudding basin for 55-60 minutes in centre of a very moderate oven (325-350°F.—Gas Mark 3). When cold cut into layers and spread with jam and a little cream. Before sandwiching together again cut a large round from centre of top layer—then sandwich all layers together. Coat sides with jam and roll in lightly browned blanched almonds. Fill centre with cherries, and make a handle by moistening strip of angelica to make it more pliable and holding in shape with two small cocktail sticks. Tie bow on top. Cover round with jam and nuts and stand at one side as 'lid' of basket.

## 581 Strawberry basket

As above, but use strawberries instead of cherries. Instead of cherry jam use redcurrant jelly to give a sharper flavour.

## 582 Mixed fruit basket

As above, but use a mixture of soft fruits. Use redcurrant jelly or apricot jam, which blends with most flavours, instead of cherry jam.

*Mixed fruit basket*

## 583 Mocha cakes

You can have an interesting combination of chocolate and coffee flavourings if you blend a chocolate cake mix with coffee instead of water as instructed on the packet. In all chocolate cakes a little coffee flavouring gives a pleasant 'bite', which takes away the richness of chocolate flavouring.

## 584 Gingerbread cottage

Make up 2 packets gingerbread mix, and bake in an oblong tin measuring $6\frac{1}{2} \times 8\frac{1}{2} \times 2\frac{1}{2}$ inches for approximately $1\frac{1}{2}$ hours in a very moderate oven (325-350°F.—Gas Mark 3). When cold shape the top of the cake to form a roof, then cover with marzipan (Recipe 385). Ice the walls with royal icing (Recipe 382) or glacé icing (Recipe 371). Shape marzipan with scissors to form eaves, windows, doors and chimney pots. Liquorice 'bootlace' strips can be used for the Tudor 'woodwork', sugar lumps for the cobbled path, and coloured coconut for the grass.

**585 *To colour coconut and nuts***

One can produce very decorative results by just colouring coconut, chopped nuts or even granulated sugar. Put 2 or 3 drops of vegetable colouring on a plate or saucer, then work this gradually into each piece of coconut (desiccated or finely grated fresh coconut), chopped blanched almonds or sugar grains.

**586 *Individual sponge flans***

1 packet ready-prepared flan mix
1 egg
1 tablespoon water
fruit of choice

Place the flan cases on a baking tray leaving a space between each. Make up the flan mix with the egg and water according to the instructions on the packet. Divide the mixture equally between the eight flan cases as shown on the packet. Bake for 10-12 minutes above centre of a moderate to moderately hot oven (375-400°F.—Gas Mark 5). Remove and allow to cool. Remove flans from baking cases. Arrange fruit in flans. Cover with the glaze supplied in packet. *(Illustrated in colour plate 1.)*

**587 *Chocolate floral cakes***

Make up a Devil's Food Chocolate mix and place in a Swiss roll tin lined with greased greaseproof paper. Bake in a hot oven (425-450°F.—Gas Mark 6-7). Turn on to a wire rack to cool. When cold cut into fingers. Decorate with flowers made from royal icing (Recipe 382)—these can be bought from good grocers—and pipe in green butter or royal icing (Recipes 387, 382) to represent foliage.

# CAKES THAT REQUIRE LITTLE COOKING

It is surprising the number of cakes that can be produced with little cooking, or if you use the biscuit or ready-made sponges, no cooking. They have, however, a flavour rather of their own and for the first time I would suggest making a small quantity.

**588 *Chocolate clusters***

4 oz. chocolate couverture, plain *or* milk chocolate
about 2 oz. breakfast cereal

Break the chocolate into small pieces and heat in a basin over hot, but not boiling, water. Remove from heat and beat well until liquid, but cool, then add the very crisp cereal gradually until well coated. Put into small pyramid shapes on a flat tin and leave to set.
**Note**
The breakfast cereal must be very crisp, so if necessary warm through for a short time in the oven.

**589 *Orange chocolate clusters***

As above, but add finely grated rind of 2 oranges. Stand the cakes on wafer thin slices of fresh orange.

**590 *Hazelnut and chocolate gâteau*
*An uncooked party cake***

12 tablespoons strong coffee
1 tablespoon sherry *or* Tia Maria
about 36 sponge fingers (Savoy *or* lady fingers)

*Filling*
3 oz. butter
3 oz. icing sugar, sieved
1½ oz. cocoa powder
1 egg yolk
2-3 oz. hazelnuts, chopped
small amount coffee *or* milk

*Decoration*
¼ pint thick cream
1 egg white
1 oz. icing sugar
few drops vanilla essence
about 12 small meringues (Recipe 420)
square of chocolate
few hazelnuts

Line an 8- or 9-inch cake tin with a round of paper. This cake is easier to remove if a tin with a loose base is used. Pour the coffee and sherry or Tia Maria into a shallow dish. Dip enough sponge fingers into this to cover the bottom of the tin—you will need to cut some to fit. Take care you do *NOT* make the sponge fingers too soft.
Cream the butter and icing sugar, then beat in the sieved cocoa, egg yolk and nuts. Add just enough coffee or milk to make a soft consistency. Spread half of this over the sponge fingers top with another layer of sponge fingers. Cover with the rest of the filling, then a final layer of the sponge fingers. Leave for several hours, or this cake can be stored in a refrigerator for some days. Turn out, and remove the paper.
Whip the cream and the egg white until very stiff. Fold the egg white into the cream, then add the sugar and vanilla essence. Coat top and sides of cake with this, and press meringues round the sides. Decorate with grated chocolate, hazelnuts and, if any cream mixture remains, with whirls of this on top of the cake. Serve as cold as possible.
*(Illustrated in colour plate 24.)*

**591 *Refrigerator chocolate cake***

8 oz. digestive biscuits
3 oz. margarine
1 oz. castor sugar
1 tablespoon golden syrup
1 tablespoon cocoa powder
vanilla icing (Recipe 592)
chocolate drops

Roll digestive biscuits into fine crumbs. Brush a 7-inch flan ring with a little melted margarine and stand it on a flat plate or dish. Take margarine from the refrigerator and cream with sugar and syrup in a mixing bowl. Work in the cocoa and stir in the biscuit crumbs. Pack the mixture into the prepared ring, smoothing over the top. Chill in the refrigerator for 2-3 hours or leave overnight. Make the icing and smooth over the top and sides of the cake. Mark with a fork and decorate with chocolate drops.

**592 *Vanilla icing***

2 oz. margarine
4 oz. icing sugar
few drops vanilla essence
2 teaspoons milk

Take margarine from the refrigerator for the icing and work in the sieved icing sugar. Beat in the essence and milk.

**593** *Almond and chocolate gâteau*
*An uncooked party cake*

Recipe as Hazelnut and Chocolate Gâteau (Recipe 590), but use 3 oz. ground almonds and a few drops of almond essence instead of hazelnuts for the filling. Decorate with browned almonds instead of hazelnuts.

To brown almonds, blanch the nuts by putting into boiling water for 1 minute, removing the skins, then drying well on a cloth. Put the nuts on to baking tins and brown for a few minutes in the oven or under a moderately hot grill.

**594** *Chestnut and chocolate gâteau*

Recipe as Hazelnut and Chocolate Gâteau (Recipe 590), but use either 3 oz. cooked sieved chestnuts and a little almond essence to give flavour, or 2-3 oz. chestnut purée (obtainable in cans or tubes). As this is rather sweet reduce the amount of icing sugar slightly.

Decorate with the grated chocolate, and one or two marrons glacés, cut into small pieces.

**595** *Rum and coffee gâteau*

1 sponge round, about
  7-inches in diameter
  (it can be a stale cake)
4-5 oz. butter
4-5 oz. castor sugar

2 egg yolks
½ pint *strong* coffee
1 tablespoon rum
2-4 oz. split browned almonds
  *or* finely chopped almonds

Line a cake tin the same size as the sponge with greased paper. Split the cake across to make about 4 layers. Cream together the butter and sugar until very soft and light, then work in the 2 egg yolks and 4 tablespoons of the coffee and rum. The mixture will doubtless have a curdled appearance, but this does not matter. Put one layer of sponge cake in bottom of the tin, then pour over enough coffee to moisten this. Spread with a thin layer of the coffee mixture. Put the next layer of sponge over the top, moisten with coffee and spread with coffee mixture. Continue in this way until you put on the top layer of sponge. Simply moisten this with coffee. You should find you have a certain amount of the coffee mixture left, so keep this in a cool place. Put a piece of paper over the top of the cake and put a weight on top. Leave overnight. Remove the weight and paper, and gently pour away any coffee that may have come to the top of the cake. Turn out of the tin. Spread the sides and top with the last of the cream mixture, decorating the sides with the nuts, and the top with piped roses in the mixture. This cake has a moist texture that is quite delicious.

**596** *Tipsy cake*

Victoria sandwich
  (Recipe 76)
jam
sherry

1 pint custard sauce
  (Recipe 414)
whipped cream

Split each half of the Victoria sandwich through the centre and spread with jam. If possible use different flavoured jams. Put on to a plate or dish and soak lavishly in sherry. Coat with the custard sauce and decorate with cream.

**597** *Kikskage*

(*Danish chocolate biscuit cake*)
7 oz. Danish lard *or* butter
3½ oz. cocoa powder
9 oz. icing sugar
3 tablespoons cream

1 egg yolk
10 oz. plain square biscuits
glacé cherries
walnuts
slices fresh orange

Melt lard slowly in a bowl over saucepan of boiling water. Sift cocoa and icing sugar. Add to lard, stirring constantly. Remove bowl from heat. Add cream and egg yolk. Line an oblong baking tin with greaseproof paper. Pour in thin layer of chocolate mixture. Cover with a layer of biscuits. Repeat these layers, beginning and ending with the chocolate mixture. Decorate top with glacé cherries and walnuts, and orange butterflies. Place cake in a cold place to set for an hour.

**598** *Russian cake*

about 12 oz. cake (use any
  left-over cake except fruit
  cake)
2 tablespoons sugar
2 tablespoons water

2 tablespoons sherry *or* rum
water icing (Recipe 371) in
  different colours—
  chocolate, pink, etc.

Line a cake tin with greased paper, then put in the pieces of cake. The best effect is obtained if you use several different colours of cake. Boil sugar and water together until sugar has dissolved, then add sherry or rum. Pour over cake, seeing that it is evenly moistened. Put into a moderate oven (375°F.—Gas Mark 4) for 15 minutes, then leave to cool in tin with a weight on top. Turn out when cold and cover with a layer of one-colour water icing. Feather in one or two other colours (see Recipe 381).

**599** *Coconut pyramids (1)*

6 oz. desiccated coconut
1 dessertspoon cornflour
3 oz. castor sugar
2 egg whites, stiffly beaten

*To decorate*
cherries
angelica

Mix coconut, cornflour and sugar together. Work into the egg whites until a firm mixture. If egg whites are very large do not use all of them. Form into pyramids with your fingers, and either put on to a well greased baking tin or rice paper on a tin. Bake in centre of a very moderate oven (350°F.—Gas Mark 3) until pale golden brown on top. Handle carefully until cold.
Decorate with cherries and angelica.

**600** *Chocolate coconut pyramids*

As above, but omit cornflour and add 1 rounded dessertspoon cocoa powder. When set pour a little melted chocolate on to pyramids. Decorate with cherries.

**601** *Coconut pyramids (2)*

1 can full cream condensed
  milk
8-9 oz. desiccated coconut
rice paper

Mix the ingredients together, adding enough coconut to give a firm consistency. Form into pyramid shapes and stand on rice paper on baking tins or on well greased tins. The mixture can be coloured if wished. Bake for approximately 10-15 minutes in a moderate oven (375°F.—Gas Mark 4) and allow about 5 minutes in a hot oven (450°F.—Gas Mark 7) to brown tips.
Tear round rice paper carefully when quite cold.

# Index

# ACKNOWLEDGMENTS

Illustrations by courtesy of the following:

Angostura Aromatic Bitters: Black and white photograph accompanying Recipe 326.

Australian Home Recipe Service: Black and white photograph accompanying Recipe 333.

Brown and Polson, Ltd. Colour plate no. 12. Black and white photographs accompanying Recipes 212, 216.

Butter Information Council: Colour plate no. 6. Black and white photographs accompanying Recipes, 164, 251.

Blue Band Bureau: Black and white photographs accompanying Recipes 16, 43, 83, 104, 136, 148, 159, 220, 236, 305, 312, 313, 319, 328, 334, 436, 481, 537.

Cadbury's Chocolate: Colour plate no. 4, 10, 18, 24. Black and white photographs accompanying Recipes 68, 228, 334, 421, 427.

Carnation Milk Bureau: Black and white photographs accompanying Recipes 201, 219.

Colman's Semolina: Black and white photographs accompanying Recipes 116, 149, 210, 221, 241, 320, 458, 525.

Coffee Promotion Council: Black and white photograph accompanying Recipe 567.

Creda Electric Cookers: Black and white photographs accompanying Recipe 175.

Eden Vale Cottage Cheese: Black and white photograph accompanying Recipe 520.

Elders and Fyffes: Black and white photographs accompanying Recipes 217, 499, 503.

Flour Advisory Bureau: Black and white photographs accompanying Recipes 29, 74, 87, 134, 145, 185-190, 230-232, 240, 470, 474, 475, 516, 520, 551.

Fowler's Golden Syrup Jelly: Black and white photograph accompanying Recipe 242.

Fowler's West India Treacle: Colour plate no. 9. Black and white photograph accompanying Recipe 440.

J. W. French, Co., Ltd.: Black and white photograph accompanying Recipe 15.

Fruit Producers' Council: Colour plates no. 5, 7, 11, 14, 15, 17. Black and white photograph accompanying Recipe 286.

Gale's Honey: Colour plates no. 3, 13, 16, 23.

Gale's Peanut Butter: Colour plate no. 19.

H. J. Green Co. Ltd.: Colour plate no. 1.

Kenwood Manufacturing Co., Ltd: Black and white photograph accompanying Recipe 3.

Kraft Foods, Ltd: Black and white photographs accompanying Recipes 32, 140, 141, 142, 144, 166, 167, 180, 208, 247, 290, 295, 314, 317, 330.

Lard Information Bureau: Colour plates no. 2, 20, 22.

McDougall's Cookery Service: Colour plate no. 8.

Nabisco Foods Ltd.: Black and white photographs accompanying Recipes 174, 243, 332, 580-582.

Playing Cards Bureau: Black and white photograph accompanying Recipe 191.

Potato Marketing Board: Black and white photograph accompanying Recipe 59.

Prestige Group, Ltd: Black and white photograph accompanying Recipe 44.

Spry Cookery Centre: Black and white photographs accompanying Recipes 11, 20, 108, 128, 157, 160, 173, 195, 198, 225, 245, 253-256, 259, 276, 281, 282, 294, 318, 325, 345, 350, 407, 481, 533, 534.

Stork Cookery Service: Black and white photograph accompanying Recipes 194, 300, 552.

Summer County Margarine: Black and white photograph accompanying Recipe 76.

T. Wall & Sons, Ltd: Black and white photograph accompanying Recipe 272.